In Dialogue:
Tradition and Interaction in the Mesolithic–Neolithic Transition

Edited by

Jolene Debert
Mats Larsson
Julian Thomas

BAR International Series 2809

2016

Published in 2016 by
BAR Publishing, Oxford

BAR International Series 2809

In Dialogue: Tradition and Interaction in the Mesolithic–Neolithic Transition

ISBN 978 1 4073 1478 5

COVER IMAGE *Digital reconstruction of the Early Neolithic timber structure, Whitehorse Stone, in Kent, UK (image by Jolene Debert)*

Printed in England

BAR
PUBLISHING

BAR titles are available from:

BAR Publishing
122 Banbury Rd, Oxford, OX2 7BP, UK
EMAIL info@barpublishing.com
PHONE +44 (0)1865 310431
FAX +44 (0)1865 316916
www.barpublishing.com

Contents

Preface   v

Section 1: The House   **1**

1   HOUSE SOCIETIES AND THE BEGINNING OF THE BRITISH NEOLITHIC   3
Julian Thomas

2   THE EMPTY HOUSE: EARLY NEOLITHIC SETTLEMENT STRUCTURE IN
SOUTHERN SCANDINAVIA   11
Mats Larsson

3   WHEN ARTEFACTS CAN'T SPEAK: TOWARDS A NEW UNDERSTANDING OF
BRITISH EARLY NEOLITHIC TIMBER STRUCTURES   19
Jolene Debert

Section 2: Monumentality   **27**

4   CONSTRUCTED OR CONCEIVED LANDSCAPES – SOME THOUGHTS ON THE SUBJECT OF
HUMAN EXPERIENCES IN THE NEOLITHIC, AND HISTORIC LANDSCAPES   29
Anna-Karin Andersson

5   NEOLITHISATION AND INTRODUCTION OF CAUSEWAYED ENCLOSURES.
TWO STRUCTURALLY RELATED PROCESSES   37
Lutz Klassen

Setion 3: Materiality   **45**

6   BOTH ARTEFACT AND PHENOMENON: A MATERIAL APPROACH TO ENGAGEMENTS
WITH FIRE IN THE LATE MESOLITHIC OF BRITAIN   47
Ellen McInnes

7   POTS IN CONTEXT: ASPECTS ON POTTERY PRODUCTION AND USE IN THE
EARLY NEOLITHIC FUNNEL BEAKER (TRB) CULTURE ON ÖLAND, SE SWEDEN   55
Ludvig Papmehl-Dufay, Ole Stilborg, Anders Lindahl and Sven Isaksson

Section 4: The Transition   **67**

8   TIMING AND PROCESS IN THE FIFTH AND EARLY FOURTH MILLENNIUM CAL BC   69
Frances Healy

9   LATE MESOLITHIC-EARLY NEOLITHIC IN SOUTHERN SCANDINAVIA:
TRADITION AND INTERACTION   77
T. Douglas Price

10   IN DIALOGUE: FROM SOCIAL ANALYSIS TO EPISTEMOLOGICAL CONCERNS   87
Irene Garcia-Rovira

Preface

This book is the result of two conferences, one in Manchester in 2012 and one in Iceland in 2013. They were both parts of a project "North-West Europe in Transition: The Early Neolithic in Britain and Scandinavia" which began in 2009 and ended 2014 at the EAA conference in Istanbul. It was financed by The Swedish Foundation for International Cooperation in Research and Higher Education (STINT) as an Institutional Grant (IG). Prof. Mats Larsson at the Linnaeus University in Kalmar administered it with the cooperation of Prof. Julian Thomas, University of Manchester. A special thank you goes to Dr. Jolene Debert. Without her help in organising fieldtrips, conferences and co-editing books the result would not have been this good!

The aim of the project was the organization of conferences, seminars, books and papers, fieldtrips as well as lectures and seminars by visiting lecturers. It was highly successful and the collaboration has only continued and deepened after the ending of the grant.

Section 1

The House

Chapter 1

House Societies and the Beginning of the British Neolithic

Julian Thomas

University of Manchester, UK

In this contribution, a social mechanism is offered for the transformation from Mesolithic to Neolithic modes of organisation in Britain. It is noted that the large timber halls that have been recognised over the past forty years did not represent the characteristic form of dwelling structure throughout the Early Neolithic, or even the first four centuries of that period. Instead, they represented a stage or phase of development, following shortly after the first appearance of Neolithic things and practices in a given region. An explanation for this pattern is found in the notion of the 'house society', a characteristic social form that it often associated with communities undergoing abrupt change, in which the shared identity of a bounded group of persons is reinforced by their common attachment to a physical structure and an estate of material and immaterial property. This attachment both brings the community into being, and ensures its durability over time. It is argued that the change from extensive networks of hunting bands to bounded house societies claiming shared descent from a common group of ancestors facilitated the collective ownership of a body of wealth, which included domesticated animals and cultivation plots.

Keywords: Neolithic, house societies, ancestors, wealth, halls, long barrows

Introduction

Throughout the European continent, the transition from the Mesolithic to the Neolithic involved economic change, cultural change, and social change, and these developments were generally closely interlinked. Hunter-gatherers and farmers are not two different kinds of human beings, with dissimilar capabilities and capacities, as earlier generations of anthropologists and archaeologists would sometimes have had us believe (e.g. Sollas 1911). Despite this, more than the presence or absence of domesticated species separates them. This is because certain aspects of hunter-gatherer social organisation are hard to reconcile with the tending of plants and animals and the accumulation of material wealth (Woodburn 1982). Whether we choose to attribute the beginning of the Neolithic in Britain to the transformation of indigenous societies or population movement from the continent, it is clear that a very different kind of social formation emerged in the early fourth millennium BC. This contribution will seek to identify some of the mechanisms involved, and in the process to locate the principal social dynamic of early Neolithic society in Britain.

To begin with hunters and gatherers, Marshall Sahlins (1972: 171) once argued that the fundamental element of the foraging economy is generalised reciprocity, in which all give gifts to all without the expectation of a return. Nurit Bird-David (1990: 184) elaborated on this theme to describe a 'cosmic economy of sharing', in which the environment is understood to provide limitless goods,

like a caring parent, while humans are required to provide for each other, like siblings. One critical element of this arrangement is 'demand sharing', the imperative to hand over whatever food or goods one has on request (Peterson 1993: 860). The sharing economy reduces the risk of starvation by ensuring that all will have food except in the most dire of famines. It also limits the ability of successful hunters to build up prestige and authority, and it chronically restricts the accumulation of wealth, so that typically people own no more goods than they can carry on their person (Kelly 1995: 187). However, where delayed-return strategies are practiced and effort has to be invested in subsistence activities in advance of a return being achieved, a tension typically develops between the need for groups to collectively own their subsistence technology and tended wild resources, and the demand to share with a wider range of persons. This tension is greater still once domesticated resources are brought into the picture. As James Woodburn (1982: 447) points out, hunter-gatherers such as the !Kung typically find it very difficult to begin farming, since their kin and neighbours simply descend on them and eat up the seed-corn or slaughter the breeding stock.

Yet in some cases, classically the American northwest coast, sharing relationships were eclipsed and corporate descent groups emerged within hunter-fisher societies, monopolising key resources and developing highly unequal social structures, without agriculture being practiced (Kelly 1995: 163; Rosman and Rubel 1971). In Britain, the situation was rather different, for the Late Mesolithic was characterised by economic diversity, with practices ranging from intercept hunting of ungulates to the firing of upland vegetation, the selective harvesting of plant foods, freshwater and marine fishing, and the hunting of marine mammals. There is little indication that the kind of residential stability and social elaboration that have been suggested for southern Scandinavia were common in Britain (Milner 2006). British Mesolithic societies were not progressing independently toward sedentism and social stratification, although they doubtless contained unresolved tensions between those who sought personal advancement and traditional levelling mechanisms. Change was therefore brought about through contact with continental Neolithic societies: the present author would prefer to say through intensified interaction, while others would favour the actual arrival of small groups of colonists (Sheridan 2010; Thomas 2013). In either case, we have to account for the process by which indigenous communities were restructured, enabling domesticated resources to contribute to subsistence, and prestigious artefacts to be acquired, circulated, or retained within communities as inalienable wealth (Weiner 1992).

Settlement and buildings

Such an explanation can best be found by looking at settlement evidence, and particularly the difficulties that archaeologists have found in interpreting it. Since the identification of causewayed enclosures as special-purpose sites used for gathering, exchange and feasting rather than nucleated settlements, the comparative lack of Early Neolithic dwellings has been a nagging problem for prehistorians in Britain (Smith 1971; Bradley 1987). Between the 1960s and 1980s, a small number of large, isolated timber buildings of Early Neolithic date were discovered at Fengate (Pryor 1974), Llandegai (Lynch and Musson 2004) and Balbridie (Ralston 1982), but at the same time a conviction was growing that for the most part Neolithic habitation practices had been only semi-sedentary, and structures had been informal and flimsy. This picture shifted somewhat during the 1990s, particularly in Ireland, where fieldwork in advance of extensive infrastructure projects led to the discovery of large numbers of rectangular oak-built Early Neolithic houses (Grogan 2004; Smyth 2010). Further structures were also now identified in Britain, at sites including White Horse Stone, Claish and Yarnton, but the rate of discovery remained much lower than in Ireland.

Peter Rowley-Conwy (2004: 95) presented the Early Neolithic houses of Britain, Ireland and southern Scandinavia as a unified phenomenon, but the contrasts between these regions are actually quite instructive. The Danish and Swedish houses are very numerous, and lightly constructed (Larsson and Rzepecki 2003), while the 80 or so Irish structures are relatively small, but very stoutly built, often with plank walls set in slots. In Britain, far fewer buildings are known, and many of these were much larger in scale, representing 'halls' rather than 'houses'. Most striking is the restricted chronology of the structures in Britain and Ireland, which are not distributed evenly

throughout the millennium or so of the Earlier Neolithic. In Ireland, the recent Bayesian analysis of Whittle, Healy and Bayliss (2011: 598) suggests that all of the houses were built within a century, and perhaps in a period of as little as 55 years, a generation or two after the start of the Irish Neolithic. A comparable pattern can be discerned on the British mainland. Here, the process of Neolithisation took a rather different form. Whilst in Ireland the appearance of Neolithic artefacts and practices seems to have been broadly contemporaneous throughout the island (Whittle, Healy and Bayliss 2011: 662), in Britain the Neolithic expanded from the southeast to the northwest over a period of more than three centuries. If we imagine this process as a wave, gradually progressing across the British landmass, then the building of halls or houses seems to have followed in its wake, a generation or so after the first appearance of Neolithic entities in a given region (see Fig. 1). Many of these buildings had relatively short use-lives, some were deliberately destroyed by fire, and most were not replaced in their immediate surroundings. So, rather than representing the characteristic form of dwelling throughout the Early Neolithic, hall-building seems to have been a phase that communities went through, and conceivably a distinct part of 'becoming Neolithic'.

One explanation for this development is offered by Alison Sheridan (2008: 3), who suggests that the halls were 'designed as 'pioneer' settlement sites, to house extended families who had just arrived from the continent'. This argument has the virtue of addressing the relatively short period during which these buildings were in use. However, the largest and most impressive of the halls were built in lowland Scotland, two or three hundred years after the first Neolithic presence in southeast England. This would require that any process of maritime colonisation would have been very protracted indeed. An alternative interpretation begins with the suggestion made by both Gabriel Cooney (2000: 52) and Jessica Smyth (2010: 2), to the effect that in the Irish context Early Neolithic communities were 'house societies'. However, it takes the argument in a slightly different direction.

House societies

The term 'house society' comes from the work of Claude Lévi-Strauss (1982: 164), who identifies the 'house' as a distinctive form of social organisation, which can be recognised in contexts ranging from Native North America to feudal Europe and Japan. In each case, the term 'house' refers both to the physical structure *and* those who claim affiliation to it. Lévi-Strauss first coined the term to account for groups like the northwest coast Kwakiutl and the California Yurok, whose kinship systems did not seem to follow normal rules. Instead, the house represents a corporate group who all claim descent from a founding ancestor (although this is often actually fictive), and who collectively own an estate of material and immaterial property (Gillespie 2000: 22). This may include resources, prestige valuables and heirlooms, the house itself, as well as names, titles, rituals and dances.

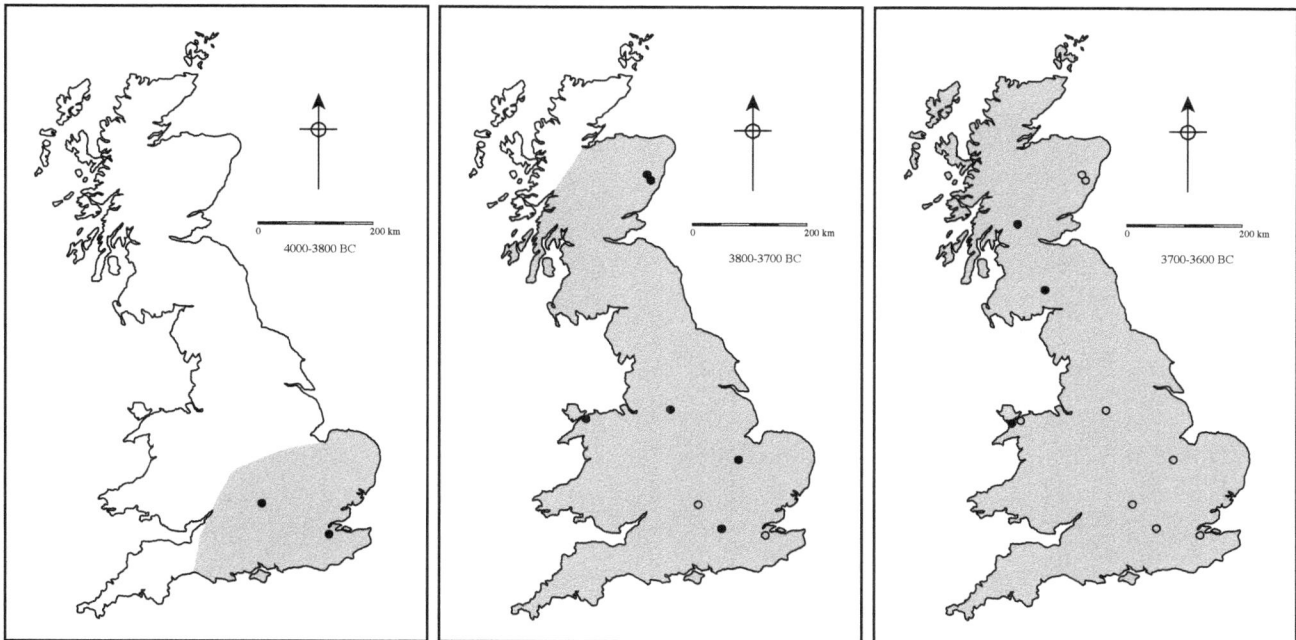

Fig. 1: The locations of timber halls in Britain, related to the progressive expansion of Neolithic things and practices, as charted by Whittle, Healy and Bayliss (2011).

The effect of this collective holding of material things, customs and memories is to maintain the identity of the community across the generations. Indeed, Lévi-Strauss argues that the house acts as a 'moral person': it is a social actor, which owns property and engages in collaboration and competition with other houses (Beck 2007: 6).

Critically, the house structure and the estate of material wealth do not simply reflect the identity of a pre-existing community. The building of the house brings the community into being, and establishes the conditions for the accumulation of wealth (Carsten and Hugh-Jones 1995: 3). The body of possessions that the house builds up continues to exist beyond the lifetime of any single person, so that the durability of the community is embedded in material things (Watson 2000: 182). But these things are not just symbols, in that they are both used and inhabited. Having said that, the 'houses' of house societies are often not lived in by the whole community, but may represent 'origin houses' maintained by a caretaker group. The community as a whole may be more dispersed, only returning to the house at key junctures during their lives.

In his book 'The Way of the Masks' (1982), Lévi-Strauss presented house societies as something rather like an evolutionary stage, located between kin-based and class-based formations, in which the language of kinship and affinity is used to express growing social inequality. But authors such as Susan Gillespie (2007: 30) have pointed out that 'housification' is actually a process that can occur in radically different societies, although it is generally a symptom of rapid social and economic change. 'Houses' generally emerge where property relations are transformed, and more bounded and competitive social formations develop (Sissons 2010: 383). House societies are stable social units created in unstable times, which

build their coherence and continuity on a relationship with the past which is vested in both collective memory and the durability of material things.

This relationship with the past is often expressed through a concern with ancestors, in the very specific sense of the person or persons who founded the house. Although the profligate use of the concepts of 'ancestors' and 'ancestry' within prehistoric archaeology has received some criticism (Whitley 2002), it is important to note that the notion is employed here in a quite specific way. As we have seen, all of the members of the community claim descent from the house ancestors, irrespective of their actual parentage. The house itself may be understood as the dwelling-place of the founding ancestors, or as embodying the life force of an ancestor, or even as the ancestor's body (Waterson 1995: 54). But despite this, other material entities can substitute for the house as the physical focus of the community: a boat, a set of regalia, a tomb or a shrine. Indeed, for house societies there is a degree of overlap between houses, tombs and shrines, as the bodies of the ancestors are often interred within or beneath houses, and their bones may be kept in niches or house shrines, while the homes of the ancestors can gradually become objects of veneration (Kirch 2000: 109).

House societies, then, are corporate groups whose material equipment represents at once a store of collectively owned value, a reminder of origins in the past, and an enduring core to which people attach themselves. The potential relevance of this set of ideas to the Eurasian Neolithic is obvious, for here social life was characterised by the emergence of an environment rich with made things: not only houses, but also pottery, figurines, polished stone tools, beads, gardens, tombs and monuments (Hodder 2006: 60). Houses compete against one another, and their material wealth is at once the medium of their competition and the measure of their success. Since the construction of the house and the initiation of the community are one and the same thing, the symbolism of building is often very rich for house societies, with much stress being placed on the erection of the principal house-posts, which Richard Fox (1993: 172) describes as 'ritual attractors', about which symbolically-charged acts cluster. House rituals provide a context for both celebrating the ancestors and incorporating outsiders as kin, so that house societies may be expansionary structures (Waterson 1990: 123). This will be of particular importance in situations where the accumulation of wealth depends upon the amount of labour that can be deployed, which may be the case where domesticated resources are in the process of being adopted.

'Houses' and the inception of the British Neolithic

The argument proposed here is that the beginning of the British Neolithic involved the creation of house societies, and that house organisation represented a framework by which hunters and gatherers, who had previously been resistant to the accumulation of wealth, formed themselves into property-owning corporate groups. This transformation would make it more practicable for communities to herd cattle, grow cereals, and circulate prestige goods, although it would not dictate the specific form that subsistence practice might take. It is suggested that the construction of substantial timber halls and houses in Britain and Ireland shortly after the first appearance of Neolithic practices and artefacts within any region was the means by which bounded social units were brought into being, and their existence signalled to others. Further, it seems plausible that earthen long barrows and chambered tombs, which became more numerous as houses and halls began to decline, had a similar role, in that they represented structures that contained the physical remains of ancestors and served as an enduring focus for the collective identity of social groups.

On the British mainland, fewer than twenty timber halls are known, ranging between nine and thirty metres in length, with the Scottish examples generally the largest. They do not form extensive settlements, like those of the European *Bandkeramik*, although they are sometimes found in dispersed pairs: Warren Field and Balbridie, Llandegai and Parc Bryn Cegin, White Horse Stone and the possible structure at Pilgrim's Way. As some distance separates each of these pairs of halls, it is conceivable that they were not built by the same communities, and that if they were contemporary they were effectively in competition with each other. This much is suggested by Warren Field and Balbridie, which were radically distinct from each other in architectural terms, and contained entirely different assemblages of cereals, suggesting the consumption of different foodstuffs by the communities involved (Thomas 2013: 398). An exception to this pattern lies in the four quite small timber buildings identified at Kingsmead Quarry, Horton in Berkshire, which appear more similar to the small groups of scattered buildings known in some parts of Ireland (Nichols 2013). The earliest known example in Britain is White Horse Stone in Kent, probably dating to the fortieth century BC and comparatively lightly built, with internal aisles and outer walls defined by gullies (Booth et al. 2011: 71). Taking this site as a point of departure it is clear that while there is great diversity in form and size, some of the British halls became larger and more structurally elaborate as time progressed. While White Horse Stone can be claimed to have taken inspiration from the very rare Michelsberg structures at Hautes Chanvières at Mairy in the Ardennes (Marole 1989), British halls also gradually became more remote from any continental parallel (Last 1996: 27). Arguably, we can see the development of this insular tradition as having been driven by competitive emulation and prestige display.

Some of the British halls have evidence for a raised floor at one end, and this may suggest that part of the wealth that they embodied took the form of stored foodstuffs or seed grain (Kenney 2008: 21). White Horse Stone had little positive evidence for internal partitioning, but most of the later structures seem to have been sub-divided in some way. Warren Field, Claish, Llandegai, Balbridie, Parc Bryn Cegin and Yarnton all appear to have contained at least one comparatively large open space, located toward the principal entrance. In most cases, this space was not directly visible from the entrance, being obscured by either screens or, at Warren Field, by a large upright (Murray, Murray and Fraser 2009: 62). There may thus have been a preoccupation with the seclusion of some of the activities that took place inside these buildings.

Many of the British halls had a central, axial passage, defined by pairs of posts. These effectively form a series of 'doorways', which in some cases run between sets of lateral bays that flank the axial passage. Interestingly, this arrangement of a central passage with a series of bays on either side was later replicated by the stalled cairns of Orkney, where the side compartments held benches which received the remains of the dead (Davidson and Henshall 1989). One possible implication of this organisation of space is that the bayed areas were each associated with a particular social segment. Amongst the timber halls, it is likely that these pairs of large uprights would have been the first element of the building that was constructed, establishing the hall and its community. In the Scottish halls, very large posts became a more emphatic theme, enhancing the principal entrance at Warren Field, for example. While Warren Field and Lockerbie had a central aisle and lateral bays (Kirby 2011: 7), Claish and Balbridie had a very different structure. Entering these buildings, the visitor is confronted by lateral screens, which turn them to either left or right, so that they would have to progress around the inside of the outer wall (Topping 1996: 164). Further internal partitions them defined a series of graded lateral spaces. While it is entirely possible that Claish and Balbridie were inhabited by at least a caretaker community, the comparison with White Horse Stone demonstrates that over time the priorities of hall-building had shifted in favour of the structured organisation of movement and experience, establishing very particular conditions for social encounters and performances. As Kenneth Brophy (2007: 86) has observed, these were not simply farmhouses.

At Warren Field, the two largest posts were set at either end of the central aisle, and the excavators argue that these were non-structural timbers, which were dug out and removed before the building was deliberately destroyed by fire (Murray, Murray and Fraser 2009: 58). Similarly at Claish, two large postholes were positioned within the central northern space (Barclay, Brophy and MacGregor 2002: 72). So in both cases the principal social activities of the community were bracketed between two large timber uprights. The largest assemblages of pottery sherds and cereal grains in each hall had been deliberately placed in these postholes after the removal of the upright, evidently as part of the decommissioning of the buildings (Murray, Murray and Fraser 2009: 44). It is entirely possible that these timbers were then reused in some other kind of structure, having achieved a particular kind of importance and value through their use in the halls. The purposeful deposition of cereals in these significant contexts and as part of the destruction of the buildings does fatal damage to the interpretation of the plant remains from these sites as a representative sample of stored material preserved by accidental combustion (Jones and Rowley-Conwy 2007: 404; Rowley-Conwy 2000: 48).

Single large non-structural posts can also be identified inside the halls at Lockerbie and Balbridie, and these can be compared with focal posts at the post-defined cursus monuments of Douglamuir and Holywood North (Kendrik 1995; Thomas 2007), and the axial pits in the timber enclosures of Littleour and Balfarg (Brophy 2007: 86), all of which are rectilinear structures that arguably refer to or elaborate upon the idea of the timber hall. These examples provide further support for the idea that placing large timbers in the ground was a symbolically charged act during the earlier Neolithic, which expressed the coming-into-being of a human community of a certain sort. In particular, the pairing of posts to enclose inhabited spaces within the halls clearly relates to themes of boundedness and exclusion. The removal of the large posts from Warren Field and Claish, and of the gable posts at Parc Bryn Cegin (Kenney 2008: 21) suggests that these timbers were understood as valuable or efficacious in their own right, condensing the life force or identity of the hall community, or their ancestors.

Houses and the dead

It is therefore highly significant that paired oak uprights also took on a focal role in another architectural form of the Early Neolithic, the timber mortuary structures found beneath earthen long barrows (Kinnes 1975: 19; Whittle 1991: 93). These were composed of a linear trough or embanked zone on which human remains were laid out, perhaps with a wooden 'lid', with a substantial wooden post at either end. In many cases, these consisted of a single tree-trunk that had been split down the middle,

enhancing the theme of boundedness and containment. The similarity with the pairs of posts at Warren Field and Claish suggests that these structures were explicitly related to houses and halls, and that they shared an emphasis on the initiation of community, as expressed through the erection of the wooden posts. Architectural connections with halls and houses are also evident in other structural elements found beneath long barrows, including timber façades and avenues of posts. Various authors including Ian Hodder (1984: 59) and Richard Bradley (1996) have suggested that Neolithic mortuary monuments represented 'houses of the dead', often on the basis of the formal similarities between long barrows and the long houses of central Europe. These include an easterly orientation, a trapezoidal ground plan, the presence of flanking pits or ditches, and an entrance at one end. However, the argument pursued here is slightly different. Rather than the living and the dead being assigned to separate spheres of practice, it is suggested that in some senses tombs *were* houses. Obviously, they were not inhabited, but as permanent structures containing the remains of the ancestral dead they served as the enduring material referent for a particular social group.

This suggestion has some bearing upon a long-running debate regarding Neolithic funerary practice. Richard Atkinson (1968: 92) pointed out that although long barrows and chambered tombs often contained numerous human skeletons, these were rarely enough to suggest that all of a community's dead had been deposited there over any substantial period of time. By implication, the majority of the deceased must have been dealt with in some other, archaeologically invisible manner throughout the Earlier Neolithic. If these structures had been used over an extended period, some criterion must have been employed to decide who was interred inside them, and it is possible that these represented a social elite of some kind. Conversely, if the funerary deposit had accumulated very swiftly, it is possible that everyone who died during this time had been introduced into the mortuary facility (Saville et al. 1987: 117). A series of Bayesian analyses on human remains from long barrows and cairns shine some light on these issues. Despite the evidence that monuments that were morphologically similar to each other were being built over hundreds of years, the deposition of skeletal material at each was of quite short duration. At sites such as Wayland's Smithy and West Kennet, all of the bodies and body parts were introduced into the chamber areas in no more than one or two generations (Whittle et al. 2007: 133). At Hazleton North in Gloucestershire, the burials are estimated to have accumulated over a period of 30 to 65 years. However, it is possible that the period was as little as five to twenty years if some of the stray funerary elements from the chambers represented 'ancestral' remains that had been brought to the site from elsewhere, already in a skeletal state (Meadows et al. 2007: 6).

The implication of this new information is that earthen long barrows and chambered long cairns were not 'cemeteries', in the sense of formal disposal areas that had been set aside for the burial of the dead over protracted periods.

Instead, they were locations at which a distinct episode of interment took place, lasting for a period ranging between a single year and as much as a century. Thereafter, it appears that these sites continued to be venerated, as they were still visited, and offerings of various kinds deposited in and around them. The finite character of funerary practice suggests that the persons who were laid out in these monuments were house ancestors, the founding generations who brought the community into being, and who were subsequently venerated by their descendants. The basis for their inclusion was not necessarily that they represented members of a group, but simply that they had lived and died at a time when a bounded social group was being brought into being, and that they thereafter served as the progenitors from whom future generations traced their descent. In a sense, it may be a mistake to imagine that the tombs and barrows were built to honour these dead. Rather, their presence lent legitimacy to the monument as a durable signifier of collective identity.

Conclusion

Halls and houses were a distinctive development during the very first phase of the Neolithic in Britain. People who were adopting domesticated plants and animals and using new forms of material culture, including prestige goods, found themselves in conflict with the established norms of hunter-gatherer society. The accumulation of collective wealth and prestige was incompatible with sharing and social levelling mechanisms. The formation of bounded and exclusive corporate groups was the means by which this contradiction could be overcome, and large timber halls were the innovation by which the transformation was effected. However, it appears that the process was short-lived. In each region, timber halls belong to the first century or two of the Neolithic, and they then declined (Whittle, Healy and Bayliss 2011: 840). But this decline was matched by a complementary growth in the numbers of mortuary monuments. Although some of these can be very early in date, they generally became more numerous shortly after the disappearance of the halls.

It was not quite that long barrows and megalithic tombs 'replaced' timber halls, so much as that they did a more restricted range of things in a more emphatic manner. Rather than being dwelling-places, meeting-places, places for subsistence activities, places of ritual and social foci, mortuary monuments were massively durable symbols of collective identity and containers for the founding generations. As the continental innovations of the Neolithic began to be 'bedded down' and adapted to the insular context, it may be that these became a more suitable kind of 'house' for Neolithic societies.

References

Atkinson, R. J. C. 1968 Old mortality: some aspects of burial and population in Neolithic England. In: J. Coles & D. D. A. Simpson (eds.) *Studies in Ancient Europe*, 83-94. Edinburgh, Edinburgh University Press.

Barclay, G. J., Brophy, K. and McGregor, G. 2002 Claish, Stirling: an early Neolithic structure in its context. *Proceedings of the Society of Antiquaries of Scotland* 132, 65-137.

Beck, R. A. 2007 The durable house: material, metaphor, and structure. In: R. A. Beck (ed.) *The Durable House: House Society Models in Archaeology*, 3–24. Carbondale, Center for Archaeological Investigations.

Bird-David, N. 1990 The giving environment: another perspective on the economic system of gatherer-hunters. Current Anthropology 31, 189-196.

Booth, P., Champion, T., Glass, H., Garwood, P., Munby, J. and Reynolds, A, 2011 *On Track: The archaeology of the Channel Tunnel Rail Link in Kent.* Oxford, Oxford Wessex Archaeology.

Bradley, R. J. 1987 Flint technology and the character of Neolithic settlement. In: A. Brown and M. R. Edmonds (eds.) *Lithic Analysis and Later British Prehistory*, 181-186. Oxford, British Archaeological Reports 162.

Bradley, R. J. 1996 Long houses, long barrows and Neolithic enclosures. *Journal of Material Culture* 1, 239-56.

Brophy, K. 2007 From big house to cult house: Early Neolithic timber halls in Scotland. *Proceedings of the Prehistoric Society* 73, 75-96.

Carsten, J. and Hugh-Jones, S. 1995 Introduction. In: J. Carsten and S. Hugh-Jones (eds.) *About the House: Lévi-Strauss and Beyond*, 1-46. Cambridge, Cambridge University Press.

Davidson, J. L. and Henshall, A. S. 1989 *The Chambered Cairns of Orkney: An Inventory of the Structures and their Contents.* Edinburgh, Edinburgh University Press.

Fox, J. J. 1993 Memories of Ridgepoles and Crossbeams: The Categorical Foundations of a Rotinese Cultural Design. In: J.J. Fox (ed.) *Inside Austronesian Houses: Perspectives on Domestic Designs for Living*, 140-79. Canberra, Australian National University.

Gillespie, S. 2000 Beyond kinship: an introduction. In: R. A. Joyce and S. D. Gillespie (eds.) *Beyond Kinship: Social and Material Reproduction in House Societies*, 1-21. Philadelphia,University of Pennsylvania Press.

Gillespie, S. 2007 When is a house? In: R. Beck (ed.) *The Durable House: House Society Models in Archaeology*, 25-50. Carbondale, Centre for Archaeological Investigations.

Grogan, E. 2004 The implications of Irish Neolithic houses. In: I. A. G. Shepherd and G. J. Barclay (eds.)

Scotland in Ancient Europe, 91-102. Edinburgh, Society of Antiquaries of Scotland.

Hodder, I. R. 1984 Burials, house, women and men in the European Neolithic. In: D. Miller and C. Tilley (eds.) *Ideology, Power and Prehistory*, 51-68. Cambridge, Cambridge University Press.

Hodder, I. 2006 *Catal Höyük: The Leopard's Tale*. London, Thames and Hudson.

Jones, G. and Rowley-Conwy, P. 2007 On the importance of cereal cultivation in the British Neolithic. In: S. College and J. Conolly (eds.) *The Origins and Spread of Domestic Plants in Southwest Asia and Europe*, 391-420. Walnut Creek, West Coast Press.

Kelly, R. L. 1995 The *Foraging Spectrum: Diversity in Hunter-gatherer Lifeways*. Washington, Smithsonian.

Kendrik, J. 1995 Excavation of a Neolithic enclosure and an Iron Age settlement at Douglasmuir, Angus. *Proceeding of the Society of Antiquaries of Scotland* 125, 29-67.

Kenney, J. 2008 Recent excavations at Parc Bryn Cegin, Llandygai, near Bangor, North Wales. *Archaeologia Cambrensis* 157, 9-142.

Kinnes, I. 1975 Monumental function in British Neolithic burial practices. *World Archaeology* 7, 16-28.

Kirby, M. 2011 *Lockerbie Academy: Neolithic and Early Historic Timber Halls, A Bronze Age Cemetery, an Undated Enclosure and a Post-Medieval Corn-Drying Kiln in South-West Scotland*. Edinburgh, Scottish Archaeological Internet Report 46.

Kirch, P. V. 2000 Temples as 'holy houses': the transformation of ritual architecture in traditional Polynesian societies. In: R. A. Joyce and S. D. Gillespie (eds.) *Beyond Kinship: Social and Material Reproduction in House Societies*, 103-14. Philadelphia, University of Pennsylvania Press.

Larsson, M. and Rzepecki, S. 2003 Pottery, houses and graves. The earliest TRB culture in Southern Sweden and Central Poland. *Lund Archaeological Review* 2003/4, 1-21.

Last, J. 1996 Neolithic houses - a central European perspective. In: T. C. Darvill and J. S. Thomas (eds.) *Neolithic Houses in Northwest Europe and Beyond*, 27-40. Oxford: Oxbow.

Lévi-Strauss, C. 1982 *The Way of the Masks*. Vancouver, University of British Columbia Press.

Lynch, F. M. and Musson, C. 2004 A prehistoric and early medieval complex at Llandegai, near Bangor, North Wales. *Archaeologia Cambrensis* 150, 17-142.

Marole, C. 1989 Le village Michelsberg des Hautes Chanvières à Mairy (Ardennes). I: Etude préliminaire des principales structures. *Gallia Préhistoire* 31, 93-117.

Meadows, J., Barclay, A. and Bayliss, A. 2007 A Short Passage of Time: the Dating of the Hazleton Long Cairn Revisited. *Cambridge Archaeological Journal* 17, S1, 45-64.

Murray, H. K., Murray, J. C. and Fraser, S. 2009 *A Tale of Unknown Unknowns: A Mesolithic Pit Alignment and a Neolithic Timber Hall at Warren Field, Crathes, Aberdeenshire*. Oxford, Oxbow.

Nichols, K. 2013 Southern England's first housing development. *Wessex Archaeology Online*. http://www.wessexarch.co.uk/blogs/news/2013/03/05/southern-england%E2%80%99s-first-housing-development

Peterson, N. 1993 Demand sharing: reciprocity and the pressure for generosity among foragers. *American Anthropologist* 95, 860–874.

Pryor, F. M. M. 1974 *Excavation at Fengate, Peterborough, England: The First Report*. Toronto, Royal Ontario Museum Archaeology Monograph 3.

Ralston, I. M. B. 1982 A timber hall at Balbridie Farm. *Aberdeen University Review* 168, 238-49.

Rosman, A. and Rubel, P. G. 1971 *Feasting with Mine Enemy: Rank and Exchange among Northwest Coast Societies*. Prospect Heights, Waveland.

Rowley-Conwy, P. 2000 Through a taphonomic glass, darkly: the importance of cereal cultivation in prehistoric Britain. In S. Stallibrass and J. Huntley (eds), *Taphonomy and interpretation*, 43-53. Oxford, Oxbow.

Rowley-Conwy, P. 2004 How the west was lost: a reconsideration of agricultural origins in Britain, Ireland, and southern Scandinavia. *Current Anthropology* 45s, 83-113.

Saville, A., Gowlett, J. and Hedges, R. E. M. 1987 Radiocarbon dates from the chambered tomb at. Hazleton (Glos.): a chronology for Neolithic collective burial. *Antiquity* 61, 108-119.

Sheridan, A. 2008 'Halls', houses and 'huts' in the carinated bowl Neolithic of Britain and Ireland: origins, identity, symbolism and functionality. Paper presented at the World Archaeological Congress, Dublin.

Sheridan, A. 2010 The Neolithization of Britain and Ireland: the big picture. In: B. Finlayson and G. Warren (eds.) *Landscapes in Transition*, 89-105. Oxford, Oxbow.

Sissons, J. 2010 Building a house society: the reorganisation of Maori communities around meeting houses. *Journal of the Royal Anthropological Institute* 16, 372-86.

Smith, I. F. 1971 Causewayed enclosures. In: D. D. A. Simpson (ed.) *Economy and Settlement in Neolithic and Early Bronze Age Britain and Europe*, 89-112. Leicester, Leicester University Press.

Smyth, J. 2010 The house and group identity in the Irish Neolithic. *Proceedings of the Royal Irish Academy* 111C, 1-31.

Sollas, W. J. 1911 *Ancient Hunters and Their Modern Representatives*. London, MacMillan.

Thomas, J. S. 2007 *Place and Memory: Excavations at Pict's Knowe, Holywood and Holm. Oxford, Oxbow.*

Thomas, J. S. 2013 *The Birth of Neolithic Britain.* Oxford, Oxford University Press.

Topping, P. 1996 Structure and ritual in the Neolithic house: some examples from Britain and Ireland. In: T. Darvill and J. Thomas (eds.) *Neolithic Houses in Northwest Europe and Beyond*, 157-70. Oxford, Oxbow.

Waterson, R. 1990 T*he Living House: An Anthropology of Architecture in South-East Asia.* London, Thames and Hudson.

Waterson, R. 1995 Houses and hierarchies in island southeast Asia. In: J. Carsten and S. Hugh-Jones (eds.) *About the House: Lèvi-Srauss and Beyond,* 47-68. Cambridge, Cambridge University Press.

Weiner, A. 1992 *Inalienable Possessions: the Paradox of Keeping-While-Giving.* Berkeley, University of California Press.

Whitley, J. 2002 Too many ancestors. *Antiquity* 76, 119-26.

Whittle, A. 1991 Wayland's Smithy, Oxfordshire: excavations at the Neolithic tomb in 1962-3. *Proceedings of the Prehistoric Society* 57, 61-102.

Whittle, A., Barclay, A., Bayliss, A., McFadyen, L., Schulting, R. and Wysocki, M. 2007 Building for the dead: events, processes and changing worldviews from the thirty-eighth to the thirty-fourth centuries Cal. BC in southern Britain. *Cambridge Archaeological Journal* 17 (supp.), 123-47.

Whittle, A., Healy, F. and Bayliss, A. 2011 *Gathering Time: Dating the Early Neolithic Enclosures of Southern Britain and Ireland.* Oxford, Oxbow.

Woodburn, J. 1982 Egalitarian Societies. *Man* 3, 431-451.

Chapter 2

The Empty House: Early Neolithic Settlement Structure in Southern Scandinavia

Mats Larsson

Linnaeus University, Sweden

This essay is about the Early Neolithic settlement structure in S. Scandinavia and the changes that occurred between the late Mesolithic and the Early Neolithic. There is a marked difference between the settlements of the two periods; sites full of debris and implements characterize the late Mesolithic while the houses in the Early Neolithic are more or less clean. However, outside the houses we find cultural layers and pits full of waste and implements.

Keywords: Late Mesolithic, Early Neolithic, houses, waste, Southern Scandinavia

Introduction

During the last couple of decades our understanding of the Neolithic settlement structure and how people used their landscape in southern Scandinavia has fundamentally changed. The foundation for this marked change is to a large degree based on the development of contract archaeology. Large-scale excavations, stretching in several cases over years, have given us evidence for complex Neolithic settlements that was unheard of only a decade ago.

In this article I will discuss Neolithic settlement structure, focussing on the spatial arrangement of settlements, especially the spacing of house structures, culture layers and different types of pits. I will argue that there is a fundamental break in the way people perceived the world during the late Mesolithic and the Earliest Neolithic in Southern Scandinavia and elsewhere.

The end of Late Mesolithic settlements

The large coastal sites inhabited during the Ertebølle period (c.5400-4000 BC[1]) were more or less abandoned as permanent settlements after having been in use for about 1000 years. For instance, the Björnsholm shell midden in northern Jutland was in use from c. 5050-4050 BC (Andersen 1991). The only substantial features found in the midden were hearths: there were no traces of huts, pits or postholes. Yet late Mesolithic houses and huts have recently been excavated at Tågerup in western Scania. The presence of Ertebølle pottery from House III suggests a late Ertebølle date (c. 4600-4000 BC) (Cronberg 2001; Hallgren 2004).

An interesting fact is that no elaborate ceremonial activities are documented in the Ertebølle Culture. Burials are simple, although the graves are sometimes richly furnished. Almost all burials – Vedbæk/Bøgebakken, Skateholm – are from the *early* Ertebølle Culture, c. 5000 BC.

Regional differences have also been observed within the Ertebølle Culture, with pointed based vessels in Jutland, Funen and Zeeland and vessels with tap-shaped bases on Scania and Bornholm (Jennbert 1984; Andersen 2011; Vang Petersen 1984; 2001). There seems to be a regional border at Öresund. Another border is observed at the Storebælt, which is based on the distribution of T-Shaped antler axes (Jutland) and Limhamn axes (Zeeland and Scania).

The Early Neolithic

Pit sites

These regional differences seem to disappear during the Oxie phase, when the same vessels are found all over Southern Scandinavia. A few centuries later, differences in the vessels and their ornaments are observed in Jutland (Volling), Zeeland (Svaleklint) and Scania (Svenstorp), thus showing the same regional pattern and borders at Storebælt and Öresund, which were observed during the Ertebølle Culture.

In all of this we can see people as active agents in the way in which the settlement sites, the farming plots and so on were chosen. In the earliest part of the Early Neolithic new areas inland, away from the Late Mesolithic sites, located on sandy soils and close to water were preferentially chosen. Not that many inland sites have been excavated so the expansion is mainly shown in the distribution of archaeological stray finds, such as pointed butted flint axes. These clearly indicate a huge potential of many undiscovered Early Neolithic inland sites located on easily-worked arable soils (Sørensen and Karg 2012).

People also mixed their material culture bringing in both new items while still preserving some old ones. In a way this is a form of 'creolisation' (Cohen & Toninato 2010:1 ff). The existence of transverse arrowheads, flake axes and singular core axes has been noted and discussed as evidence for a close connection between the people of the late Ertebølle and the earliest Funnel Beaker culture, the Oxie group (M Larsson 1984). This close connection actually only exists in the earliest Neolithic (Oxie/Svenstorp) and is obviously gone in the later stages (Bellevuegården/Virum).

People thus developed a sense of group identity as well as a self-identity. This might be seen in the development of the Oxie group pottery discussed above.

What I would like to suggest in the following that people in the Early Neolithic changed their perception of the surrounding world and this is visible in the arrangement of settlement sites. There is a huge difference if we look at some late Mesolithic structures like Bredasten and Tågerup in the way that these were arranged and used compared to the early Neolithic house sites (M Larsson 1986; Cronberg 2001). The Mesolithic houses are full of flint waste, pottery, bone and so forth while the early Neolithic ones are kept almost completely clean. Why this is so is discussed below.

In the period preceding the discovery of the first long houses most of the then known early Funnelbeaker (TRB)

sites were made up of different types of pits, sometimes in the hundreds, and little else. Several of these sites were situated on ridges or small hills in the undulating landscape. These pits were frequently recut and reused, and contained large amounts of flint debris as well as unused implements like flake axes, flake scrapers and in some cases even complete vessels or axes. So why discard complete vessels and implements? We cannot just see the pits as waste pits but as evidence for something much more profound. The notion that we here have what has been called 'structured deposits' is maybe not that easy to uphold. In most cases there is no obvious pattern for the placement of the artefacts in the pits (see Figure 1).

Some of the pits with complete axes or vessels have been re-interpreted though, as ritual pits (Karsten 1994; Andersson 2003:169; Rogius *et al* 2003).

These pits and their content might be interpreted as an example of what is called structured deposits. The term describes the ways in which material culture is organised at the time it is deposited in the ground (Bradley 2000:118). To perform rituals were an important part of the structuration

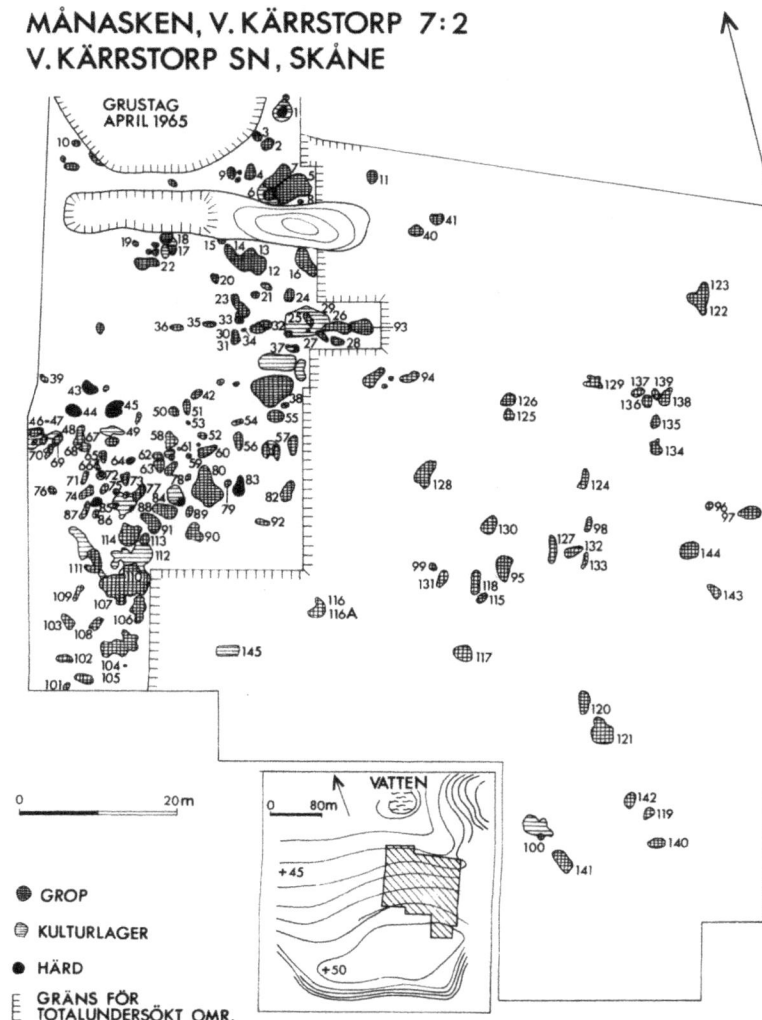

Figure 1: Example of a typical "pit site" (Larsson 1984).

of society and they helped people to not only connect and re-connect with the ancestors, but also with the future.

Ritual deposits have often been interpreted 'as a new aspect' within Neolithic features, pits, destruction of artifacts etc. In the Mesolithic there are plenty of examples of artifacts (ornamented antler axes, stray finds of human bones, unused Limhamn axes or shoe-last-axes) found in Late Ertebølle and Early Neolithic kitchenmiddens/lake shore sites, which could be interpreted as ritual depositions. There is obviously a continuation in the deposition of artefacts between the late Mesolithic and the Earliest Neolithic but the use of new areas away from the coast indicates new habits and a changed view of the world.

Something of the same picture emerges in Ireland and Britain. Pits are found alone or in some cases in the hundreds. In Ireland pits are sometimes associated with houses as well. In Britain they are in a few cases associated with both the large EN timber halls but also with smaller houses. (Hillary, K. et al 2009; Chaffey, G. & Brook, E. 2012)

For example Ireland's several Neolithic houses have been excavated during the last decade and the evidence points towards some sort of settlement agglomeration with clusters of two or more houses in contemporary use (Grogan 1996:56 f; Cooney 2000:62 ff)).

As Darvill (2012:38) asked a couple of years ago 'There is the question of how these pits and shafts were used and what they were for'. In later years there have been a lot of questions asked, as well as some plausible answers. Richard Bradley has said, referring to Britain that these artefacts were being returned to the elements from which they were formed (Bradley 2000:131). According to Julian Thomas (1999:72 f) the digging of pits is associated with feasting and the items deposited in the pits are a sort of remembrance of these feasts. By bringing together different elements, the sites eventually became a microcosm of the landscape as a whole.

Houses

Most of the early excavations that mention houses or huts in Scandinavia are hard to interpret and most of the Danish ones were also to a large degree discarded in an article some years ago (Eriksen & Madsen 1984). Classic examples of re-interpretations are Barkaer and Stengade in Denmark. Both sites were interpreted as long houses but were later convincingly re-interpreted as being Long Barrows. In both cases they were erected on top of earlier settlement sites, thus marking a historical connection to the particular area, indicating that the placement of the monument was deliberate and used as territorial markers in the landscape.

Probably the first time a proper long house was excavated was in 1986 at Mossby in southern part of Scania (M. Larsson 1992). The Mossby house, now a 'type site', was c 12m by 6m in size, with three large postholes in the centre

to support the roof. The remains of the wall were made up of rather shallow postholes and the form of the house was elliptical. A layer consisting of sooty sand and occupational debris covered an area of about 70m^2, largely within the walls and fitting the shape of a floor depression. There were few artefacts, but these included cord-decorated pottery and flint waste. Some ten meters east of the house a 280m^2 area was excavated, rich in occupation debris including pottery and flint. Beneath the debris pits, patches of soot and postholes were found, but it was not possible to delimit any houses in this area (The pottery found in the layer and in the pits was identical to that found in the layer that covered the house. The five available radiocarbon dates are all in the range of 4100-3900 BC, putting them among the earliest in Southern Scandinavia (see Figure 2).

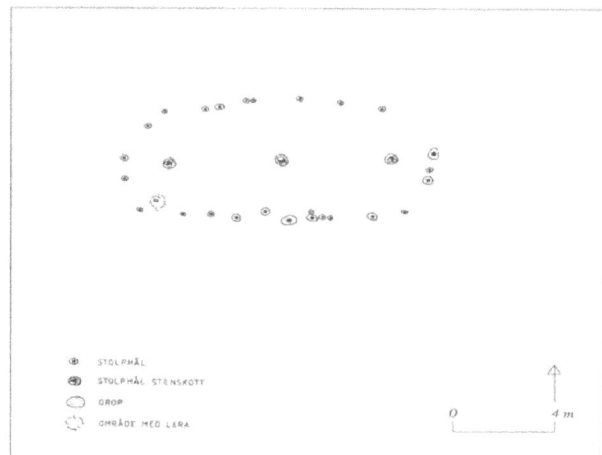

Figure 2: The Early Neolithic Mossby house. Stolphål=posthole, grop=pit område med lera=claypit (Larsson 1992).

Large-scale rescue excavations have for many years been important in bringing forward new material. In connection with the extensive excavations performed in western Scania for a new railway at the end of the 1990s a large number of early Neolithic settlements were excavated. On several of these sites houses have been found. In the vicinity of the village of Dagstorp outside the city of Lund, on slightly undulating farmland along a river valley, here a large number of Neolithic houses have been excavated (Andersson 2003; 2004; Svensson 2003). The settlements make up a sequence from the earliest Neolithic to the central part of the Middle Neolithic. 17 of the 36 houses currently known from Early and Middle Neolithic in southern Scandinavia are Mossby-type houses, and these can be dated from the earliest Neolithic up until the early Middle Neolithic. The size of these buildings varies between 36 and 128m^2. The large-scale excavations have demonstrated that settlements could be very large: up to several thousand square metres. We can also note that the houses, as Mossby, were more or less cleaned out. Outside the houses, beneath a culture layer, several pits were excavated with pottery and flint (see Figure 3).

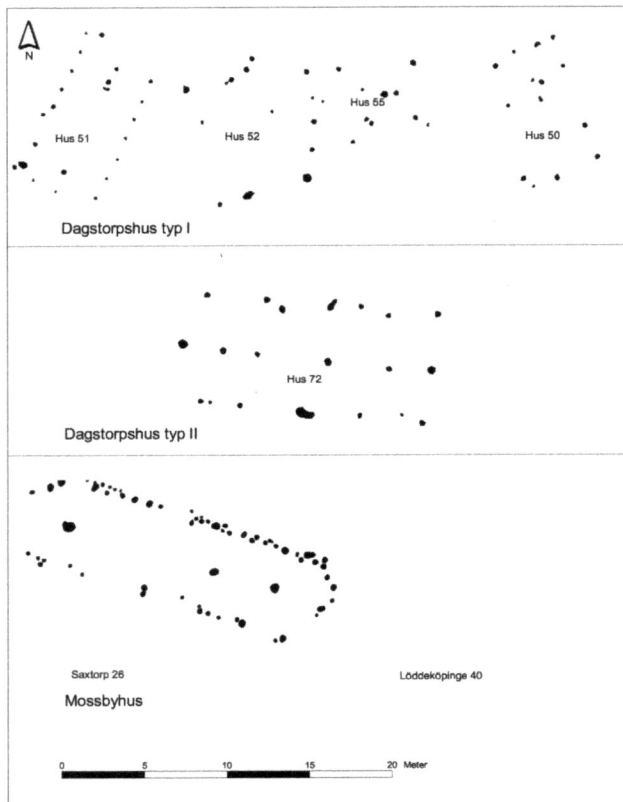

Figure 3: Early Neolithic housetypes (Andersson 2003).

good examples of how the sites were organised. We can discern the same pattern in other parts of Scandinavia too (M Larsson 1994; Carlsson 2004; Stenvall 2007)(see Figure 4).

In the western part of the county of Östergötland a settlement dating to the early Neolithic as well as the iron age was excavated (M Larsson 1994). The early Neolithic house was 9x4m large and had one row of roof supporting posts. The roof supporting construction was made up three posts. Based on sherds found in the postholes of the house it dated to the later part of the period c. 3400/3300 BC. The finds were rather sparse and were made up of pottery, quartz and some flint. About 20 meters from the house itself a rather small cultural layer was excavated. In this the same type of pottery as well as some flint and quartz were found. In the vicinity of the house some small pits were also found. We might see the cultural layer and the pits as the activity area of the house.

The site at Kimstad was excavated in 2006. At the site a 15.5 x 6.5m large house of the (Figure 5) Mossby type was excavated (Stenvall 2007). A cultural layer, interpreted as a trampled floor, was found between the wall posts. In a corner of the house a 4.9 x 2.2m large pit was excavated. It contained a lot of early Neolithic Funnelbeaker pottery. Material from the pit is radiocarbon dated to 3790-3630 BC. It was interpreted as a storage pit.

At all sites mentioned above a single house of the Mossby type was excavated. The houses were more or less empty, obviously cleaned out, while an area with pits, and/or cultural layer was found close by. In the pits and culture layers pottery, flint and stone were found that clearly dates the sites to the Early Neolithic (see Figure 6).

If we go further north to Eastern Sweden we have more or less the same picture. In the district of Östergötland several Early Funnelbeaker sites have been excavated during the last decades and they all show the same picture; more or less empty houses and surrounding areas with culture layers or pits. Sites like Brunneby, Bleckenstad and Kimstad are

Figure 4: Reconstruction of an Early Neolithic settlement (Larsson 2012).

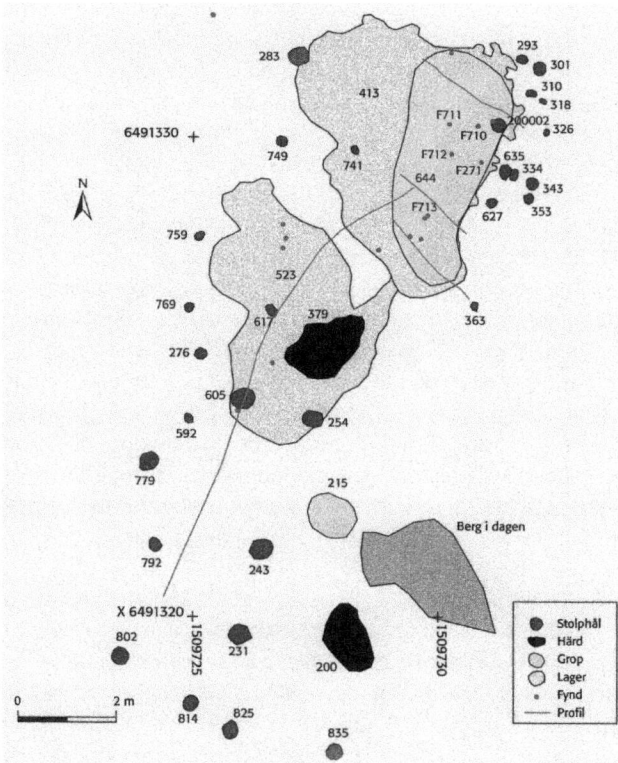

Figure 5: Early Neolithic settlement at Kimstad, Eastern Middle Sweden. Red=posthole yellow=pit black=hearth greenish=culture layer (Stenvall 2007).

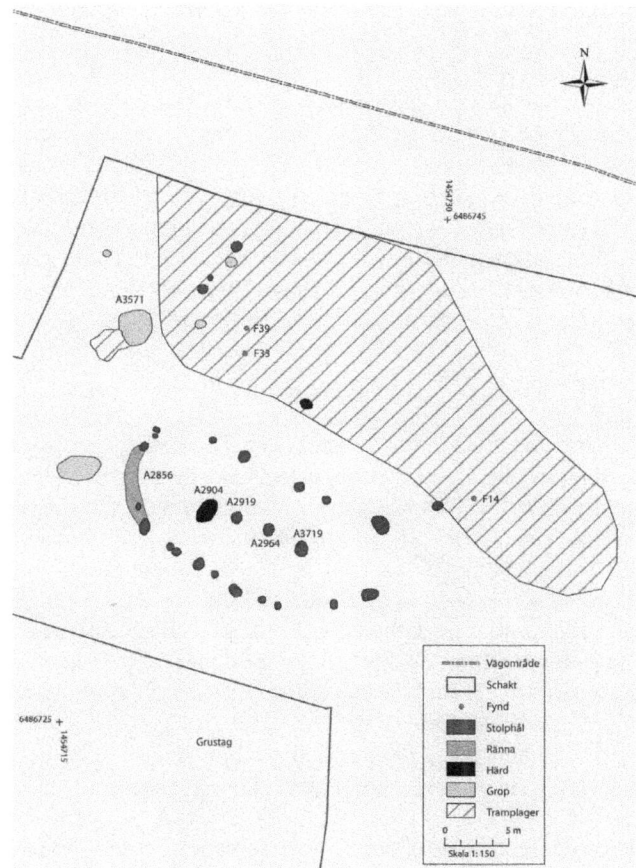

Figure 6: Early Neolithic settlement at Nyckelby, Eastern Middle Sweden. Red=posthole yellow=pit black=hearth stripped=culture layer (Helander 2011).

Further north at sites like Skumparberget, Skogsmossen and Fågelbacken we have single houses surrounded by activity areas with pits and cultural layers. The site Skogsmossen is situated in the county of Västmanland in eastern Middle Sweden (Hallgren 1997). During the course of the investigation a house of the Mossby type was found. It was rather fragmented though. The area with the house was initially seen as a stone free area with few or no finds. North of this area a 10 x 10m large cultural layer was excavated. In this a lot of finds were found. This area has been interpreted as an activity area (Hallgren 1997:101). The house itself is rather incomplete but the interpretation of the site with house and activity areas are conclusive. There is also evidence for a votive fen in which a large number of vessels were found. Fågelbacken is different as we here have evidence for a cemetery with cremation graves as well (Hallgren 2008). The site was located on an island. At the site four D-shaped huts have been excavated. If we put the huts together we obviously have a Mossby type house. The dating of the site falls between 3800 and 3600 BC. The settlement site has a clear spatial structure and has been interpreted as a gathering place for a number of inland farming sites. The site was visited regularily over the year.

Settlement evidence from Denmark is similar. In many cases the excavated areas around the structures are too small to draw comparisons with the Swedish evidence (cf. Buus-Eriksen 1992), but there are exceptions, like the Mossby-type house excavated at Skraeppekaergård on Northern Zealand (Kaul 1997). Areas of occupation debris

(including pottery and flint) were situated 4-8m from the house and covered areas of 25 by 25m and 20 by 20m. In the last couple of years this has changed though. One such example is Ullerödgård on the Island of Zealand. The excavated area is very large, c 20, 000m2. The site could be divided into three areas; two separate areas with pits of various sizes and a large area in which a total number of 19 small houses were excavated. They are all two aisled houses of the Mossby type with 2-3 roof supporting posts. It is however difficult to with any certainty say if the houses are contemporary. Some of them overlap though. The site might have been in use for about 240-400 years in the earliest Neolithic (Rosenberg 2008).

In connection with excavations in the vicinity of the causewayed enclosure Sarup on the Island of Funen in the last decade some houses of the Mossby type have been excavated (Andersen 2009:25 ff). Interestingly enough two of the houses were found underneath long dolmens. Small amounts of sherds and flint were found in, or around the houses. No pits were found. Niels Andersen (2009:37) suggests that the Neolithic population very knowingly manipulated the waste material for use in other contexts, for example in enclosures or dolmens.

If we for a moment leave Scandinavia and have one more look at the settlement evidence from Britain there is one newly excavated site that is comparable to the

Scandinavian ones; Horton in Berkshire. (Chaffey and Brook 2012:200 ff). The rectangular house is dated to c 3800-3640 BC and is, if not devoid of finds, rather empty. Foundation gullies were excavated but gave very little in the way of artefacts. Inside the house a few pits that contained very fragmented pottery sherds were excavated. In addition to pottery, flint and stone, cereals were also found. About 25m NE of the house some pits with a lot of material culture was excavated. These pits are however younger than the house proper (Chaffey and Brook 2012:205 ff).

Discussion

What I have tried to put forward here is how people created a 'New World' that was very distinct from the preceding late Mesolithic. It is very obvious that there is a huge difference in the structuring of space between the late Mesolithic and the earliest Neolithic and this is seen throughout Southern Scandinavia as well as in Britain and Ireland. At a regional and community level the adoption of agriculture and other Neolithic traditions and practices, individual and collective motivations - reasons and justifications for doing things - must have been formulated into strategies by people who had a certain level of knowledge about their social and natural environment - 'knowledgeable social actors'.

How did then come about? This is something I am going to discuss further below.

How can, as Bhabba stated (1994:154), the question of authority, power and presence be studied in the material from the settlements of the earliest Neolithic? What does the obviously empty houses and the pit areas represent? These are some of the issues that I intend to explore further in the coming pages.

Tim Ingold (2000:193) in a discussion of temporality and landscape has written, 'In short, the landscape is the world as it is known to those who dwell therein, who inhabit its places and journey along the paths connecting them'. This he calls a 'taskscape'. The landscape is thus both agency and time embodied (Ingold 2000). As mentioned above Mesolithic man had of course both previously moved and dwelled in the landscape but it was now much more important to secure an identity and to make a lasting impact on the landscape.

The location of the settlement sites in the landscape and their relation with other sites is in this way very important. Information and stories regarding for example features in the landscape is in this way connected and in a way a mental landscape is created. In performing certain actions in a regular way a pattern is created in which rituals, different tasks and meeting become part of a cyclical story of the landscape.

Chris Tilley (1994:35) stated that to try and understand and interpret some of the similarities and differences in the relationship between people and the land, and the manner in which it is culturally constructed is of great importance for the understanding of the power and significance invested in a 'natural' environment. The building of a house, or a monument, involves an important change which significantly alters people's roles in the landscape and their view of it. 'Building' means transforming a place; a 'place for something' emerges. Myths are then woven about it and the place thus becomes historical (Thomas 1996:89). Buildings and placing might be thought of as a kind of naming process (Whittle 2002:195). Social structures have a dialectical relationship with human actions as structures are both the medium and the outcome of social practices (Parker Pearson and Richards 1994:3). This notion has rather elegantly been expressed by Matthew Johnson (1994:170) as follows 'Landscape is all about a sense of place; architecture is simultaneously a moulding of landscape and the expression of a cultural attitude towards it'.

The construction of a house, as well as the abandonment of it, can be seen as an important mechanism of social reproduction in both a temporal and an ancestral perspective. Ian Hoddder and Graig Cessford (2004) suggested in the case of Catal Hoyuk that consistencies in the organization and use of domestic space served to produce broadly shared social practices related to the politics of collective memory.

Possibly this also represents a shift from kinship-based to household-based societies (Levi-Strauss 1982:174), where the house constitutes a 'corporate body holding an estate that reproduces itself through the transmission of its name, goods, and titles' (Hodder and Cessford 2004:31).

The very nature of a house, or for that matter a monument, means that it can be very active in direct control over people, their access, movement and interaction in architectural space. Vicki Cummings (2002:107) has stated that the first monuments fitted into a landscape already filled with potent and symbolic places. The presence of monuments in the landscape began to transform peoples´ understanding of the world; in other words the beginning of the dualism between nature and culture. John Barrett has introduced the concept of inhabitation, or inhabiting a landscape, that involves an understanding of the landscape that involves earlier experiences (Barrett 1999:29).

There are obviously different opinions regarding the degree of ideological transformation and changes in the landscape at the Mesolithic and Neolithic transformation

The obvious spatial demarcation between activity areas and living areas seen at several sites like Mossby, Brunneby and many others can be interpreted in structural terms like for example clean/unclean and wild/tame. The houses were obviously kept clean and for example tool making was performed some distance from the house. Gosden (1994) distinguishes between the day-to-day activities of people, which were governed by habit, and the long term continuities expressed by monuments and similar structures. This he calls public time. This is a very useful concept when we look at the early Neolithic settlement system. It is rather obvious that if we look at the evidence discussed above there were some sort of 'rules' that governed people's use of space. Some areas, like the house, were kept clean while other areas were not.

Another issue of great importance is the interpretation of different activity areas, or lack of them, that we can distinguish on the sites themselves. We might assume that every task was undertaken in the 'correct' place and through time spatial meaning was created. We may in this context think about Niels Andersens notion that material culture was manipulated at the sites, as they according to him were brought somewhere else for example causewayed enclosures or megaliths. Here we can bring back the pit sites. There is a possibility that these sites represent exactly this. Material culture items in the form of pottery, flint and stone were brought to pits away from the house itself. This might have, in reference to things said above, been the 'correct' way of doing things. It was also a way for people to mark both their self identity as well as group identity. It created a sense of 'belonging' to a place or region and understanding of a new landscape.

This is what Bhabba said (1994:154) authority, power and presence was thus created.

References

Andersen. N. H. 2009. Sarupsområdet på Sydvestfyn i slutningen av 4. årtusendet f.Kr. In:Schülke, A. (ed.). *Plads og rum i tragbægerkulturen*. 25-45. Copenhagen, Det Kongelige Nordiske Oldskrifselskab.

Andersen, S. H. 1991. Björnsholm. A stratified Kökkenmödding on the Central Limfjord, North Jutland. *Journal of Danish Archaeology* 10, 59-96.

Andersen, S. H. 2011 *Kitchen middens and the early pottery of Denmark. Bericht der Römisch-Germanischen Kommission*, Band 89, 2008. Philipp von Zabern 2011, 193-215.

Andersson, M. 2003. *Skapa plats i landskapet. Tidig- och mellanneolitiska samhällen utmed två västskånska dalgångar*. Malmö, Acta Archaeologica Lundensia 8, 22.

Barrett, J. 1999. Chronologies of Landscape. In A. Ucko and R. Layton, (eds.) 21-30. *The Archaeology and Anthropology of Landscape. Shaping your landscape. One World Archaeology*. London, Routledge.

Bhabha, H. K. 1994. *The Location of Culture*. London, Routledge.

Bradley, R. 2000. *An archaeology of natural places*. New York, Routledge.

Buus-Eriksen, L. 1992. Ornehus på Stevens. Tidligneolitisk hustomt. *Aarbøger for Nordisk Oldkyndighed og Historie*, 1991, 7-19.

Carlsson, T. 2004. Neolitisk närvaro. En nästan fyndlös tidigneolitisk gård vid Bleckenstad i Ekeby socken, Östergötland. *Fornvännen* 99:1-8.

Chaffey, G. and Brook, E. 2012. Domesticity in the Neolithic: excavations at Kingsmead Quarry, Horton, Berkshire. In: H. Anderson-Whymark. and J. Thomas, (eds.). *Regional Perspectives on Neolithic Pit Deposition. Beyond the Mundane*, 200-216. Oxford, Oxbow Books.

Cooney, G. 2000. *Landscapes of Neolithic Ireland*. London, Routledge.

Cronberg, C. 2001. Husesyn. In: P. Karsten and B. Knarrström (eds.) *Tågerup specialstudier*. 82-154. Skånska spår-arkeologi längs Västkustbanan. Stockholm, Riksantikvarieämbetet.

Cummings, V. 2002. All cultural things: actual and conceptual monuments in the neolithic of western Britain. In C. Scarre (ed.) *Monuments and landscape in Atlantic Europe. Perception and society during the Neolithic and Early Bronze Age*. 107-122. London, Routledge

Darvill, T. 2012. Sounds from the underground: Neolithic ritual pits and pit-clusters on the Isle of Man and beyond In: H. Anderson-Whymark. and J. Thomas, (eds.). *Regional Perspectives on Neolithic Pit Deposition. Beyond the Mundane*, 29-42. Oxford, Oxbow Books.

Eriksen, P. and Madsen, T. 1984. Hanstedgård. A Settlement site from the Funnel Beaker culture. *Journal of Danish Archaeology* 3, 63-83.

Gosden, C. 1994. *Social being and time*. London, Blackwell.

Grogan, E. 1996. Neolithic houses in Ireland. In: T. Darvill, and J. Thomas (eds.) *Neolithic houses in Northwest Europe and beyond*, 41-60. Oxford, Oxbow.

Hallgren, F 1997. Skogsmossen, an early Neolithic settlement site and sacrificial fen in the northern borderland of the funnel-beaker culture. *Tor*, 49-111.

Hallgren, F. 2004. The introduction of ceramic technology around the Baltic Sea in the 6th Millennium. In: H. Knutsson (ed.) *Coast to Coast. Arrival*. Coast to coast books no. 10. Uppsala, 123-143.

Hallgren, F. 2008. *Identitet i praktik. lokala, regionala och överregionala sociala sammanhang inom nordlig trattbägarkultur*. Uppsala.

Helander, A. 2011. *En tidigneolitisk boplats vid Nyckelby*. UV Rapport 2011, 146. Riksantikvarieämbetet.

Hillary, K., Murray, J., Murray, C. and Fraser, M. S. 2009. *A tale of the unknown unknowns. A Mesolithic pit alignment and a Neolithic timber hall at Warren Field, Crathes, Aberdeenshire*. Oxford, Oxbow.

Hodder, I. and Cessford, C. 2004. Daily Practice and Social Memory at Catal Höyuk. *American Antiquity* 69, 17-40.

Ingold, T. 2000. *The Perception of the Environment. Essays in livelihood, dwelling and skill.* London, Routledge.

Jennbert, K. 1984. Den produktiva gåvan. *Acta Archaeologica Lundensia* 4, 16. Lund.

Johnson, M. H. 1994. Ordering houses; creating narratives. In: M. Parker-Pearson and. C. Richards (eds.) *Architecture and Order. Approaches to social space,* 170-178. London: Routledge.

Kaul, F. 1997. Et tidligneolitisk hus ved Skrœppekœrgård, Nordssjœlland. *Aarbøger for Nordisk Oldkyndighed og Historie* 1996, 7-21.

Larsson, M. 1984. Tidigneolitikum i Sydvästskåne. Kronologi och bosättningsmönster. *Acta Archaeologica Lundensia* 4, 17. Lund.

Larsson, M. 1986. Bredasten-An Early Ertebølle Site with Dwelling Structure in South Scania. *Meddelanden från Lunds universitets historiska museum* 1985-1986, 5-25.

Larsson, M. 1992. The Early and Middle Neolithic Funnel Beaker Culture in the Ystad Area. Economic and Social Change 3100-2300 BC. In L. Larsson, J. Callmer and B. Stjernquist, (eds.) *The Archaeology of the Cultural Landscape.* 17-91 Acta Archaeologica Lundensia 4, 19.Lund.

Larsson, M.,1994 *Ett tidigneolitiskt hus från Brunneby i Östergötland.* Arkeologi i Sverige 3, Stockholm.

Larsson, M. 2007. I was walking through the wood the other day. Man and landscape during the late Mesolithic and early Neolithic in Scania, Southern Sweden In: B. Hårdh, K. Jennbert and D. Olausson (ed) *On the road. Studies in honour of Lars Larsson,* 212-217. Stockholm, Almqwist and Wiksell International.

Larsson, M. 2012. *En ny värld. Yngre stenålder i Sverige.* Studentlitteratur. Lund.

Lévi-Strauss, C. 1982. *The Way of the Masks.* London, Johnatan Cape.

Nielsen, P. O. 2009 Den tidligneolitiske bosættelse på Bornholm. In: A. Schülke, (ed.) *Plads og Rum i Tragtbœgerkulturen.* Nordiske Fortidsminder Serie C, Copenhagen, 9-24.

Parker-Pearson, M. and Richards, C. 1994. Architecture and order: Spatial representation and archaeology. In M. Parker-Pearson and C. Richards (eds.) *Architecture and Order. Approaches to social space.* 38-73. London, Routledge.

Petersen-Vang, P.1984. Chronological and regional variation in the Late Mesolithic. *Journal of Danish Archaeology* 3, 21-45.

Petersen-Vang, P. 2001 Grisby – en fangstboplads fra Ertebølletid på Bornholm. In: O. Lass Jensen., S. A. Sørensen and K. M. Hansen (eds.) *Danmarks jægerstenalder – status og perspektiver,* 161-174. Hørsholm.

Rogius, K., Eriksson, N. and Wennberg, T. 2003. Buried Refuse? Interpreting Early Neolithic Pits. *Lund Archaeological Review* 2001: 7-19.

Rosenberg, A. 2008. *Ullerødgård.* Rapport Folkemuseet, Hillerød.

Stenvall, J. 2007. *En Vråboplats I Kimstad.* UV öst Rapport 2007:45. Lund, Riksantikvarieämbetet.

Svensson, M. 2003. *I det neolitiska rummet. Skånska spår-arkeologi längs Västkustbanan.* Lund, Riksantikvarieämbetet.

Sørensen, L. and Karg, S. 2012 The expansion of agrarian societies towards the North – new evidence for agriculture during the Mesolithic/Neolithic transition in Southern Scandinavia. *Journal of Archaeological Science* 51, 98-112.

Thomas, J. 1996. *Time, Culture and Identity. An Interpretative Archaeology.* London, Routledge.

Thomas, J. 1999. *Understanding the Neolithic: a revised second edition of Rethinking the Neolithic .* Rev. 2. ed. London, Routledge.

Tilley, C. 1994. *Phenomenology of Landscape.* London, Berg.

Whittle, A. 2002. *The Archaeology of People. Dimensions of Neolithic life.* London, Routledge.

Chapter 3

When Artefacts Can't Speak: Towards a New Understanding of British Early Neolithic Timber Structures

Jolene Debert

Mount Royal University, Canada

This paper will examine the enigma that are the rectangular timber framed structures of the early Neolithic from Britain. Recent discoveries, through both research and developer funded projects, have significantly increased the number and variety of these buildings. However, they remain relatively rare and confined in date to the very early part of the Neolithic - the initial Neolithic (4050-3650 BC). There is mass disagreement about the meaning and function of these structures; few artefacts have been recovered associated with the structures. As such, those seeking the function and meaning of the structures have proposed multiple equally supported interpretations. I would suggest that not only is the question 'What was the ultimate function of these structures?' flawed, but our concentration on what artefacts have been recovered blinds us from the more interesting immaterial. This paper examines these structures not in terms of receptacles for materials, but as stages for multiple complementing and disparate performances. The structures were digitally reconstructed and the resulting space was examined. Using these models I hope to develop an alternative understanding of the British initial Neolithic where the actors are placed back on their stage.

Keywords: Early Neolithic, timber structures, structured space, movement through space, British Neolithic

Introduction

The British Neolithic started in the 4th millennium BC and stretches for roughly two thousand years (Fairen-Jimenez 2007: 84; Tilley 2007). This period can be seen as a microcosm of cultural change as several major innovations date to this period: the start of agriculture, stone monument building, manufacture of pottery, the development or refinement of polished stone industries and the early Neolithic timber structure to name just a few. These were undoubtedly the material manifestation of profound ideological changes (Bradley 2005; Thomas 1991; Warren 2009).

People's implicit knowledge, habitual practice and material culture can be seen as forms of cultural inheritance that are passed between generations and are modified by innovation. In this process materials are not merely the outcomes of human action, but the media through which human projects are propagated. As such, the forms of archaeological evidence available to us are not simply the ordered residues of acts, but were integral to the changing traditions that we seek to investigate. The architecture built within this cultural framework is therefore bound to the community just as it is representative of its identity. This paper seeks to use the architecture in place of the material culture, which is lacking at the structures, to develop a robust discussion of created space within the structures.

The ways in which people negotiate new identities and integrate new customs through reference to the past becomes tangible through material culture. The material world is one context in which personhood and identity are understood, created, expressed and transformed. Cultural values and tradition are animated through their interactions with the material world; it is only through this dynamic relationship that a generational dialogs can ensue. The space in which these actions take place informs customs and shapes its very sense of place. The space can be the natural landscape, the built environment, or more likely a highly intertwined combination. It is this created space that will be discussed below, as the material culture of the timber structures remains silent or at least quiet.

Timber Structures

The timber structures cluster in date between 4050-3650 BC, what will hitherto be referred to as the initial Neolithic, and have numerous physical and material culture similarities (Barclay et al. 2002; Brophy 2007; Debert 2010; Garton 1991; Hayden and Stafford 2006; Hey and Bell 2000; Kenney and Davidson 2006; Lynch and Musson 2004; Ralston 1982). The length of the structures vary roughly from 30-10 m and from 15-5 m in width (Debert 2010). There is also internal division of space within the structures and evidence to suggest that the structures were roofed. The possibility of a first floor has been suggested in the majority of the structures. Construction methods involved oak posts often with wall trenches. Walls were constructed often using wattle and daub, plank techniques or a combination (Barclay et al. 2002; Brophy 2007; Debert 2010; Garton 1991; Hayden and Stafford 2006; Hey and Bell 2000; Kenney and Davidson 2006; Lynch and Musson 2004; Ralston 1982).

The structures are not grouped into villages like the LBK. Instead the structures were found alone or within 500-700 m of another timber structures or a closer smaller auxiliary building (Barclay et al. 2002; Brophy 2007; Debert 2010; Garton 1991; Hayden and Stafford 2006; Hey and Bell 2000; Kenney and Davidson 2006; Lynch and Musson 2004; Ralston 1982). This pairing of structures and the extended distance between structures has not been explored at any length in the literature. One possible explanation for this is the inability to determine if the structures were contemporaneous or represent relocation. Another complexity is the limited number of finds recovered during the excavations of these structures. This dearth of refuse has been interpreted as domestic cleaning and as evidence for ritual use. This is by no means an exhaustive description of the timber structures however; it should form a solid basis to discuss internal space creation.

Background

Much time and argument has been spent suggesting how these structures might fit into the new identity being created at this time in Britain (Darvill 1996; Darvill and Thomas 1996; Ralston 1982; Whittle 1996). It is not the intention of this paper to present an in-depth examination of possible uses or their roles (for this see (Debert 2010)). Instead this paper suggests that it is only by first putting them in their context that we can begin to understand. It is during this time that people are negotiating new ideologies, materials and lifeways. In this context the initial Neolithic is defined as 4050-3650 BC, which coincides with the construction of the structure but predate all other monument classes including causeway enclosures.

These changes aren't solely concealed in material culture but can be illuminated in the way in which people viewed and interacted with their landscape. In this context the landscape including the built environment represents a microcosm for the mitigation of the associated stresses. How the timber structures fit into this new worldview is incredibly important to our understanding of the negotiations that took place.

Any attempts to pigeon hole the timber structures as domestic, ritual or social space is unnecessarily strict and offers little to the current discussion. Ethnographic accounts show that, 'ritual is superimposed on, or interdigitated with, productive routines, not divorced from them' (Bogaard and Jones 2007: 357). It should be noted that several authors have discussed the intricate nature of the interplay between ritual and every day activities, with regards to the timber structures (e.g. Sherratt 1999; Thomas 1999).

Thus, the timber structures are not receptacles of material but a stage in which the new identity of the Neolithic was developed, enacted and reinforced for several generations; until they suddenly were abandoned, burnt down and never rebuilt again. It is this change in architecture that defines the material manifestation of the period and thus we must appreciate its importance to the people who conceived of them, built them, and used them to order and comprehend their changing worldview.

The timber structures were the first large monuments built in Britain and are in stark contrast to earlier and later ephemeral structures. The act of building one of these large timber structures would have involved many people, large amounts of materials, time and effort. The collection of the necessary materials and the transportation of them to the site would have required greater planning and organisation then anything before. After the initial Neolithic, once the negotiations had finished, the cultural landscape changed again. Timber structures were no longer needed, is that stress had passed. Instead we see a move from single multifunctional spaces to multiple types of reduced function monuments. It is only when the final timber structures are being burnt down and no new timber structures built to replace them that we see the start of causewayed enclosures, long barrows and megalithic tomb construction (Whittle 2007; Whittle and Bayliss 2007).

Even though the use of the timber structures was relatively short lived, the act of burning them down does not appear to be final, as the sites are revisited many generations later in the late Neolithic and early Bronze Age. As noted, causewayed enclosures, long barrows and megalithic tombs all begin to be built in Britain as the timber structures are being burnt down and abandoned (Whittle 2007; Whittle and Bayliss 2007). Similarities in the timber construction of these monuments with the timber structures has long been noted, but function has been hard to correlate, as these monuments are often associated with the dead. To date, there are no known burial associations at any of the timber structures. However, suggesting that the only function of the causewayed enclosures, long barrows and megalithic tombs was burial would be a dramatic over simplification (Bradley 1996; Brophy 2005; Edmonds 1999). These monuments were as much for the living as the dead. They were the site of important ritual activity and community affirming (Bradley 2005; Brophy 2007). In this sense they were probably very similar to the timber structures. Thus, some of the importance and activities that were focused at the timber structures were transferred to those monuments; but not all.

Several others (e.g: Barclay et al. 2002; Brophy 2007) have also suggested that the function(s) and meaning(s) of the timber structures were transferred to later monuments. The similarities in external form of the timber structures to later Neolithic unroofed structures such as Littleour, Balfarg Riding School and Carsie has been used to create a kind of shared architectural vision (Barclay et al. 2002; Barclay and Maxwell 1998; Brophy 2007). These later unroofed structures 'seem to have been the focus of ceremonial activity, mortuary activity and ritual' (Brophy 2006: 37). Possibly, by extension then it could be said that the timber structures had a similar role in the developing ritual life of the community. In other words, it is possible that some of the multiple functions of the timber structures were transferred to other later monuments. This great diversification of monuments and building signals the end of the initial Neolithic and the start of the early Neolithic.

Richards (1993) has argued that a cosmological model is represented in the plans of structures in Orkney; those of Barnhouse settlement, Maes Howe burial mound and Stenness henge. This argument relies on the restriction of movement and the emphasis on certain directions and themes that span these different monument types. These kind of studies have moved architecture into the realm of the 'socially significant and symbolically-loaded' (Barclay et al. 2002: 124). Monuments, and now houses, are being seen as part of the process of creating identity and place (Barrett 1994; Whittle 1996). These structures would have aided formalized behaviour and reinforced the emerging habitus.

Combining

Thus, I suggest that the oak posts used in these buildings may have retained a sense of their original location and perhaps the people who were involved in their felling. With groups taking leadership in the acquisition and working of individual timbers, the structure could become personalised. This would have created a modified landscape within the structures and transcended the individual as they moved through the structure (Barclay et al. 2002; Bradley 2003). For example the structure could tell a story of the people - ancestors who built it - keeping them in memory and folklore. In a very real sense the structures built the community as the community constructed the structures. Therefore, with the proper movement into and through the structure an individual can be transformed into another realm, possibly of the ancestors. And helped separate space into communal/private, and ancestral/present while fostering a new identity (Whittle 1996). In other words: we

are different now. Therefore, we could look at the timber structures not as a single entity resulting from construction, but instead as an amalgamation resulting from an act of transformation which is maintained in memory and recurrently preformed; all necessitated by a changing world view.

The interior, though lit with hearths, was still dark. Timber posts supported a high roof, blackened from smoke (Figure 1). The firelight would play against the potentially carved posts and beams of the walls and thatched roof, creating an altered space/ reality. It would be quite easy to see how in a world without other large enclosed spaces like these structures would invoke a sense of other worldliness.

The timber structures without large quantities of bone, flint or ceramics have puzzled archaeologists since the first one was identified in the 1980s. The large quantity of grain at a handful of the structures also complicated the picture. Original questions focused on the timber structures, dealt primarily with function in relation to the large Neolithic debates origin / dissemination, and residence / mobility. Thus the timber structures were discussed in terms of domestic or ritual, permanent or transient. I believe these questions are restrictive and limit our interpretation of meaning and function. In fact the timber structures with their multiple functions should not be defined in simple terms. And the questions we should pose should relate to the use of these structures to negotiate changes occurring.

Movement

To better envision the created space within the timber structures I built a digital model of each of the structures. These digital models were constructed from the plan view maps of the location of postholes, pits, trenches and other features. The models were constructed using the program called 'Sweet Home 3D'. This is a freeware program designed for several operating systems but used on a Macintosh operating system.

There are often several different ways in which the interior can be divided. The number of internal spaces created

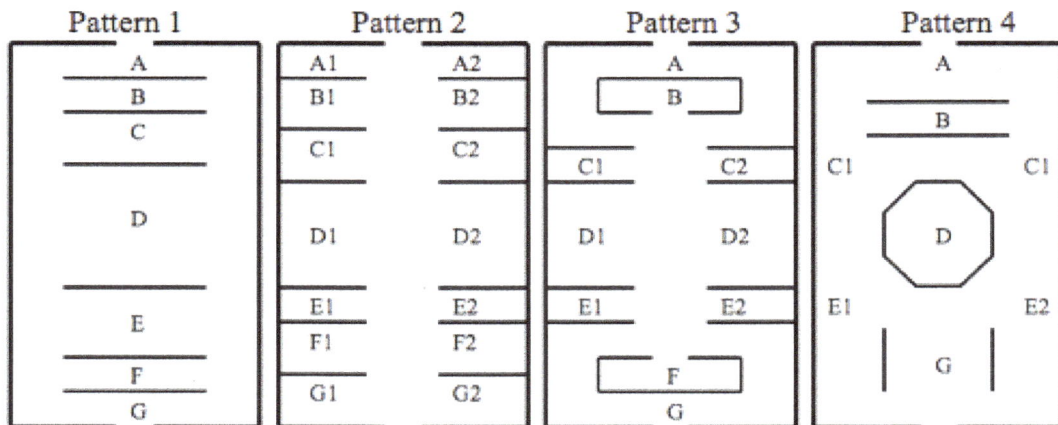

Figure 1: Proposed internal spatial patterns for Early Neolithic timber structures

ranges from four to seven. These patterns (Figure 2) are presented as schematic representations. The number and size of spaces can vary between individual structures, but the overall patterns are maintained. The construction of these internal divisions through the erection of partitions restricts movement within the structure and possibly creates socially appropriate and inappropriate movement (Bradley 2005; Ethington 2007; Guitian 2007; Parker Pearson and Richard 1994). These patterns of movement are hard to identify archaeologically, but their discussion adds further insight into the structures and the people who built them.

Pattern 1

Pattern One has two lateral corridors running the length of the building. The number of internal walls that run perpendicular to these corridors can vary and as a result so does the number of internal spaces. The important features of this division of space are that every space is accessible from both sides and that there are no fully enclosed spaces. In other words there are no spaces that are contained within three walls. Visibility within Pattern One structures is limited, as on entering visitors are met by a wall that restricts lines of sight between interior and exterior. The visitor must choose a direction of movement immediately upon entering the building. Since there are no enclosed spaces, movement can be continuous, and the visitor would never have to turn around to exit a space (Kalogirou 1992; Scott 1976). The use of the small lateral corridors meant that people would not see an area until immediately before they entered it. These small corridors would be dark and would provide a notable contrast with the central area, which would presumably have been lit by a hearth.

The feeling of restricted space is not the only possible rationale for the two lateral corridors. The selection of a path at the entrance may have been dictated by some social rule of behaviour (Blomberg 1992; Parker Pearson and Richard 1994). However, as both directions led to the same areas, there could have been different meanings

attached to the direction of approach (Bruck 2001; Parker Pearson and Richard 1994). In fact, upon entering the building visitors could have been divided into two groups, each taking a different path through the structure, although, both need not have been used, and one could have be reserved for sprits, ancestors, etc. Additionally, as there are lateral corridors originating at both entrances, there are actually four potential paths into and out of the structure; from that point on the possible combinations of directions dramatically increase. This arrangement gives the possibility of the segregation of people into four groups (Hodder and Cessford 2004; Kacerauskas 2008).

Pattern 2

Pattern Two has only one central corridor, which runs the full length of the structure. This central corridor again provides access to every space created by the perpendicular walls. The major difference between Pattern One and Pattern Two is that in the latter there are several spaces that are fully enclosed. With a central corridor, the perpendicular walls extend inward from the exterior walls, thus creating a series of three-sided enclosed spaces. These enclosed spaces are better suited to storage than open spaces and could have been used for this purpose. Visibility in Pattern Two structures is much more extensive than in Pattern One structures, as the entire length of the interior can be seen from either entrance.

The corridor provides a feeling of openness throughout the structure. Upon entering the structure the visitor is able to see clearly into every space and even through to the entrance at the other end. However, the lateral spaces are enclosed on three sides the internal spaces are not visible until a person stands at their entrances.

The movement into and out of the structure could be unidirectional, entering at one end and passing through the structure, exiting the other end. Alternately, the entrances could have been used by two different groups of people. In

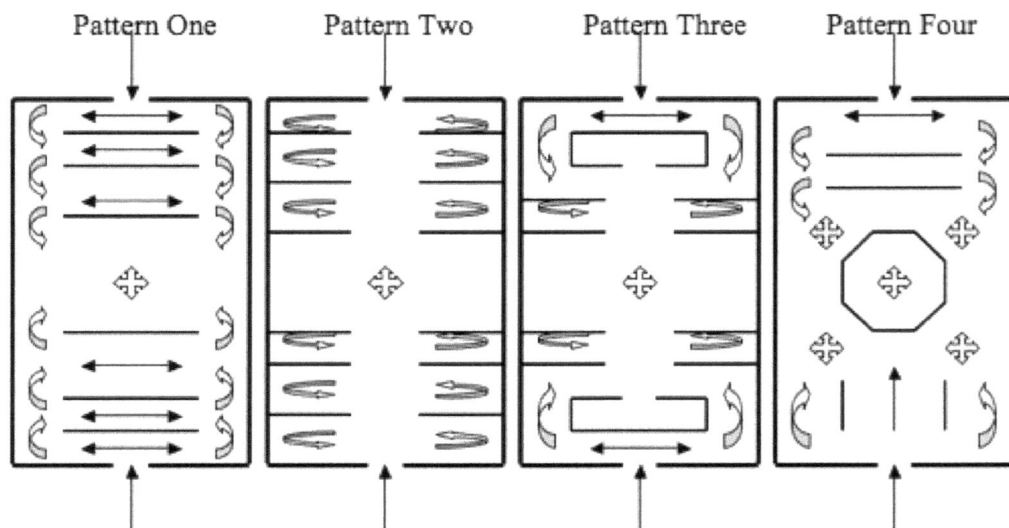

Figure 2: Proposed movement patterns through Early Neolithic timber structures

this scenario it is the behaviour of the people that restricts access to or use of the space, not the restricted space that influences movement, as is the case in Pattern One (Walker 2004).

Pattern 3

Pattern Three contains elements of both patterns One and Two, as it has both lateral and central corridors. The construction of a pair of round rooms at the entrances of the structure creates lateral corridors around the enclosed space. However, deeper into the interior a central corridor is formed, through use of lateral perpendicular walls. This pattern is quite different from the other structures as a greater number of enclosed spaces is created. Visibility is restricted until the central area of the structure is entered. Even then, it is possible that the entrances to the round rooms were narrow or obscured, and as such visibility into the rooms may have been hindered.

In this pattern both lateral and central corridors are used for movement within the structure. Also, as with Pattern One, visitors can be divided into two or four groups when they enter, owing to the lateral corridors around the round rooms (Hodder and Cessford 2004; Kacerauskas 2008). What is distinctly different from Pattern One is that once beyond the round the room, the visitor is presented with one central corridor and the interior of the structure is now visible.

A unique feature of this pattern is that there are three focal points provided by each of the round rooms and the central area. This contrasts with the first two patterns where the focal point is less apparent, but was probably the central area. Given the restricted nature of the entrances and the possible division of visitors into four groups, it could be that only certain people were allowed to enter certain round rooms or that each room was only used at certain times of the year. However, the opening of the central area of the structure into a central corridor does provide a more communal area (Villecco 1985), possibly supplying an area for the separated groups to again be reunited in one space.

Pattern 4

Pattern Four is a combination of features and spaces identified in the other three patterns. The important and unique feature of Pattern Four structures is that the central area is enclosed within a separate room. The divisions at either end probably did not mirror each other quite in the manner proposed in the diagram above. The enclosure of the central space may have had the same rational in all models. The narrow lateral corridors would have restricted the view of the interior afforded to people located outside or entering the building. Alternatively, entering at the other end, with the central corridor would have allowed easy, open access into the interior.

The spaces constituted by Pattern Four are a variation on the other three patterns and this is reflected in the potential pattern of movement within the structure. There is a distinctive asymmetry to this pattern with each end of the building containing its own mix of spaces. The enclosed central space provides a very powerful focus for movement. As such, movement can take place along any of the five paths from the entrances and although they confront other spaces on the way there is a distinct directionality towards the central room.

The unique feature of this pattern is that the asymmetry means visitors who enter the building at different points will experience the structure in very different ways. As with the other patterns there is the opportunity to separate people entering the building into several groups, reuniting them at the central space once they have experienced different paths. It is thus possible that particular groups would exit by the same path as they entered, never encountering the other end of the structure. Equally, they might continue through the structure taking another path onwards from the round room.

There is of course another reason for the enclosure of the central space, and that is to exclude (Parker Pearson and Richard 1994). Unlike the other patterns, the central space is not open and access was probably restricted to a smaller opening, which may have only been visible from one or two paths into the structure. This would create an inner sanctum for the initiated few and leave the remainder of the structure comparatively communal.

Summary of Space

Three of the four patterns described above contain a larger space. This central area may have been used as a place of gathering and feasting. It is also possible that for the majority of people feasting took place outside the structures and that only certain members of society entered the timber structures during these events. The restricted nature of most of the entrances suggest that a clear separation of interior/exterior or created/natural space was important. Thus, the architecture may not have only served to unite the community during building and seasonal feasts but also to differentiate people.

Discussion

During the initial Neolithic there were considerable cultural stresses that were mitigated with the community-based building of the timber structures. These stresses are visible in the major changes to material culture, subsistence and landscape patterns. The placement of these timber structures in the landscape was not happenstance. Instead the location of the structures already had significance and the addition of the structures would have only accentuated this.

Two prime examples of the importance of the location and orientation of the structures in the landscape are Lismore Fields and White Horse Stone. At Lismore Fields the structure was constructed in an upland area away from arable land (Garton 1991), yet large quantities of grain were transported to the site. At White Horse Stone the structure was orientated NNW-SSE, which runs perpendicular to the slope and meant that the northern and southern ends were at different heights (Hayden and Stafford 2006). Therefore, the location, orientation and probably sight lines from the structure were important enough to warrant the extra expenditure of energy at both of these sites.

As important as the area of construction was the mere act of erecting the timber structures changed the locality and further elaborated the significance of the locale. Once the timbers were erected the place was now intertwined with the memory of the building and of those involved in the construction (Edmonds 1999; Tilley 2007; Winterbottom and Long 2006). Just as the structure is an amalgamation of timbers it also consolidates individuals into a community.

A parallel can be drawn between the memory of the location of rock sources used in the production of polished stone axes and the materials used in the timber structures (Larsson 2000; Thomas 2004; Thomas 2007). The importance of polished stone axes lies not only in their form or function, but also in the material itself and its history (Bradley and Edmonds 1993; Thomas 1999). In other words, the experience and difficulty endured to obtain the material remained attached to the object after it was worked and allowed that experience of place to be transplanted and retained. 'The object itself is but an object, it is ultimately the connotations connected to this object that make an object inalienable or even sacred' (Wentink 2006: 84). A similar statement can be made about the timber structures. They are simply a combination of timber, thatch, wattle and daub, but they are also are imbued with multiple layers of meaning. A similar manifestation of place and memory may have taken place at these timber structures, with the erection of timbers taken from the far-reaching landscape.

Thus, oak beams used in the building may have retained a sense of their original location and perhaps the people who were involved in their felling. With groups taking leadership in the acquisition and working of individual timbers, the structure could become personalised. This would have created a modified landscape within the structures and transported the individual as they moved through the structure (Barclay et al. 2002; Bradley 2003). Thus the structure later tells a story of the ancestors who built it, keeping them in memory and folklore. The movement patterns that were discussed above would serve to intensify these memories and guarantee their longevity. With proper movement a sense of discovery is invoked as the individual moved through the structure; this would have been particularly strong in the patterns in which certain spaces were only revealed to view as on entered them (Patterns 1, 3, 4).

Conclusion

The timber structures were a focus for a community that was possibly dispersed though most of the year, with some following a pastoral or forging type of seasonal round and others remaining at the structures to tend the crops. These activities point to a society that was integrating the new domesticated resources into their existing life-ways. The addition of the timber structures to the landscape was a means to address a need previously unfelt. This acute stress is not only visible in the sudden construction of the timber structures, but also with their disappearance only a few centuries later.

The internal division of space within the structures reveals a number of restricted/ open, public/ private spaces. The creation of these highly ordered spaces influenced the movement into and through the structures. The rigidity of this movement fashioned a new set of cultural norms and allowed the organic creation of social division. Though short-lived the timber structures served a very important role in the creation of community, identity and in the mitigation of new stresses.

Bibliography

Barclay, G., Brophy, K. and Mcgregor, G. (2002) Claish, Stirling: An early Neolithic structure in its context. *Proceedings of the Society of Antiquaries of Scotland* 132, 65-137.

Barclay, G., Brophy, K. and Mcgregor, G. (2002) Claish, Stirling: An early Neolithic structure in its context. *Proceedings of the Society of Antiquaries of Scotland*, 132, 65-137.

Barclay, G. J. and Maxwell, G. S. (1998) *The Cleaven Dyke and Littleour: Monuments in the Neolithic of Tayside*. Edinburgh, Society of Antiquaries of Scotland Monograph.

Barrett, J. (1994) *Fragments from antiquity: An archaeology of social life in Britain, 2900-1200 BC*. Oxford, Blackwell.

Blomberg, B. (1992) Domestic Architecture and the Use of Space - an Interdisciplinary Cross-Cultural-Study. *American Antiquity*, 57, 4, 738-739.

Bogaard, A. and Jones, G. (2007) Neolithic Farming in Britain and Central Europe: Contrast or Continuity? *Proceedings of the British Academy*, 144, 357-375.

Bradley, R. and Edmonds, M. (1993) *Interpreting the Axe Trade: Production and Exchange in Neolithic Britain*. Cambridge, Cambridge University Press.

Bradley, R. (1996) Long houses, long mounds and Neolithic enclosures. *Journal of Material Culture*, 1, 2, 239-256.

Bradley, R. (2003) A Life Less Ordinary: the Ritualization of the Domestic Sphere in Later Prehistoric Europe. *Cambridge Archaeological Journal* 13, 5-23.

Bradley, R. (2005) *Ritual and Domestic Life in Prehistoric Europe*. London, Routledge.

Brophy, K. (2005) Not My type: Discourse in Monumentality. IN V. Cummings and A. Pannett, (eds.) *Set in Stone: New Approaches to Neolithic Monuments in Scotland,* 1-13. Oxford, UK, Oxbow Books.

Brophy, K. (2006) Rethinking Scotland's Neolithic: Combining Circumstance with Context. *Proceedings of the Society of Antiquity Scotland*, 136, 7-46.

Brophy, K. (2007) From Big Houses to Cult Houses: Early Neolithic Timber Halls in Scotland. *Proceedings of the Prehistoric Society*, 73, 75-96.

Bruck, J. (2001) Monuments, power and personhood in the British Neolithic. *Journal of the Royal Anthropological Institute*, 7, 4, 649-667.

Darvill, T. (1996) Neolithic Buildings in England, Wales and the Isle of Man. IN T. Darvill and J. Thomas (eds.), *Neolithic Houses in Northwest Europe and Beyond* 77-112. Oxford, Oxbow Books.

Darvill, T. and Thomas, J. (1996) *Neolithic Houses in Northwest Europe and Beyond*, Oxford, Oxbow Monographs.

Debert, J. (2010) *Functional Analysis of Lithics from British Early Neolithic Timber Structures*. Unpublished PhD. thesis. The University of Manchester

Edmonds, M. (1999) Inhabiting Neolithic landscapes. *Journal of Quaternary Science*, 14, 6, 485-492.

Ethington, P. J. (2007) Placing the past: 'Groundwork' for a spatial theory of history. *Rethinking History*, 11, 4, 465-493.

Fairen-Jimenez, S. (2007) British neolithic rock art in its landscape. *Journal of Field Archaeology*, 32, 283-295.

Garton, D. (1991) Neolithic Settlement in the Peak District: Perspective and Prospects. IN R. Hodges and K. Smith (eds.) *Recent Developments in the Archaeology of the Peak District,* 3-22. Sheffield, J.R. Collis Publication.

Guitian, D. (2007) Cultural goods in the habitable space. *Argos*, 24, 47, 28-41.

Hayden, C. and Stafford, E. (2006) The Prehistoric Landscape at White Horse Stone, Boxley, Kent. CTRL Integrated Site Report Series Unpublished, 1-224. London, Oxford Archaeological Unit, Wessex Archaeology, Joint venture for CTRL.

Hey, G. and Bell, C. (2000) *Yarnton Floodplain B Post-Excavation Analysis Research Design: Modules 3,4,5 and Overview*. CTRL Integrated Site Report Series Unpublished, 1-256. London, Oxford Archaeological Unit, Wessex Archaeology, Joint venture for CTRL.

Hodder, I. and Cessford, C. (2004) Daily practice and social memory at Catalhoyuk. *American Antiquity*, 69, 1, 17-40.

Kacerauskas, T. (2008) Body in the living world. *Problemos*, 73, 72-82.

Kalogirou, A. (1992) Domestic Architecture and the Use of Space - an Interdisciplinary Cross-Cultural-Study. *American Journal of Archaeology*, 96, 4, 764-765.

Kenney, J. and Davidson, A. (2006) *Parc Bryn Cegin Llandygai: Assessment of Potential for Analysis Report*, Unpublished report.

Larsson, L. (2000) The passage of axes: Fire transformation of flint objects in the Neolithic of southern Sweden. *Antiquity*, 74, 285, 602-610.

Lynch, F. and Musson, C. (2004) A Prehistoric and Early Medieval Complex at Llandegai, Near Bangor, North Wales. *Archaeologia Cambrensis*, 150, 17-142.

Parker Pearson, M. and Richard, C. (1994) Ordering the World; Perceptions of Architecture, Space and Time, 1-37. IN M. Parker Pearson and C. Richard (eds.) *Architecture and Order: Approaches to Social Space*. London, Routledge.

Ralston, I. M. B. (1982) A Timber Hall at Balbridie Farm. *Aberdeen University Review*, 168, 238-249.

Richard, C. (1993) Monumental Choreography: Architecture and Spatial Representation in Late Neolithic Orkney, 143-178. IN Tilley, C. (ed.) *Interpretative Archaeology*. Oxford, Oxbow.

Scott, J. A. (1976) Arrangement and Use of Domestic Space. *Humanitas*, 12, 3, 355-365.

Sherratt, A. (1999) Cash-Crops Before Cash: Organic Consumables and Trade. IN Gosden, C. and Hather, J. (eds.) *Prehistory of Food: Appetites for Change,* 13-34. London, Routledge.

Thomas, J. (1991) *Rethinking the Neolithic*. Cambridge, Cambridge University Press.

Thomas, J. (1999) *Understanding the Neolithic*. London, Routledge.

Thomas, J. (2004) Current Debates on the Mesolithic-Neolithic Transition in Britain and Ireland. *Documenta Praehistorica*, XXXI 113-130.

Thomas, J. (2007) Mesolithic-Neolithic Transitions in Britain: From Essence to Inhabitation. *Proceedings of the British Academy*, 144, 423-439.

Tilley, C. (2007) The Neolithic Sensory Revolution: Monumentality and the Experience of Landscape. *Proceedings of the British Academy*, 144, 329-345.

Villecco, M. (1985) The Renewed Importance of the Public Realm + Looking at Architecture as the Shaper of the Communal Landscape. *Architecture-the Aia Journal*, 74, 12, 46-47.

Walker, J. (2004) Ephemeral architectures: the body and landscape in augmented reality. *Digital Creativity*, 15, 2, 93-97.

Warren, G. (2009) How can we understand researchers' perceptions of key research developments? A case study focusing on the adoption of agriculture in Ireland. *World Archaeology*, 41, 4, 609-625.

Wentink, K. (2006) *Early Farming Communities in North-West Europe*. Archaeology. Leiden Univeristy.133

Whittle, A. (1996) House in Context: Buildings as Process. IN Darvill, T. and Thomas, J. (eds.) *Neolithic Houses in Northwest Europe and Beyond,* 13-26. Oxford, Oxbow Books.

Whittle, A. (2007) The Temporality of Transformation: Dating the Early Development of the Southern British Neolithic. Proceedings of the British Academy, 144 377-398.

Whittle, A. and Bayliss, A. (2007) The Times of Their Lives: From Chronological Precision to Kinds of History and Change. Cambridge Archaeological Journal, 17, 1, 21-28.

Winterbottom, S. J. and Long, D. (2006) From abstract digital models to rich virtual environments: landscape contexts in Kilmartin Glen, Scotland. Journal of Archaeological Science, 33, 10, 1356-1367.

Section 2

Monumentality

Chapter 4

Constructed or Conceived Landscapes – Some Thoughts on the Subject of Human Experiences in the Neolithic, and Historic Landscapes

Anna-Karin Andersson

Linnaeus University, Sweden

The article highlights the differences between the constructed and the conceived landscape and the effect that various landscape and theirs component has on people, particularly in relation to monuments. The article begins with questioning if some of the remains from Southern Scania really are remains of long mounds, and continues to discuss what implications could be if the remains were not monumental mounds.

Key words: Long mound, long barrow, landscape, façade structures, standing posts

During The 11th Nordic TAG 2011 that was held in Kalmar, I gave a paper called 'Bringing it all together – pits as monuments' in which the relationship between pits and long mounds was discussed. Part of the discussion in my paper addressed the inflation that can be seen in the number of long mounds found in Sweden during the last decade. Before the 1990s there were only a few known, e.g. the Giant Grave and Krångeltofta (compared to Denmark where several long mounds have been known for many years (e.g. Glob 1975; Liversage 1980; Midgley 1985)).

Several of the recently discovered long mounds in Scania, are in fact not more than post-holes in a row, interpreted as façade structures (Rudebeck and Ödman 2000; Rudebeck 2006; Nilsson and Rudebeck 2010; Jönsson and Lövgren 2003). In the best cases there are remains of grave- or grave-like features to the west of these post-holes (e.g. Rudebeck

and Ödman 2000; Larsson 2002; Gidlöf et.al 2006; 2009; Berggren et. al 2009; Jönsson and Lövgren 2009). There are only a few examples where an actual long mound is firmly demonstrated e.g. the Giant Grave (Larsson 2002) Krångeltofta (Eriksson Lagerås 1999; Lindahl Jensen 2002) and Örnakulla (Engström 1927; Sjöström and Pihl 2002).

The conclusion in the paper I gave during the 11th Nordic TAG was that pits and long mounds are inevitably connected for a number of reasons, not to be discussed in detail here. It is however important for the following discussion to recognise that at all of the sites in Scania that contains long mounds, pit digging is always present and precedes the actual mound e.g. Almhov (Gidlöf et.al 2006; Gidlöf 2009), Kristineberg (Rudebeck and Ödman 2000) and Hörlanders Väg (Berggren et. al 2009) (Figure 1).

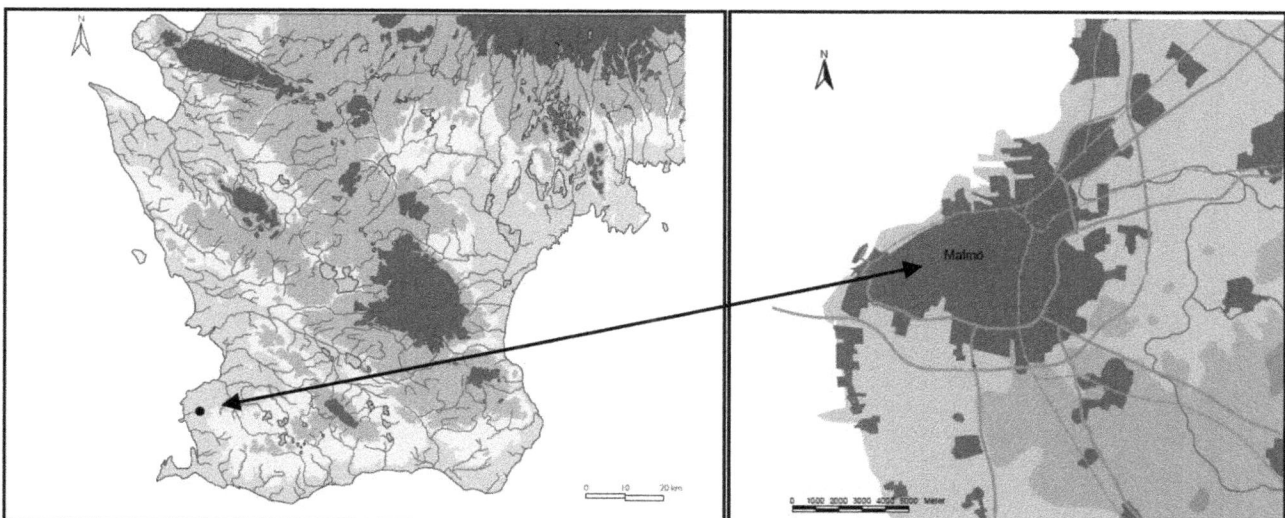

Figure 1. Scania and the study area around Malmö.

After my presentation a British colleague asked: 'Are you sure the features are long mounds?' Based on the interpretation of the alignment of the façade (see below) and the remains of graves, the alignment of the façades and the graves as well as the similarities with features underneath the actual mounds (compared to long mounds from Denmark and Europe (in particular the British Islands see Fussels Lodge (Ashbee 1966) or Gwernvale (Britnell and Savory 1984)), I replied that I did interpret the features as remain of long mounds (see Andersson 2013).

However, that question 'Are you sure they are really long mounds?' made me think of a more profound question that I intend to discuss throughout this article:

Does it matter if the features are remains of long mounds or simply remains of ritual structures consisting of a façade and graves? If it matters; in what way does it matter if the standing posts were in fact not long mounds but simply remains of standing posts or some kind of façade?

The profound question has to do with architecture, both the architecture of landscape and the architecture of buildings. It has also to do with how architecture influences and directs human life (amongst others Barrett 1994; Parker Pearson 1994; Ashmore and Knapp 1999; Ingold 2000; Carlie 2004). It is obvious with the substantial pre-monumental activities that the places themselves have been important sites in the landscape even before more long-lasting buildings were created at the sites (Midgley 1986; 2012; Gidlöf et. al 2009; Gidlöf 2010; Nilsson and Rudebeck 2010; amongst others).

Activities that pre-date the façade structures are present at all of the sites mentioned above and consist of cultural layers and pits. In that sense, there are strong indications that the sites have a long history of use before the façades or long mounds were built. Several of the depositions in pits at these sites indicate that people returned to the sites over and over again. This is exemplifies in pit 19049 at Almhov situated *ca.* 30 metres south of long mound no. 1 and measured 4.9 by 3.9 metres and had a depth of 0.74 metres (Figure 2).

A19049 contained the assemblage of at least 60 Funnelbeaker vessels and five clay discs, and a flint inventory that exceeded 20 kg mainly waste from tool manufacturing. Pit 19049 displayed a multi-phased profile, as did several other pits at Almhov, indicating that the pit had been used for deposition on several occasions. The character of the depositions opens up the possibility that the site had been a place for gathering and feasts (see also Welinder et. al. 2009; Nilsson and Rudebeck 2010).

The long mound sites

Kristineberg

Figure 3 shows the remains of two long mounds from outside Kristineberg. The site was excavated during the 1970s but the excavation report was not published until 2000 (Rudebeck and Ödman 2000). The material was interpreted as the remains of two ploughed out long mounds, several pits and the remains of cultural layers.

The features were interpreted as long mounds due to the large pits (east in the figure), which contained the marks of several standing posts in a row. The two façade pits in the northern mound measured 1.8 by 1.5 metres, and 1.8 by 1.1 meter. The pits were situated 0.15 metres apart and both

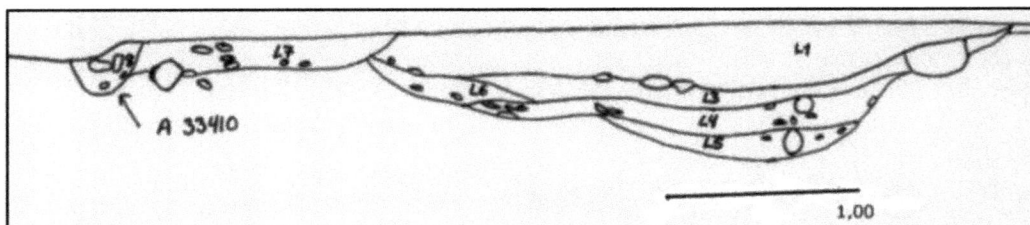

Figure 2. Profile from pit A19049 and A 33410 is an adjacent posthole.

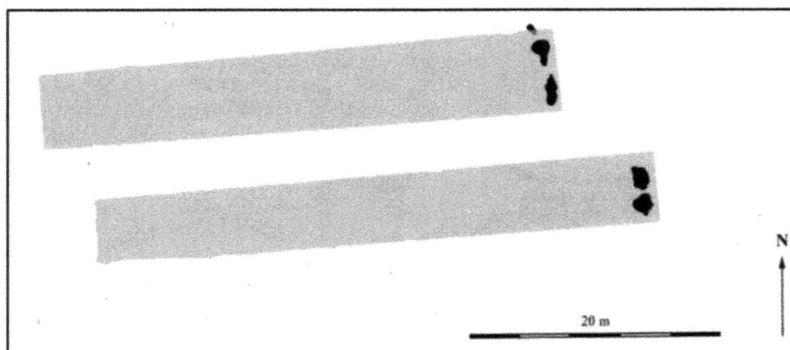

Figure 3. Kristineberg (modified after Rudebeck and Ödman 2000, 86). The shaded areas in the figure are not visible, but are the proposed extensions of the long mounds, originally interpreted by Rudebeck and Ödman 2000.

Figure 4. Internal structure of Almhov with early Neolithic pits and long mounds. The possible extension of the long mounds is indicated by hatched lines; figure not in scale (modified after Gidlöf et.al. 2006).

contained smaller stones below the surface that could have supported a total of three to five standing posts (Rudebeck and Ödman 2000, 81).

The pits were therefore interpreted as the façades for two long mounds. A possible grave was also associated with the southern long mound. This feature was aligned on the axial element to the west of the façade. The feature measured 3.5 m. by 0.6-1.3 metres in plan and had a depth of 0.3 metres, consisting of darker soil and small stones (Rudebeck and Ödman 2000). The long mounds at Kristineberg were dated to the first phase of the Funnelbeaker period based on ceramic typology. One radiocarbon sample on charcoal from feature 162, gave the date to 3942-3373 cal. BC (LuA-4304).

Almhov

Almhov is situated in the southwest of Scania just south of Malmö, in an area that today supports extensive agriculture. The site was excavated between 1999 and 2002 as part

of the City-tunnel-project (Lindhe et.al 2001). A total of 103,000 square metres of open-area excavation were undertaken with over 6500 features discovered (Gidlöf et. al. 2006; 2009). The material from Almhov is much richer but of the same character as that from Kristineberg. The site holds hundreds of Neolithic pits and four, possibly five long mounds (Gidlöf et. al. 2006; Gidlöf 2009).

The four long mounds consisted of façades with two to four pits containing smaller stones that could have supported standing posts. Long mounds number one and four displayed central graves that were aligned on the axial element. Only long mound number one displayed erosion in-filling. This infill stretched for some 85 metres to the west of the façade structure (Gidlöf et.al. 2006).

Almhov was typologically dated from ceramic and flint to the Early Neolithic with a few radiocarbon dates confirming that. Long mound number one was radiocarbon dated from an undefined grain from one of the post-hole in the façade structure to 3946-3656 cal. BC (Ua-17158). The

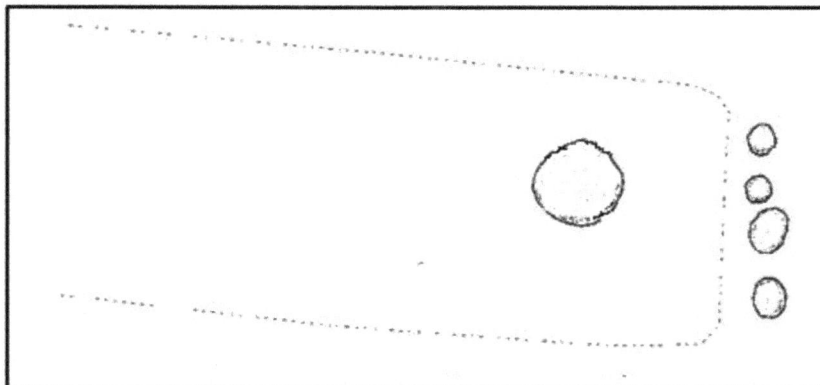

Figure 5. Long mound no.1 at Almhov. The hatched line is the imaginary limit of the former long mound(modified after Gidlöf et. al. 2006).

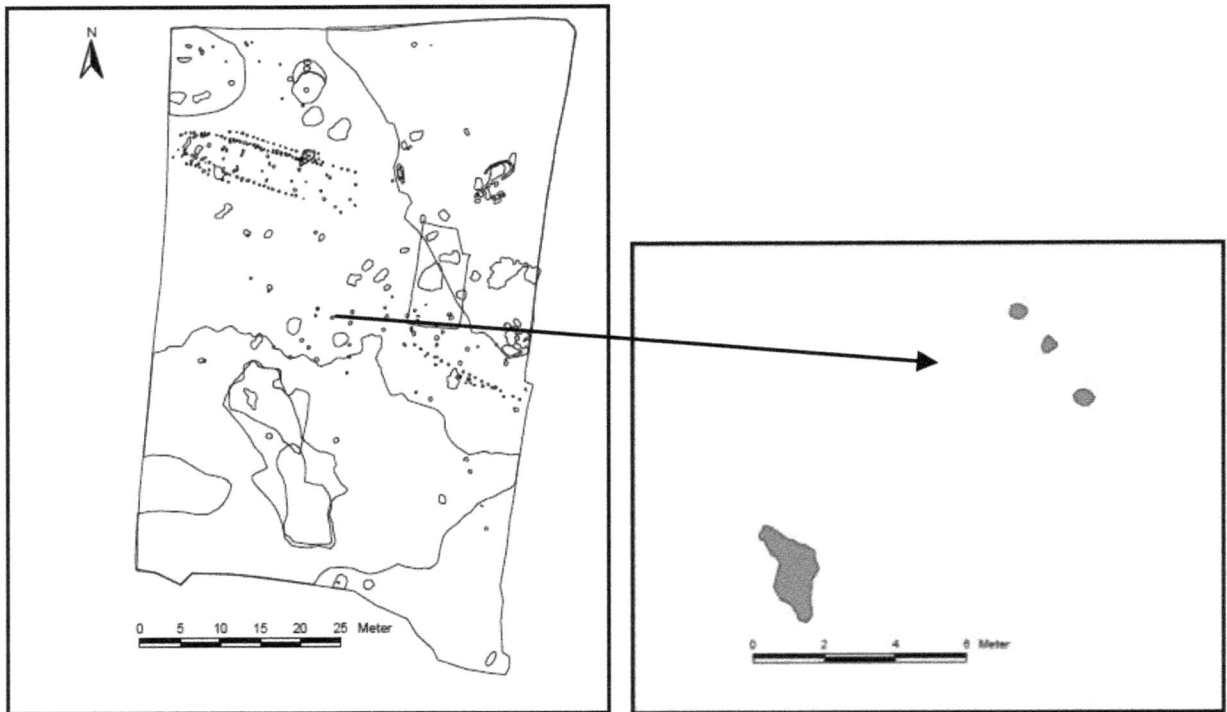

Figure 6. Plan of features at Hörlanders Väg (modified after Berggren et. al. 2009, 75)

grave to the west of the façade produced a date of 3356-3029 cal. BC (Ua-21333) on human bone. The connection between the grave and the façade can therefore be questioned. It is not possible to confirm that the grave and the façade structure belong to the same feature since these are not contemporary. If the façade and the grave are not contemporary, it is a possibility that the features at Almhov are not the remains from a long mound, but instead two different features; a grave and row of standing posts.

Hörlanders Väg

The site is situated in south western Scania on a low hill 17-20 metres above present day sea level. The archaeological material in the area includes residential sites, graves, flint-mines and offering sites (see the Ängdala area (Rudebeck 1986) and Husie 41:1 (Scnittger, 1910)). An area of 40 by 75 metres was excavated with open-area excavation at Hörlanders Väg. The archaeological remains from the earliest Neolithic consisted of a façade structure with three pits in a row (see Figure 6) and a stone packing nine metres to the west. There were also six other pits located in the central and northern parts of the site.

The pits were round to round ovate in plan, measuring 0.06-0.32 metres, and had a distance to each other between 1.30 to 1.80 metres and a depth between 0.30-0.42 metres. Nine metres to the west of the post-holes there was a stone packing consisting of small stones (Berggren et. al. 2009).

No radiocarbon samples were taken and the only artefacts found in the long mound were a sherd of a grinding stone (806 gr.) found in one of the façade pits and flint debris (4gr.) in the infilling.

The Giant Grave – one that stands

There is however evidence of long mound that is still present in Scania. A couple of these monuments are visible above ground, e.g. the Giant Grave outside Trelleborg. The Giant Grave was excavated during the 1990s by the University of Lund (Larsson 2002). The excavation was limited to the monument itself and did not include the area in front or around the structure. This makes it impossible to see whether there had been pits or other depositions in front or around the actual monument.

The long mound is rectangular with a façade structure consisting of a gully (3.4 meters long and between 0.4 to 0.6 meters wide) where at least four standing posts have been present (Larsson 2002). The posts must have been of considerable size (the post-holes measured between 0.4-0.6 meters in diameter) and could have reached several meters in height (Larsson 2002). The standing posts in the façade structure at The Giant Grave are similar to the façade structures at Almhov, Hörlanders Väg and Kristineberg.

The architecture of landscape and the architecture of place

Before I continue with further discussion regarding long mounds, I want to return to the discussion of architecture and touch upon landscape theory. During the last 15 years in archaeology, landscape theory has rested upon the thought that a place is always built otherwise it is simply space or nature (Ingold 2000). This assumption relies on the notion that building exists outside as it does inside human minds. The process of building does not have to be artificial in nature but can be a matter of how sites are structured, e.g.

according to dwelling and waste areas (see Andersen 1975; 1989; Price and Gebauer 2005).

Buildings and architecture makes people move and dwell in specific and often intended ways (e.g. Barrett 1994). In some cases the role of architecture is to ensure that the rules and norms in a society are followed and manifested. At other times architecture creates rules and norms that are not yet properly set (e.g. Barrett 1994; Parker Pearson 1994; Ingold 2000; 2011;). In that sense architecture can be said to guide and sometimes control human lives (see below in the discussion about cathedrals).

The notion that architecture guides human lives draws on the structuration theory of Giddens (1979) as well as the Habitus of Bourdieu (1977). People are both created by- and creating the world by living their lives.

> '(…) worlds are made before they are lived in (…) that acts of dwelling are preceded by acts of worldmaking' (Ingold 2000, 179).

From the every-day practice, specific and particular meanings grow. In the sense of 'we build because we are', the human body (the human experience) is intimately connected to architecture. We cannot live without continuously building and structuring sites; continuously turning space into place. In the same way, the structure of the house reflects the structure of society (Carlie 2004). Architecture is part of human experiences and cannot be separated from the self (see e.g. Bollnow 1994; Ingold 2000), in the same way people and the environment are indisputably connected (Merleau-Ponty 1945; Hägerstrand 1973; Carlstein 1982; Edmonds 1999; Ingold 2000; Bradley 2002 amongst others). People turn nature into culture and spaces into places as they routinely live their lives. From this routine, specific meanings can crystallise (e.g. Bourdieu 1977; Ingold 2000; 2011). As a consequence here off monuments could be seen as a prolonging of earlier activities in the landscape and at the sites (Barrett 1994; Bradley 1998; Andersson 2013).

But, besides the architecture that is created from routine movements, there is another architecture that is designed, planned and created with the *intention* to guide human life. This stems from the intentions of not only controlling movements, but also controlling human lives. A distinct example of this is the architecture in e.g. cathedrals (e.g. Trimen 1856; Bulzan 2008). The architecture for most of the medieval cathedrals in Europe is characterised by a main entrance in the far west. The altar is placed in the far east, and in between these there is the charcel, the crossing, the north- and the south trancept, the Nave and the narthex. Cathedrals often have the form of a cross, built into their very architecture (e.g. Mjöberg 1995).

The architecture of cathedrals and churches are outlined to ensure that norms and rules are being solidly manifested (Mjöberg 1995-). The architecture works in a restricted way, creating division amongst people, drawing lines between areas where the public are permitted to go and areas where only religious elite have access. People brought back a correct way of moving from the architecture in the cathedral to their ordinary life (see e.g. Barrett 1994 for a similar discussion). One distinct example of this is the sharp division between women and men, supported by the architecture that placed women and men on either side of the aisle and in that they had separate entrances to the cathedrals.

Another example of this controlling architecture is from Vreta monastery in Sweden. The monastery began to be built in the 10th century A.D. It was in use until 1528 A.D. (Gustavi 1998). The church in Vreta had an architecture that effectively separated the nuns from the rest of the visitors in the church during services. The front of the church was screened off so that the nuns could participate in the service without having to either be seen or involved with other people. This was an isolation that was vivid during their every-day life as well as the nuns were not allowed to move or speak in any way that contravened the rules of the monastery (Ibid)

El Camino

The architecture of cathedrals created and maintained divisions and rules between people. But architecture can also work the other way around. Places, sites, tracks, paths and landscape features can be planned and built with the aim of creating a sense of belonging and drawing people together. This is exemplified through a present day landscape: the pilgrim trail to Santiago de Compostella in Northern Spain, *El Camino*.

El Camino de Santiago is the pilgrimage route to the cathedral of Santiago de Compostella in the Galicia region of north western Spain. According to tradition the remains of the apostle *St. James* were buried there after having been killed in the year 42 A.D. (Andersson 1989). The bones were then transported by boat from Jerusalem to northern Spain and the city of Santiago de Compostella and buried in the church (the church was rebuilt during the 11th century to the cathedral that stands today). The stick of St James was housed in the cathedral and in the 13th century A.D. St James was declared the saint of all pilgrims (see e.g. Thomell 1987; Andersson 1989). The pilgrim trail to Santiago de Compostella is now a world heritage site and hundreds of thousands of people take the walk of the 800 km from St Jean de Port in France to Santiago de Compostella in Spain each year (http://whc.unesco.org/en/list/669).

By following the scallop shells along the route the modern pilgrims know that they are on the right path. Along the route there are numerous monuments, statues and buildings; many are built with the aim to make people recall a specific historical person, or a specific event. In *Roncevalles, there* is a pilgrim hospice dating back to the 11th century A.D. It is situated right next to a monastery that still has a cemetery for pilgrims. Numerous pilgrims have ended their days in the earth of the cemetery and the place is signposted to ensure that the present day pilgrims can easily recall the hardship of the hundreds of thousands of pilgrims that went on the trail before them (Andersson 1989).

One of the famous crucifixes that line the route is in Foncebadón; pilgrims throughout history have placed a stone on a cairn (www.galiciaguide.com). These crucifixes are for the most part placed on higher and visible ground in the landscape and tradition has it that every pilgrim should add a stone to the cairn. This incorporates the action of past people into the lives of the pilgrims of today. By adding a stone to a historical monument the landscape is not only incorporated into the minds of people but people also contribute to the formation of the landscape in the present day landscape (www.galiciaguide.com; Andersson 1989).

The landscape of the *El Camino* creates a sense of belonging and being part of history. The scallop shells, the statues, monuments and landmarks, directs and focus people's mind on a shared goal; the cathedral in Santiago de Compostella. In that sense the pilgrims both create and are created by the landscape of shared meanings and the remembrance of common hardships of the historical pilgrims.

Returning to the prehistoric landscape

In contradiction to the constructed landscape stands the 4000 cal. BC landscape in south west Scania. This displays a topography and environment that is constituted by small sites often located to higher areas in the interior of the landscape (e.g. Larsson 1984; Andersson 2004). Some sites might solely had been places where people stopped for hunting, others would have been places where people spent a great part of their every-day life, and others again might have been sites where people got together for special occasions (Strömberg 1976; Larsson 1984; 1997; 2007; Karsten 1994; Tilley 1996; Persson 1999; Andersson 2004; Hadevik 2009; amongst others). At all three sites; Almhov, Hörlanders Väg and Kristineberg there were pits with rich deposition (see Rudebeck and Ödman 2000; Gidlöf et. al. 2006; Gidlöf 2009; Hadevik et.al. 2009; Berggren et.al. 2009 for further discussions on pits see Thomas 1996; Garrow 2006; Lamdin-Whymark 2008; Brophy and Noble 2011 amongst others). The space in this article has not allowed for a thorough discussion regarding dates, but it can be concluded that in most cases the pits pre-date the façade/long mound structures.

Landscapes create undoubtedly identities (identity is used here in the sense of '...a complex of different scales of statuses and roles, including personal, social, and cultural attributes.' (Kealhofer 1999, p. 59)) and stipulates how relations between people, groups and landscapes might look like. The constructed landscape, as opposed to the conceived one (e.g. Ashmore and Knapp 1999) directs people to look at and understand the world in a pre-determined and specific way. In the cases of the habitual created landscape, like the Neolithic, places have grown out of the daily round and a repetitive pattern and not through a pre-determined or created architecture. Familiar places and paths created a sense of belonging and an understanding of how life was to be understood (Tilley 1994; Bradley 2000; Ingold 2000; 2011). Kealhof (1999) stated that the landscape was used to 'establish, negotiate, and maintain community and individual social identity.' (p. 76). Following that thought, it is not the actual architecture of monuments in prehistoric landscapes that is most important. That is instead the sites themselves that:

'(...) have acted primarily as symbolic reference and ritually important ceremonial meeting-points on paths of movement, drawing attention to the relationship between local groups and the landscape (...)' (Tilley 1994, 109).

The most prominent features at the long mound sites in Scania are pits and depositions in close relation to the façade structures and the possible long mounds. This suggests that the actual façade structure or long mounds were not the most important features. Instead it was people's continuous engagement with the sites; the returning and the repeated deposition that was most important and shaped the character of the site.

Long mounds or not: does it matter?

Building monumental structures that consisted of façades, graves, pits and stone-packings, could have enforced the formation of a more unified comprehension of how the world worked. It would not however have mattered if the row of pits and postholes were façade structures in long mounds or some kind of entrances or shielding to screen off certain parts of the sites. The architecture could have functioned in a similar way in both scenarios; some people had the right to access all parts of a monumental structure or site while others were excluded (e.g. Barrett 1994).

Whether the standing posts are in fact long mounds or simply façade structures is therefore subordinate to the more profound question of how human experiences at these sites shaped and created the understanding of the Neolithic world.

References

Andersen, S. H. 1975. Ringkloster, en jysk inlandsboplads med Ertebøllekultur. *KUML* 1973-74, 11-94.

Andersen, S. H. 1989. Norsminde. A køkkenmødding with late Mesolithic and Early Neolithic occupation. *Journal of Danish Archaeology* 8, 13-40.

Andersson, L. 1989. *Pilgrimsmärken och vallfart: medeltida pilgrimskultur i Skandinavien.* Lund studies in medieval archaeology 7, Lund.

Andersson, A-K. 2013. Bringing it all together – Pits as monuments, in *NW Europe in Transition. The Early Neolithic in Britain and South Sweden.* In (eds.) M. Larsson and J. Debert, BAR Series 2475, Oxford.

Andersson, M. 2004. S*kapa plats i landskapet. Tidig- och mellanneolitiska samhällen utmed två västskåska dalgångar.* Acta Archaeologica Lundensia Series in 8. No 42, Lund.

Andersson, M. and Wallebom, B. 2010. *Grav- och samlingsplats från början av yngre stenålder. Skåne, Håslövs Socken, Håslöv 10:1 och 13:1, RAÄ 47. Väg E6 Trelleborg-Vellinge Dnr 423-2457-2007 och 423-4455-2007.* Rapport 2010:30, UV-Syd.

Ashbee, P. 1966. The Fussell's Lodge Long Barrow Excavations 1957. *Archaeologia* (Second Series) 100, 1-80.

Ashmore, W. and Knapp, A. 1999. *Archaeologies of Landscape: Contemporary Perspectives.* London, Wiley.

Barrett, J. C. 1994. *Fragments From Antiquity. An Archaeology of Social Life in Britain, 2900-1200 BC.* Oxford, Blackwell.

Berggren, Å., Brink, K., and Skoglund, P. 2009. *Bolagsbacken, Nummertolvsvägen and Hörlanders Väg. Undersökningar inför villabyggelse. Södra Sallerups Socken i Malmö Stad. Skåne län.* Malmö, Malmö museer arkeologienheten.

Bradley, R. 1998. *The Significance of Monuments: On the Shaping of Human Experience in Neolithic and Bronze Age Europe.* London, Routledge.

Bradley, R. 2000. *An Archaeology of Natural Places.* New York, Routledge.

Britnell, W. J. and Savory, H. N. 1984. *Gwernvale and Pennywyrlod: Two Neolithic Long Cairns in the Black Mountains of Brecknock.* Cambrian Archaeological Monograph 2. Cardiff, Cambrian Archaeological Society.

Brophy, K. and Noble, G. 2011. Within and beyond pits: deposition in lowland Neolithic Scotland. *In Beyond the Mundane: Regional Perspectives on Neolithic Pit Deposition.* In (eds.) H. Lamdin-Whymark and J. Thomas, Neolithic Studies Group Seminar Papers, 63-76. Oxford, Oxbow.

Bollnow, O. F. 1994. *Mensch und Raum.* Kohlhammer Verlag, Stuttgart.

Bourdieu, P. 1977. *Outline of a theory of practice.* Cambridge, Cambridge University Press.

Bulzan, O.S. 2008. *Church Architecture and Baptist Missions in Transylvania 1871-1918.* PhD Thesis North Carolina University, North Carolina.

Carlie, A. 2004. *Forntida byggnadskult. Tradition och regionaliteter i södra Skandinavien.* Riksantikvarieämbetet Arkeologiska undersökningar, skrifter no. 57, Stockholm.

Carlstein, T. 1982. *Time Resources, Society and Ecology: On the Capacity for Human Interaction in Space and Time.* Lund, Institutionen för kulturgeografi.

Edmonds, M. 1999. *Ancestral Geographies of the Neolithic. Landscapes, Monuments and Memory.* London, Routledge.

Engström, B. 1927. *Berättelser över undersökning av långdös vid Örnakulla, Skabersjö Socken, Bara Härad, Skåne.* Stockholm, ATA.

Ericsson Lagerås, K. 1999. *En långhög vid Krångeltofta.* Riksantikvarieämbetet, UV syd Rapport 1999:44, Malmö.

Garrow, D. 2006. *Pits, Settlement and Deposition during the Neolithic and Early Bronze Age in East Anglia.* BAR British Series 414, Oxford.

Giddens, A. 1979. *Central Problems in Social Theory. Action, Structure and Contradiction in Social Analysis.* Los Angeles, University of California Press.

Gidlöf, K. and Hammarstrand Dehman, K. and Johansson, T. 2006. *Citytunnelprojektet – Delområde 1 Almhov.* Malmö, Malmö Kulturmiljövård.

Gidlöf, K. 2009. En Tidigneolitisk smalingsplats. In *Tematisk Rapportering av Citytunnelprojektet.* In C. Hadevik and M. Steineke (eds.), 91-136. Malmö, Malmö museer.

Glob, P. V. 1975. De dödes lange hus. *Skalk.* vol 6, 10-14.

Gustavi, P. 1998. *Vreta Kloster under tusen år. Ansgårdskommissionen.* Vadstena Affärstryck AB, Linköping.

Hadevik, C. 2009. Trattbägarkulturen I Malmöområdet. In *Tematisk rapportering av Citytunnelprojektet.* In C. Hadevik and M. Steineke (eds.) Malmö , Malmö Museer.

Hägerstrand, T. 1973. The domain of human geography. In *Directions in geography.* In (ed.) R. Chorley, 67-87. London, Methuen.

Ingold, T. 2000. *The Perception of the environment. Essays on Livelihood, Dwelling and Skil.* London, Rouledge.

Ingold, T. 2011. *Being Alive. Essays on movement, knowledge and description.* Oxon, Routledge.

Jönsson, L. and Lövgren, k. 2003. *Öresundsförbindelsen Fosie 9A-B. Rapport över arkeologisk slutundersökning.* Malmö, Malmö Kulturmiljö.

Karsten, P. 1994. *Att kasta yxan i sjön. En studie över rituell tradition och förändring utifrån skånska neolitiska offerfynd,* Stockholm, Almqvist and Wiksell.

Kealhof, L. 1999. Creating Social Identity in the Landscape: Tidewater, Virginia, 1600-1750. In *Archaeologies of Landscape: Contemporary Perspectives.* In (eds.) W. Ashmore and A. Knapp. London, Wiley.

Lamdin-Whymark, H. 2008. *The Residue of Ritualised Action: Neolithic Deposition Practices in the Middle Thames Valley.* BAR British Series 466, Oxford.

Larsson, M. 1984. *Tidigneolitikum i Sydvästskåne. Kronologi och bosättningsmönster.* Lund, Gleerup.

Larsson, M. 1997. *Från det vilda till det tama. Aspekter på neolitiseringen i sydsverige.* Stockholm, Stockholm archeological Reports.

Larsson, M. 2007. I was walking through the wood the other day – Man and landscape during the late Mesolithic and early Neolithic in Scania, Southern Sweden, in *On the road – Studies in honour of Lars Larsson.* (eds.) K. Hårdh, K. Jennbert, and B. Olausson. Lund, Almqvist and Wiksell.

Lindahl Jensen, B. 2002. Långhögen i Krångeltofta. En redogörelse för undersökningarna av en tidneolitisk långhög. In *Monumentala gravformer i det äldsta bondesamhället.* In (ed.) Larsson, L. Report series No. 83, Lund, 111-117.

Lindhé, E., Sarnäs, P., Steineke, M., (eds.) 2001. *Citytunneln och spåren i landskapet. Projektprogram och undersökningsplaner för arkeologiska slutundersökningar för Citytunnelns spårsträckningar och Hotelltomten.* Malmö, Malmö Kulturmiljö.

Liversage, D. 1980. Neolithic monuments at Lindebjerg, Northwest Zealand. *Acta Archaeologica* Vol 51, 85-152.

Midgley, M. 1985. *The Origin and Function of the Earthern Long Barrows of Northern Europe.* BAR International Series 259, Oxford.

Nilsson, B. and Rudebeck, E. 2010. *Arkeologiska och förhistoriska världar; fält, erfarenheter och stenåldersplatser i Sydvästra Skåne.* Malmö, Malmö Kulturmiljö.

Parker-Pearson, M. and Richards, C. 1994. *Architecture and order; Approaches to social space.* London, Routledge.

Persson, P. 1999. *Neolitikums början: undersökningar kring jordbrukets introduktion i Nordeuropa.* Göteborg, GOTARC.

Price, D and Gebauer, A, B 2005. *Smakkerup Huse. A Late Mesolithic Coastal Site in Northwest Zealand, Denmark.* Gylling, Narayana Press.

Rudebeck, E. 1985. *Rapport Arkeologisk Huvudundersökning Ängdala, Område B:2 MHM:6655S.* Sallerup Sn. Skåne, Malmö kommun, Malmöhus län.

Rudebeck, E. 2006. Kulthus och huskult – aspekter på de tidneolitiska långhögarna. In *Kulthus and dödshus. Det ritualiserade rummets teori och praktik.* In (eds.) M. Anglert, M. Artursson, and F. Svanberg. 9-20. Stockholm, Riksantikvarieämbetet.

Rudebeck, E. 2002. En tidneolitisk långhög I Kristineberg. In *Monumentala gravformer I det äldsta bondesamhället.* Ed L. Larsson. Lund, University of Lund.

Rudebeck, E. and Ödman, C. 2000. *En gravplats under 4500 år.* Malmö, Malmöfynd.

Schnittger, H. 1910. *Förhistoriska flintgruvor och kulturlager vid Kvarnby och S. Sallerup i* Stockholm, *Skåne.*

Sjöström, A. and Pihl, H. 2002. Undersökning av Örnakulladösen, in *Monumentala gravformer i det äldsta bondesamhället.* In (ed.) L. Larsson. Departement of archaeology and ancient history. Report Series NO.83, Lund, 47-77.

Strömberg, M. 1976. *Forntid I Sydostskåne.* Föreningen för fornminnes- och hembygdsvård i sydöstra Lund, Skåne.

Thomell, K. 1987. *Vägen till Santiago de Compostella. En resehandbok för turister och pilgrimer.* Stockholm, Catholica förlag.

Tilley, C. 1994. *A phenomenology of landscape: places, paths, and monuments.* London, Berg.

Tilley, C 1996. *An ethnography of the Neolithic – Early Prehistoric Societies in Southern Scandinavia.* Cambridge, Cambridge University Press.

Trimen, A. 1856. *Church and Chapel Architecture.* London, Longman, Brown, Green, and Longmans.

Welinder, S. Hadevik, C. Gidlöf, K. and Rudebeck, E. 2009. Grismönster I gropkaos, In *Tematisk rapportering av Citytunnelprojektet.* In (eds.) C. Hadevik and M. Steineke. Malmö, Malmö Museer.

Unpublished sources

http://whc.unesco.org/en/list/669 visited 2014-02-14

www.galiciaguide.com visited 2014-02-03

Chapter 5

Neolithisation and Introduction of Causewayed Enclosures.
Two Structurally Related Processes

Lutz Klassen

Museum of Eastern Jutland, Denmark

In this paper, the neolithisation of Great Britain and South Scandinavia as well as that of some central European regions around 4000 BC is compared to the introduction of causewayed enclosures in South Britain and South Scandinavia as well as the large scale construction of these sites in central western France, northern central Germany as well as Bavaria between 3750 and 3500 BC. It is argued that both processes were structurally related, as both represent related, contemporaneous developments in geographically separated and widespread parts of Central and Western Europe. From this observation it is concluded that Neolithic groups of Central and Western Europe played an active and decisive role in the neolithisation of both Great Britain and South Scandinavia, including the immigration of smaller or larger groups of farmers.

Keywords: Neolithisation, causewayed enclosures, South Scandinavia, Great Britain, structurally related processes

The neolithisation has been and still is one of the most debated topics in both British and South Scandinavian archaeology, as evident from among others the present publication. Especially since the general abandonment of simplistic colonization models from the 1960s onwards, a bewildering amount of divergent explanations has been proposed for a historical process, which in importance only is matched by the industrial revolution in the 18th and 19th centuries and probably by the currently ongoing IT revolution. The discussions in Britain and Scandinavia in general are well comparable to each other, not least because many theoretical models developed by British scholars have been taken over and adapted to the local evidence (with some delay) by the Scandinavians. This of course not least is conditioned by the fact that the historical development in both regions follows a related course: both saw a major and lasting introduction of domesticates (with possible, earlier exceptions of regionally restricted importance) around the transition between the fifth and fourth millennium and both had been comparatively close neighbors to fully developed agricultural groups for long times (between one and one and a half millennium) previous to the neolithisation.

At present, the large number of different contributions to the debate roughly can be grouped in two different categories. Papers assuming a decisive and active role of Neolithic populations outside Great Britain and South Scandinavia make up the first category. Practically all of these operate with lesser or greater amounts of early farmers moving in from the south, often combined with a subsequent acculturation of the local Mesolithic population (e.g. Sheridan 2010 and Bayliss et al. 2011 for the British Isles, Klassen 2004 for South Scandinavia). Papers in the second category favor an indigenous adaption model and thus assume a much more important role played by the local Mesolithic population, either in form of a 'balanced interaction' with Neolithic groups, or with complete dominance of Mesolithic decision making (e.g. Thomas 2003; 2007 for the British Isles, Fischer 2002 for South Scandinavia).

The present authors' opinion on the matter clearly can be categorized as belonging to the first category (Klassen 1999a; 2002; 2004). This opinion not least is derived at by an attempt not to view the neolithisation of South Scandinavia (and Great Britain) in a local perspective, but in a European context. Explanation models that operate with a decisive role of the Mesolithic populations in the two regions in question are completely acceptable – as long as they are viewed in isolation each on their own. But in a larger geographical and historical framework they are not convincing to the present author. Should it really be a coincidence that the Mesolithic groups in the south of England decided to integrate Neolithic practices in their life more or less exactly at the same time as Scandinavian Ertebølle groups did? Not to mention several groups in the alpine forelands of central Europe that faced the same historical development at the same time? The Mesolithic groups in question all had a very different character, population density, natural habitats and subsistence economies. Still, they all underwent a closely related process at the same time.

Furthermore, especially Britain and South Scandinavia show a number of closely related specific traits, which seem to indicate closely related developments. For example, the neolithisation in both regions appears to begin not only around the same time in the very late fifth millennium BC, but in both cases it can be observed that domesticates and Neolithic pottery types first appear in a sub-region of restricted size located closest to the Neolithic neighbors to the south, from where they spread throughout the entire region. For Great Britain, a recent comprehensive investigation of this question is available (Bayliss et al. 2011), while such an investigation hasn't yet been done for South Scandinavia. However, in this area, radiocarbon dates of the earliest TRB pottery in the southernmost part (Schleswig-Holstein) generally are ca. 100-150 years earlier than those of TRB groups further north (Hartz 2011) and the earliest radiocarbon dates for bones of domesticated animals show the same trend (compare the dates for Denmark (Noe-Nygaard 2005, 856f. Tab. 1; Fischer and Gotfredsen 2006) with those for northern Germany, especially the dates for bones of goat/sheep from Wangels LA 505 (Hartz and Lübke 2004, 136 Tab. 1)). It should be noted that the conclusion drawn here only relates to the process of large scale, lasting neolithisation of the entire regions. This does not exclude more sporadic, earlier events of neolithisation as those proposed by Sheridan (2010), which only seem to have affected restricted (coastal) regions of the British Isles. Strictly speaking it is thus the emergence of the TRB in South Scandinavia that is compared to that of the "Carinated Bowl Neolithic" in the British Isles.

The earliest Neolithic pottery in both regions (again, disregarding potential sporadic earlier developments as those possibly indicated by the Castellic-vessel from Achnacreebeag in western Scotland, Sheridan 2010, 94 Fig. 9.3.1) furthermore appear fully or at least partly to belong to the same general tradition characterized by the use of largely undecorated vessels of northern French ancestry. Such a geographic relation hardly is surprising for the south of Britain, while in South Scandinavia it can be explained by the dynamics of the Michelsberg Culture expanding eastwards from the Paris Basin (Schier 1993; Jeunesse 1998; Klassen 2004).

One last example of parallel developments shall be mentioned here. It recently (Sheridan and Pailler 2012) has been proposed that the appearance of alpine jade axes in the British Isles closely is connected to the neolithisation. The authors assume these axes to have been the treasured possessions of Neolithic groups from the continent that took them across the Channel when they set out to colonize the British Isles. While the available evidence for the dating of these artifacts is scarce and in itself doesn't allow proving the proposition, it nevertheless appears rather likely – at least for part of the axes. There is very little evidence for exchange relations between late Mesolithic people in Britain and Neolithic farmers to the south, making it unlikely that the axes crossed the Channel prior to neolithisation. The same conclusion can be reached by the investigation of meaning and function of these sacred objects throughout Europe (Pétrequin et al. 2012), which appears to be related to agricultural societies. The latest

type of alpine jade axes, the Puy type, is missing almost completely from the British inventory, giving an upper limit for the movement of the axes across the Channel in the early fourth millennium BC.

In south Scandinavia there is massive evidence for exchange of artifacts between the Mesolithic Ertebølle groups and Neolithic groups in different parts of Europe (Klassen 2004). Therefore, the comparatively few alpine axes with production dates in the fifth millennium known in south Scandinavia (Klassen in press) earlier have been assumed to have reached the area in Ertebølle times (Klassen 1999b). None of the axes have been found in any archaeologically relevant context, but an increasing number of local imitations do. All of these date to the Early Neolithic. A find from the very earliest part (Oxie-group with type 0-beakers) from Lisbjerg Skole in eastern Jutland (Skousen 2008, 131) provides evidence for the appearance of axes of alpine jade at the time of neolithisation in South Scandinavia.

It can thus be stated that the neolithisation of Britain (with the possible exceptions referred to above) and South Scandinavia not only occurred at approximately the same time, but that it also involved closely related events that hardly can be explained by independent actions of Mesolithic people. Consequently it must be assumed that the cause of events must be looked for outside Great Britain and South Scandinavia, in the distribution area of Neolithic groups further south on the continent. The dynamics of the Michelsberg Culture already referred to above leaves little doubt that powerful historical developments were at play at the time in question, and that these easily could have affected Mesolithic groups in neighboring regions. In the absence of sufficient aDNA evidence it is at present not possible to prove that the movement of smaller or larger groups of Neolithic farmers into Great Britain and South Scandinavia was part of the process, but at least for South Scandinavia an argument can be made that this in fact was the case. Here, the earliest Neolithic settlement almost completely is confined to a zone only stretching few km from the coast inland (e.g. Madsen 1982, 213 Fig. 11). This in general is the same coastal zone that was inhabited by people in Ertebølle times. The material culture of these early Neolithic groups shows clear evidence of continuity from the Mesolithic, like the presence of core axes in early Neolithic contexts (Ravn 2005, 6; Fischer 2002, 351 Fig. 22.5p) or the appearance of Ertebølle type lamps in Early Neolithic context (Meurers-Balke 1983, 55; Fischer 2002, 353 Fig. 22.7c). Even more illustrative are transitional pottery types found in relevant stratigraphic contexts as those described by S.H. Andersen (2011, 211; 1993, 87 Fig. 32). Furthermore, many Ertebølle sites, among them probably all or almost all kitchen midden sites, continued to be used in the Early Neolithic. This pattern certainly indicates the taking over of Neolithic habits by the local Ertebølle population.

However, a few sites diverge from this pattern. These are located high in the landscape and further away from the coast, in topographical settings completely atypical for the Ertebølle Culture. The ceramic inventory of these sites, e.g. Stilling in eastern Jutland (Andersen, N.H. 1977, 208 Fig. 8) or Flintbek in northern Germany (Zich 1993, 21f. Figs. 5-6) diverges from that of the coastal sites by the lack of any Ertebølle-elements or transitional types and by the presence of a strong Michelsberg-component. This component is considerably more pronounced than that which can be identified in the material culture of Early Neolithic sites in the coastal zone. The Flintbek site furthermore has delivered the earliest radiocarbon dates for the TRB in Scandinavia - apart from one date published by Zich (1993, 20), another, unpublished even slightly earlier (D. Mischka, written comm.). These observations all seem to indicate the presence of (small) immigrated groups originating in the distribution area of the Michelsberg Culture and settling outside the region occupied by Ertebølle groups.

In the following, the neolithisation in Great Britain and South Scandinavia will be compared to a development that can be observed in the same regions a few hundred years later: the introduction of causewayed enclosures. While these intriguing monuments have been the topic of intense research ever since they first were discovered in the 19th century, the process behind their first appearance in different parts of Europe hasn't gotten nearly as much attention. At least this is true for South Scandinavia, where a paper by T. Madsen (1988) represents a remarkable exception. The explanation presented by Madsen exclusively operates with social and economic developments inside local TRB groups as cause of events. No active role of Neolithic groups, which in other parts of Europe constructed and used causewayed enclosures prior to their introduction in South Scandinavia, is assumed. Taken the striking resemblance not only in architecture, but obviously also in the actions

that have taken place in the enclosures (as evident from specific traits like recuttings and refillings of the ditch segments and depositions of human bones) into account, this assumption at least can be questioned. In a recent research project funded by The Carlsberg Foundation (Klassen in preparation), the problem has been investigated in detail by comparative studies of enclosure chronology and architecture. Given the space limitations of this paper, only the results of the chronological investigations will be presented shortly in the following.

Causewayed enclosures of the general type known from Britain and South Scandinavia seem to appear for the first time in the Linear Pottery Culture in Central Europe in the later parts of the 6th millennium (Jeunesse 2011). At present, only a few, geographically spread sites are known from this phase as well as from the early 5th millennium. Between 4700 and 4400 BC, a regional concentration of this type of monument emerges in the Cerny Culture of Northern France (Fig. 1). As apparent from the course of events in the following time, the Cerny enclosures represent the start of the development that led to the construction of enclosures in Britain and South Scandinavia almost one millennium later. Between 4400 and 4000 BC, the number of enclosures increases drastically (Fig. 2). From northern France they spread rapidly eastwards, a development that is connected to the emergence and development of the Michelsberg Culture. The easternmost of these sites is located at Kly in Central Bohemia. Even further to the east, comparatively few late Lengyel sites have been mapped in southern Poland. These belong to a slightly deviating architectural tradition characterized by considerably fewer interruptions of the ditches. The enclosures of the Münchshofen group in the valley of the Danube and its tributaries in Bavaria also belong to this tradition. In the

Figure 1: Distribution of causewayed enclosures built between ca. 4700 and 4400 BC.

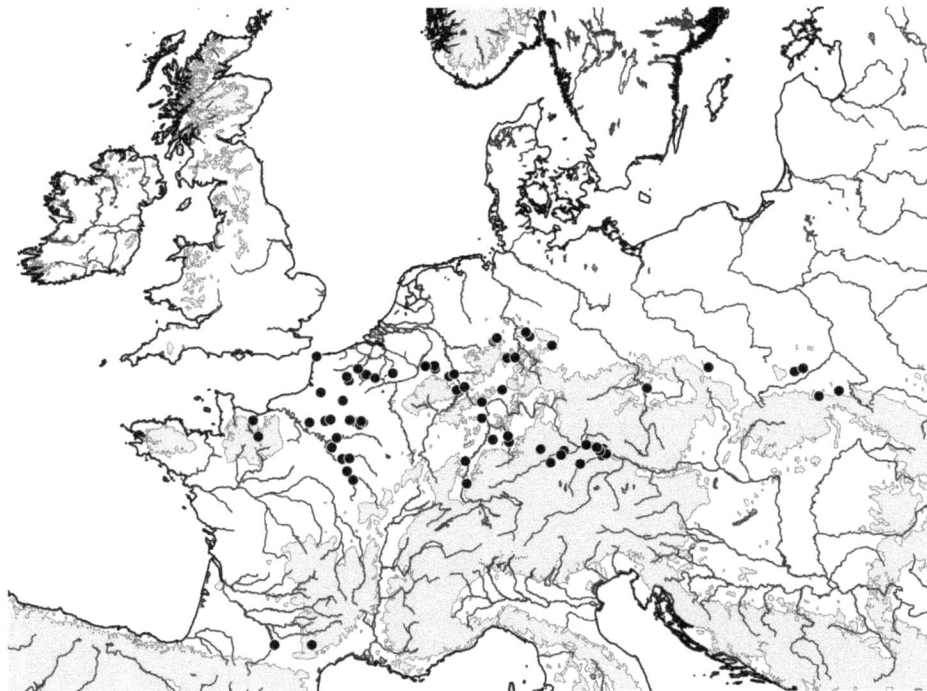

Figure 2: Distribution of causewayed enclosures built between ca. 4400 and 4000 BC.

Chasséen Culture of southern France, the first enclosures also seem to appear at this time. These monuments probably must be seen in relation to the development in northern France.

The next map shows enclosures that were constructed between 4000 and 3750 BC (Fig. 3). The number of sites is lower than in the preceding horizon, also when the different length of the two periods is taken into account. Apart from the Middle Rhine area, new enclosures were

built in the entire distribution area of the earlier sites. An enlargement of the distribution area towards the north in central Germany and first of all towards the Atlantic coast in the west can be observed. The Magheraboy enclosure in northwestern Ireland seemingly represents the first site in northwestern Europe as indicated by the radiocarbon dates (Cooney et al. 2011, 574ff.). However, due its geographically and chronologically isolated position, it won't be taken into consideration in the following.

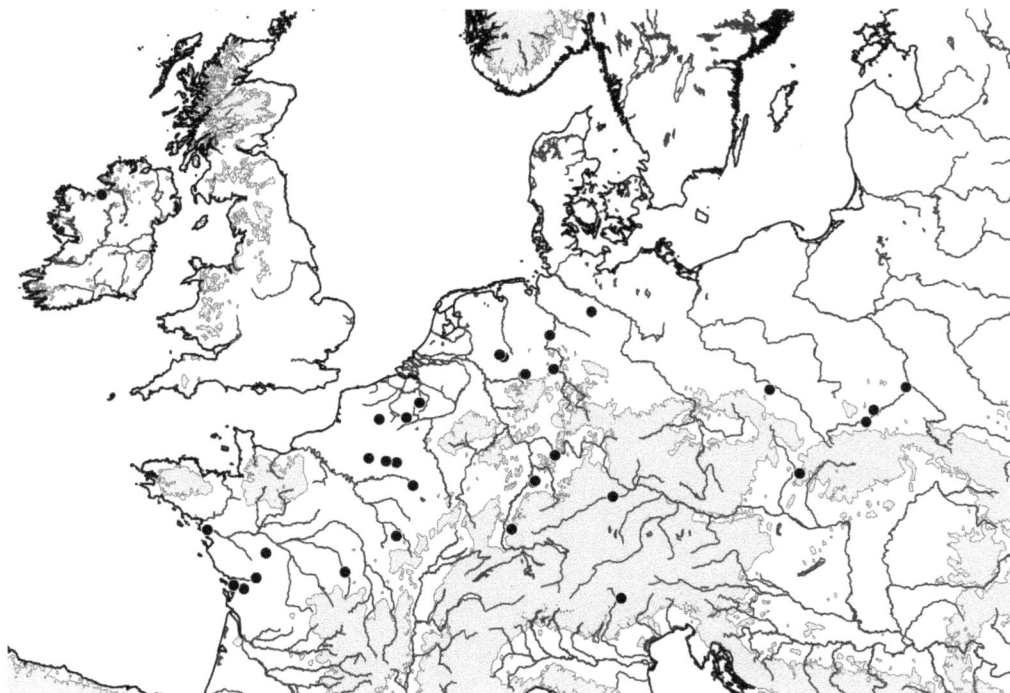

Figure 3: Distribution of causewayed enclosures built between ca. 4000 and 3750 BC.

Within the last chronological horizon of interest here, the time between 3750 and 3500 BC, a dramatic development in enclosure construction takes place in Europe (Fig. 4). Intense building activity can be registered in central western France, in South Britain, in northern central Germany and in the valley of the Danube in Bavaria. Within the former core area of enclosure construction, all building activity seems to stop, apart from a number of sites that are located on a linear path between the valley of the Neckar in south-western Germany and northern central Germany. Even further to the north, and located on the same linear path, the first sites appear in the TRB Culture of South Scandinavia. In the latter region, the state of research in enclosure chronology is very poor, as radiocarbon dates relating to the time of construction of the enclosures only are available for three of the total of 39 known sites. While several enclosures certainly weren't constructed until after 3500 BC, a number of the yet undated sites may well belong to the horizon depicted in Fig. 4.

In Britain and Ireland, only enclosures that have been dated by radiocarbon dates (Whittle et al. 2011) have been depicted in Fig. 4. The number of enclosures belonging to the time horizon in question here without any doubt is much higher than apparent from the illustration, as all but one (the Magheraboy site referred to above) of the radiocarbon-dates enclosures belong to the time between 3750 and 3500 BC, making it likely that at least the vast majority, if not all of the yet undated sites are contemporaneous.

In central Europe, a number of the sites depicted in Fig. 4 has been radiocarbon-dated, but most have been included here based on archaeological dates derived from pottery chronology (sites of the Altheim Culture in Bavaria) or based on enclosure design (northern central Europe – see Geschwinde and Raetzel-Fabian 2009).

While the quality and precision of the available enclosure chronology in the different parts of Europe thus is very inhomogeneous and some of the continental sites may belong to a different time horizon, there can generally seen be no doubt that the development reflected in Fig. 4 represents a historical reality. Enclosure construction in large parts of the former core area of building seized completely between 3750 and 3500 BC, and intense building activity started at the western and northern periphery of this region. The only parts of the former core area of enclosure construction where considerable building activity can be observed are located in the parts of Bavaria and the western parts of Germany.

There can hardly be any doubt that people in all regions that saw massive enclosure building for the first time between 3750 and 3500 BC had knowledge of enclosures in the centuries preceding the construction boom. What is reflected in Fig. 4 thus is the activation of a passively present concept. It is worth noting that this development from the very beginning led to individual design principles in the different regions. While considerable variation is present, each of the four major regions of construction appears to have a typical "standard" type of enclosure. In Britain, comparatively small (1-2 ha) enclosures of slightly oval, nearly round shape with frequent interruptions of the often widely spaced enclosures ditches are frequent (Oswald et al. 2001, 58 Fig. 4.6). The Altheim sites in Bavaria are very small, often below 1 ha in size, have a rounded rectangular outlay and few interruptions of the ditches (Matuschik 1991). The enclosures of the older Les Matignons group in

Figure 4: Distribution of causewayed enclosures built between ca. 3750 and 3500 BC.

central western France show a very complex design, with few interruptions of the ditches, ditches separating different parts of the interior and characteristic, crab-claw shaped entrances (Cassen 1987, 313ff. Figs. 103-107). Finally, in northern central Germany, monumental sites with sizes over 20 ha and a specific pear-shape with one flattened side (façade) frequently were constructed (Geschwinde/ Raetzel-Fabian 2009, 211 Abb. 156).

There can't be much doubt that the contemporaneous construction of large numbers of enclosures in many spatially separated parts of Europe was triggered by the same historical development or event and doesn't reflect regionally independent evolutions. The latter could be argued for in case of Britain and South Scandinavia due to the latter two regions related history of the earliest parts of the Neolithic. However, the development apparent from Fig. 4 also affected regions with completely different Neolithic histories, like Bavaria and northern central Germany. All of the regions that witnessed an enclosure building boom seem have been interconnected by a net of long distance roads through which the information that triggered the development could have been relayed quickly (Klassen in preparation).

The structural similarities between the neolithisation of Great Britain, South Scandinavia and a number of other regions in Europe around 4000 BC on one side and the introduction of enclosures in central western France, south Britain, northern central Germany and South Scandinavia in the 38th to 36th centuries BC on the other side are striking. Both are simultaneous processes occurring in spatially separated regions throughout large parts of western and central Europe. And in both cases the innovations that were introduced in the different regions had been known and been used actively by Neolithic groups in neighboring regions for long times prior to their introduction in course of the processes discussed here. Knowledge to the innovations in question must be assumed to have been present in all cases long time before they actually occurred. The case of the enclosures demonstrates without doubt that historical developments in Neolithic Cultures of Europe could trigger simultaneous events in distant peripheral regions. The similarity between this process and that of the neolithisation a few centuries earlier is thus another argument for the assumption of a decisive and active role of Neolithic groups in the neolithisation.

References

Andersen, N.H. 1977. Arkæologi Langs Den Østjyske Motorvej, Skanderborg-Århus. *KUML* 1976, 199-219.

Andersen, S.H. 1993. Bjørnsholm. A Stratified Køkkenmødding on the Central Limfjord, North Jutland. *Journal of Danish Archaeology* 10, 1991, 59-96.

Andersen, S.H. 2011. Kitchen middens and the early pottery of Denmark. *Berichte der Römisch-Germanischen Kommission* 89, 2008, 193-215.

Bayliss, A., Healy, F., Whittle, A. and Cooney, G. 2011. Neolithic narratives: British and Irish enlosures in their timespace. In A. Whittle, F. Healy and A. Bayliss (eds.), *Gathering Time. Dating the Early Neolithic Enclosures of Southern Britain and Ireland vol 2, 682-842.* Oxford, Oxbow.

Cassen, S. 1987. *Le Centre-Ouest de la France au IVème millénaire av. J.C.* British Archaeology Reports International Series 342. Oxford, BAR.

Cooney, G., Bayliss, A., Healy, F.,Whittle, A., Danaker, E., Cagney, L., Mallory, J., Smyth, J., Kador, Th. and O'Sullivan, M. 2011. Ireland. In A. Whittle, F. Healy and A. Bayliss (eds.), *Gathering Time. Dating the Early Neolithic Enclosures of Southern Britain and Ireland vol 2,* 562-669. Oxford, Oxbow.

Fischer, A. 2002. Food for feasting? An evaluation of explanations of the neolithisation in Denmark and southern Sweden. In A. Fischer and K. Kristiansen (eds.), *The Neolithisation of Denmark. 150 years of debate,* 343-393. Sheffield, J.R. Collis Publications.

Fischer, A. and Gotfredsen, A.B. 2006. Da landbruget kom til Nordvestsjælland – tidligt tamkvæg i Åmosen. *Fra Nordvestsjælland. Årbog for kulturhistorien i Nordvestsjælland* 2005/6, 35-54.

Geschwinde, M. and Raetzel-Fabian, D. 2009. *EWBSL. Eine Fallstudie zu den jungneolithischen Erdwerken am Nordrand der Mittelgebirge.* Beiträge zur Archäologie in Niedersachsen Band 14. Rahden/West. , Verlag Marie Leihdorf.

Hartz, S. and Lübke, H. 2004. Zur chronostratigraphischen Gliederung der Ertebølle-Kultur und frühen Trichterbecherkultur in der südlichen Mecklenburger Bucht. *Bodendenkmalpflege in Mecklenburg-Vorpommern, Jahrbuch* 52, 119-143.

Hartz, S. 2011. From pointed bottom to round and flat bottom – tracking early pottery from Schleswig-Holstein. *Berichte der Römisch-Germanischen Kommission* 89, 2008, 241-276.

Jeunesse, Ch. 1998. Pour une origine occidentale de la culture de Michelsberg? In J. Biel, H. Schlichterle, M. Strobel and A. Zeeb (eds.), *Die Michelsberger Kultur und ihre Randgebiete - Probleme der Entstehung, Chronologie und des Siedlungswesens. Kolloqium Hemmenhofen 21.-23.2. 1997.* Materialhefte Zur Archäologie In Baden-Württemberg 43, 29-45. Stuttgart, Konrad Theiss.

Jeunesse, Ch. 2011. Enceintes à fossé discontinu et enceintes à pseudo-fossé dans le néolithique d'Europe centrale et occidentale. In A. Denaire, Ch. Jeunesse and Ph. Lefranc (eds..), *Nécropoles et enceintes danubiennes du Ve millénaire dans le Nord-est de la France et le Sud-Oust de l'Allemagne.* Actes de la table ronde internationale de Strasbourg organisée par l'UMR 7044 (CNRS et Université de Strasbourg). Maison Interuniversitaire des Sciences de l'Homme-Alsace

(MISHA), 2 juin 2010, 31-71. Strasbourg, Université de Strasbourg.

Klassen, L. 1999a. The debate on the Mesolithic-Neolithic transition in the western Baltic: A central European perspective. *Journal of Danish Archaeology* 13, 1996-97,171-178.

Klassen, L. 1999b. Prestigeøkser af sjældne alpine bjergarter - en glemt og overset fundgruppe fra ældre stenalders slutning i Danmark. *Kuml* 1999, 11-51.

Klassen, L. 2002. The Ertebølle Culture and Neolithic continental Europe: traces of contact and interaction. In A. Fischer and K. Kristiansen (eds.), *The Neolithisation of Denmark. 150 years of debate*, 303-317. Sheffield, J.R. Collis Publications.

Klassen, L. 2004. *Jade und Kupfer. Untersuchungen zum Neolithisierungsprozess im westlichen Ostseeraum unter besonderer Berücksichtigung der Kulturentwicklung Europas 5500-3500 BC.* Højbjerg, Jutland Archaeological Society Publications Vol. 47.

Klassen, L. in press. Axes of Alpine jade from southern Scandinavia and northernmost Germany. *Danish Journal of Archaeology* 1, 2013,

Klassen, L. in preparation. *Detecting causewayed enclosures in South Scandinavia. A case study from Djursland, Denmark.* Research project funded by The Carlsberg Foundation.

Madsen, T. 1982. Settlement Systems of Early Agricultural Societies in east Jutland, Denmark. A Regional Study of Change. *Journal of Anthropological Archaeology* 1982-1, 197-236.

Madsen, T. 1988. Causewayed Enclosures in South Scandinavia. In C. Burgess, P. Topping, C. Mordant and M. Maddison (eds.), *Enclosures and defences in the Neolithic of Western Europe vol. 2*, 301-336. British Archaeological Reports International Series 403. Oxford, BAR.

Meurers-Balke, J. 1983. *Siggeneben-Süd. Ein Fundplatz der frühen Trichterbecherkultur an der holsteinischen Ostseeküste.* Offa-Bücher Band 50. Neumünster, Karl Wachholtz Verlag.

Matuschik, I. 1991. Grabenwerke des Spätneolithikums in Süddeutschland. *Fundberichte aus Baden-Württemberg* 16, 1991, 27-55.

Noe-Nygaard, N., Price, T.D. and Hede, S.U. 2005. Diet of aurochs and early cattle in southern Scandinavia: evidence from ^{15}N and ^{13}C stable isotopes. *Journal of Archaeological Science* 32, 855-871.

Oswald, A., Dyer C. and Barber, L. 2001. *The creation of monuments. Neolithic causewayed enclosures in the British Isles.* London, English Heritage.

Pétrequin, P., Cassen, S., Errera, M., Gauthier, E., Klassen, L. Pétrequin and Sheridan, A. 2012. Des choses sacrées... fonctions idéelles des jades alpins en Europe

occidentale. In P. Pétrequin, S. Cassen, M. Errera, L. Klassen, A. Sheridan and Anne-Marie Pétrequin (eds.), *JADE. Grandes haches alpines du Néolithique européen. Ve et IVe millénaires av. J.-C.* Maison des Sciences de l'Homme et de l'Environment Besançon, 1354-1423. Besançon, Presses Universitaires de Franche-Comté.

Ravn, M. 2005. Fjordbønder. *Skalk* 2005-2, 5-12.

Schier, W. 1993. Das westliche Mitteleuropa an der Wende vom 5. zum 4. Jahrtausend: Kulturwandel durch Kulturkontakt? In A. Lang, H. Parzinger and H. Küster (eds.), *Kulturen zwischen Ost und West. Festschrift G. Kossack*, 19-60. Berlin, Akademie Verlag.

Sheridan, A. 2010. The Neolithisation of Britain and Ireland: the Big Picture. In B. Finlayson and G. Warren (eds.), *Landscapes in Transition*, 89-105. Oxford, Oxbow.

Sheridan, A. and Pailler, Y. 2012. Les haches alpines et leurs imitations en Grande-Bretagne, dans l'Île de Man, en Irlande et dans les l'Îles Anglo-Normandes. In P. Pétrequin, S. Cassen, M. Errera, L. Klassen, A. Sheridan and Anne-Marie Pétrequin (eds.), *JADE. Grandes haches alpines du Néolithique européen. Ve et IVe millénaires av. J.-C.* Maison des Sciences de l'Homme et de l'Environment Besançon, 1046-1087. Besançon, Presses Universitaires de Franche-Comté.

Skousen, H. 2008. *Arkæologi I Lange Baner. Undersøgelser forud for anlæggelsen af motorvejen nord om Århus 1998-2007.* Højbjerg, Forlaget Moesgård.

Thomas, J.S. 2003. Thoughts on the 'repacked' Neolithic revolution. *Antiquity* 77, 67-74.

Thomas, J.S. 2007. Mesolithic-Neolithic transitions in Britain: from essence to inhabitation. In A.W.R. Whittle and V. Cummings (eds.), *Going Over: The Mesolithic-Neolithic Transition in North-West Europe*, 423-439. Oxford, British Academy and Oxford University Press.

Whittle, A., Healy, F. and Bayliss, A. 2011. *Gathering Time. Dating the Early Neolithic Enclosures of Southern Britain and Ireland. 2 vol.* Oxford, Oxbow.

Zich, B. 1993. Die Ausgrabung chronisch gefährdeter Hügelgräber der Stein- und Bronzezeit in Flintbek, Kreis Rendsburg-Eckernförde. Ein Vorbericht. *Offa* 49/50, 1992/93, 13-51.

Section 3

Materiality

Chapter 6

Both Artefact and Phenomenon: A Material Approach to Engagements with Fire in the Late Mesolithic of Britain

Ellen McInnes

University of Manchester, UK

This paper seeks to think about the use and understanding of fire in the late Mesolithic of Britain using recent approaches to materials and materiality. Discussions that have returned materials to archaeology are drawn upon to re-evaluate our approaches to the study of fire in the past. The value of taking a new approach to the archaeology of fire is demonstrated through a detailed consideration of the late Mesolithic hearths discovered at March Hill, Yorkshire. Alongside the tangible practices in which the hearths were involved the types of fire and the active properties each would display are discussed. It is suggested that we can think about a social role for fire and the cultural qualities it may have been perceived as holding.

Keywords: Archaeology, Mesolithic, hearths, fire, materials, qualities, properties, flint

Introduction

The use of fire was prevalent in the everyday lives of communities in late Mesolithic Britain. When it has been considered the practical uses of fire, such as cooking or land clearance, have been part of economic and environmental approaches to prehistoric hunter-gatherers (*e.g.* Bennett *et al* 1990; Edwards 1990; Sergant *et al* 2006). To move beyond these functional studies this paper seeks to discuss fire as a material using a number of recent approaches to materials and materiality, predominantly Ingold (2000; 2007; 2010) and Conneller (2011) but also papers in Alberti *et al* (2013) and work by Jones (2012). Drawing on these discussions this paper explores the ways in which fire was experienced in everyday activities through a detailed consideration of the Mesolithic features found at March Hill, West Yorkshire.

A (new) material approach

The concept that material culture is active in past processes and performances is well established in archaeological accounts however, it has been argued that not enough is said of materials themselves (see Boivin 2004; Knappett 2005; Ingold 2012). More recently materiality has become a commonly used approach to study material culture yet there is no agreed understanding of what materiality is or what is meant by the term (Miller 2005). Ingold (2010) has suggested that two themes can be drawn out from the many discussions of the concept. The first pathway as recognised by Ingold (2010) involves social approaches to artefacts, including ideas of symbolism, object agency and practice theory. From this perspective, the study of an object involves considering the biography, meaning, and significance of that object and discussing it in relation to

people, society, landscapes, and other objects. The aim is to understand how things and materials influence human behaviour and how they enable, empower, and constrain people's lives (*e.g.* Graves-Brown 2000; Rowlands 2005; papers in Stevenson and White 2007).

The second approach attempts to resolve the polarization between subject and object at an abstract level however, this is where Ingold (2000; 2007; 2010; 2012) argues may studies of materiality have failed. One consequence of the divide between subject and object is that materials have been discussed as a passive resource. Artefacts have often been understood as shaped and given significance by society; things are only mobilized by the cultural meanings and values attached to them (*e.g.* Godelier 1986; Gosden 1999; Williams and Costall 2000). In Anthropology critiques of this situation have argued that many approaches to material culture only view objects as a tool with which we can pursue an understanding of cultural contexts and social life (Henare *et al* 2007, 3). Within archaeology the separation of mind and matter; the continued distinction between human and material worlds, has left materials mute and invisible in our discussions. In their recent works Ingold (2000; 2007; 2010; 2012), Conneller (2011) and Cummings (2012) have developed approaches that reject the concept of materials as inert matter onto which people impress form and meaning and instead have made the 'hard physicality of the material world' (Olsen 2003, 88) their focus.

In particular Ingold (2007; 2010; 2012) places the properties and characteristics of materials at the centre of his approach and argues that they are key to understanding objects. Rather than objective and universally observable Ingold argues for a relational understanding of properties that are experienced through action and practice in specific social and environmental contexts. The properties of a material are not all evident at once but come to the fore as materials are caught up in changing environments and interactions. It is through practical engagements and sensory perception that Ingold (2007) suggests knowledge of materials is gained and reaffirmed. Tilley (2007) however, while not denying that the properties of materials are relational, has rejected the idea that a study of these alone can get at the meaning and significance of artefacts or materials. Tilley argues, that the relationship between objects and people and their effects, would be lost in an approach that focussed solely on materials.

More recently Cummings (2012) has adopted a material approach to Neolithic archaeology that also draws on ideas from animistic ontologies. For a comprehensive discussion on the use of animistic perspectives in archaeology please see Reynolds (2010) who suggests that embracing different perspectives can offer new opportunities for interpretation. Within an animistic worldview humans and animals are conceived of as having different forms, but being the same in essence (Viveiros de Castro 1998, 478). Cummings (2012) combines a focus on the active, relational and processual nature of materials with the suggestion that an animistic belief in underlying spiritual unity may have been extended to substances, materials, things and objects. For those with an animistic worldview Cummings (2012) suggests that materials may have been understood as animate and the same in essence but in a different form. Consequently the origin, properties and essence of materials may have been key to the way they were used. By incorporating a material approach within existing discussions of animistic worldviews in the early Neolithic Cummings (2012) offers a way to explicitly maintain a focus on the relationship between materials and people.

Conneller (2011) however, has highlighted a problem with an emphasis on active properties: how does a processual and relational approach to materials allow for alternate understandings of those materials? For the Cuebo Indians of the north-west Amazon, it is the power of quartz to trigger the metamorphosis of a lay person to shaman that is seen as its most important property rather than any mechanical aspect we might measure (Pearson 2002, 142; Reynolds 2010, 90). How does this understanding of quartz fit into an approach centered on properties?

In answer Conneller (2011) draws on ideas proposed by Henare *et al* (2007) that question the division between concept and thing and suggests an approach that seeks to identify mechanical properties and cultural qualities as combined in a third thing. In relation to the Cuebo Indians and their understanding of quartz this approach would suggest that the active stony properties of quartz, such as hardness and luminescence, and its transformative power are combined to make a 'powerfully transformative stone' in a contextually specific understanding. In using this approach Conneller (2011) suggests that rather than study an object in terms of its form, function and decoration alone we should look beyond its current state to the materials, transformations, combinations and active engagements that have brought it together and through which properties emerged.

How then, might this approach be applied to fire? This paper aims to think about engagements between people and fire in a way that considers their active properties alongside the transformations it effects and the actions and interactions it is bound up in. The case studies presented below aim to use this approach to fire to suggest different ways of thinking about how fire was understood within both the Mesolithic and early Neolithic. I have elsewhere (McInnes forthcoming) discussed smoke at greater length however, this paper focuses solely on fire. Following Reynolds (2010) this paper will draw on a range of ethnographic examples in exploring the archaeological record however, these are used to open up interpretive avenues rather than provide direct analogies.

Fire as an active material

At the threshold between the forest and holy sites, the Khanty of western Siberia light a fire as part of activities that mediate the crossing of a boundary between one kind of place and another (Jordan 2003, 208). Once at the holy site a second fire is lit in front of the *labas,* the house belonging to the spirits. This fire is central to ceremonies that employ smoke from coals of the fire to cleanse the faces of the spirit idols, the interior of their house, the space beneath the structure and any sacrificial gifts (Jordan 2003, 159-208). A symbolic boundary is said to run through this main fire with smoke understood as materialising that boundary and dividing the site into gendered areas maintaining broader social divisions. The concept of purification by smoke is also exercised during visits to cemeteries where it is used to purify sacrifices left at the site of burials; to cleanse the border between the cemetery and the wider forest; and to cleanse those leaving the polluted area of the cemetery (Jordan 2003, 222).

Fire itself is understood to be a spirit and each individual fire in the world is believed to be a manifestation of the universal mother of fire, *Tyurs Nay Anjki* (Wiget and Balalaeva 2011, 113). As a spiritual being, a code of conduct is observed around all fires; rubbish cannot be thrown into the fire; no axe or knife can be placed in the flame; wood (the food of the fire) has to be carefully placed; and women are not allowed to step over the fire at any point (Jordan 2003, 149). By orientating human movements and action, fires recreate cosmological schemes and reinforce the practical knowledge and social categories that are drawn from those understandings. Within a Khanty cosmology fire is understood as animate, a vital material force, and a living spirit connected to other spirits in other realms, concepts also present in other societies (*e.g.* Chard 1963, 114; Utagawa 1992; Newland 2004; Fowler 2006; Dussart 2006, 635).

The physical nature of fire is one of movement; flames do not sit still but flicker, wave and blaze. Fire itself has a lifecycle (Sørensen and Bille 2008, 256), from first spark, to full flame, to glowing embers and finally cold ashes, fires have a temporal narrative and sense of movement. It is perhaps these dynamic properties that contribute to an understanding of fire as living and embodying a named and known spirit or ancestor. Over the course of a burning changes can be detected in the colour, temperature, intensity, smell, sound and extent of a fire. These can be further affected by context and manipulation. These changes bring to the fore a range of properties and experiences that could result in complex and changing understandings of fire as it interacts with materials, objects, places and people.

Concepts of fire as an animate material force may be bound up with a sense that fire holds transformative power. Physical transformations are experienced alongside transformations in the way materials are understood and conceptualized. Transformation of the body during cremation for example is often understood to involve more than the physical breakdown of the corpse. In many societies the body and soul of a deceased person are thought to be polluted. To complete the journey from the lived world to the next, to another realm or type of existence, the deceased person must be freed by cleansing the body and soul. Failure to do this could result in the continued existence of the deceased in the realm of the living (*e.g.* Barth 1993). Many mortuary practices employ fire to purify and transform the body, relying on its power to enact risky and important transformations (Morris 1992, 10; Downes 1999; Strassburg 2000, 241; Oestigaard 2011). Among groups in western Siberia smoke is often used to purify the dead while fire 'cooks' the body to cleanse the deceased before the journey to the ancestors (Kroll-Lerner 2007, 193). Materials and objects associated with the deceased are also often thought to be polluted through their contact or connection with the dead (Manzi and Spikins 2008, 89; Downes 1999). Their unstable state and polluted status demands similar treatment to the body and purification and transformation through fire. In cremation practices a physical transformation of the corpse or material culture, is accompanied by a transformation in the way it is understood; from polluted to purified and from dangerous to benign.

Properties of Fire

The abilities to transform and purify are among a range of properties and concepts with which fire may have been associated within the late Mesolithic. Edsman (1987) describes fire as a multifaceted phenomenon that can be discussed in terms of transformations, communication, metamorphosis and as a powerful symbol of life and the home: providing heat, light, warmth, and fuel for cooking. A fire can be gentle, comforting, and controllable, or dangerous and unruly; it can be fragile and quickly extinguished or can be destructive and terrifying (Dosedla and Krauliz 2009). This broad range of properties that can be experienced will have guided the way fire was understood. The experience of a fire is highly sensory; the temperature, colours, sounds, smells and sight of fire can all vary and contribute to interactions with fire. A spectrum of shades from yellow to red are the dominant colours of an active fire, but blues, whites and black can also be seen and enhanced by the addition of different fuels (Borić 2002). The sounds and visual experience of a fire vary with its size and intensity and can be particularly potent for those involved or in close proximity to the event.

The changeable nature of fire and the different ways in which it might have been experienced and understood has been considered in some archaeological interpretations. Lars Larsson (2000; 2002) whilst discussing Neolithic Scandinavia for instance, suggested that fire had been used as a transformative tool in spectacular performances that altered flint axes and timber houses. Larsson (2002) argued that care was taken to exaggerate aspects of these fires using built structures to raise and intensify the burning. In this context it is the visual impact of fire that Larsson (2002) suggests was been particularly powerful. This visual spectacular would be accessible by many, drawing together groups of people in an experience that may have emphasised shared beliefs and identities and encouraged a kind of sociality. In a separate practice Larsson (2000) also discusses the power of fire to change the colour of flint axes as part of another kind of key transformative event. This change however, would not be as inclusive as the firing of a wooden structure and demonstrates the intimate level at which fire can operate, perhaps emphasising boundaries, difference, or the existence of specific groups within a wider community.

Events such as those suggested by Larsson, highlight the ability of fire to enhance the creation of memories of places, people and events. Fire can also act as a socialising instrument that facilitates or demands collective practices (Tringham 2005; Gheorghiu and Nash 2007; Dosedla and Krauliz 2009). As a part of performances and group activities, fires can be a focus and choreographing feature playing a central role in dances or ceremonies (Reynolds 2010). Diviners in Aka Pygmy groups for example, read the flames and smoke of a fire during dance ceremonies to determine the cause of misfortunes (Joiris 1996). These types of interaction with fire are easily forgotten in archaeological narratives, however, I suggest that a materials based approach can allow us to consider fire in terms of its active properties and cultural qualities in specific social contexts. The following section considers the archaeology of Mesolithic hearths from this perspective to explore the active properties that would have been present and cultural qualities that might be suggested through a study of the evidence of interactions and transformations involving materials, fire and people.

Mesolithic Hearths on March Hill

Work at March Hill Carr by Spikins (1999; 2002; Spikins *et al* 2002) revealed a group of four hearths dating to the late 5th millennium BC (*c.*4800-4400 cal. BC) that had been re-used on several occasions (Spikins 1999). A number of activities were shown to have been carried out at each of the features. Hearths one and two were surrounded by stone settings and were the focus of knapping activities. Charcoal and burnt flint were found in and around the third hearth which was set into a small depression and seems to have been used solely to heat flint. Hearth four was the largest feature and its elongated shape led to an interpretation that the feature was used to slowly cook meat (Spikins 2002; Manzi and Spikins 2008). The activities centered on these hearths and their practical use are tangible in both the structure of the hearths and the material remains within and around them. Each activity would require a different sort of fire and as people manipulated and worked with these fires specific properties would have emerged.

Dating to a few centuries after those at March Hill Carr a further hearth accompanied by a small number of lithics was located 200m to the north of the cluster at a prominent location in the landscape on March Hill Top (Spikins 2002). The lack of an obvious role for this fifth hearth challenged the excavators to consider the feature from a social perspective: an approach that was extended to all the hearths discovered. At March Hill Carr the stone settings around hearths one and two, for example, are suggested to have been constructed to contain the fire and stray embers allowing people to move around the features and gather together while they work, as reflected in the lithic refit patterns (Fig. 2 in Spikins 2010). In addition to enabling movement and congregation, I suggest that the stone settings reflect fires that made certain tasks possible through the provision of light and warmth. Cores, knapping debris and microliths recovered from the area in and around these hearths represent actions that were facilitated by a fire that was in close proximity to people and this enabling characteristic may have encouraged people to draw together around the fire.

These were intimate experiences that involved aspects of the fires that left no trace. The intensity and colour of the flames, amount of smoke, direction of the wind, and shadows cast by the light of the fire, are transient properties that are easily forgotten when considering the archaeological record. Similarly the interactions between people that a hearth requires, such as the collecting of firewood, the regular addition of fuel, the actions of tending a fire and the interactions fire enables, are experiences little mentioned in our interpretations. As a focus, these hearths would encourage people to interact and engage in conversation producing a kind of sociality that was brought into being, and perhaps embodied by, the fire. For those at March Hill Carr the experience of light, warmth, sociality and a central role in the lived world will have guided how the fires in hearths one and two were understood; perhaps as familiar and enabling, bound up with activities that transformed stone, with ideas of making, and concepts of the group and community.

In a similar manner, hearth four contained fire that enabled transformations, in this case of animal bodies and produced

a kind of conviviality among people as food was shared. Alongside a number of fire-cracked stones, the hearth contained significantly more charcoal than any other feature suggesting it may have been used to cook meat (Spikins 2002). The type of fire required for this process would differ from the other three hearths at the site and different fuels are likely to have been used to ensure the desired properties came to the fore. An emphasis on heat rather than light, on the longevity of the fire, and on containing the heat produced in stones and embers would require the skilled manipulation of both fire and hearth. The transformation of food would have been hidden and rather than light, the power of fire would have been expressed through high temperature and the material transformation of the cooking process.

The relationship between animals and humans in the late Mesolithic is unlikely to fit into the nature/culture dualism of modern western thought. Within animistic ontologies for example, animals can be considered to be persons, relatives, or supernatural beings that enter into social relationships with people often based on systems of reciprocity (*e.g.* Descola 1994; Ingold 2000). Despite such anthropological insights, Conneller (2011) has highlighted the continued perpetuation of the nature/culture dualism in archaeological studies of animal materials through their analysis as environmental resource or symbolic media. These two approaches are routinely separated and both neglect the animality of the beings from which the materials originate (Conneller 2011, 50). Instead Conneller (2011) uses an approach that emphasises human-animal relationships as key to considering the processes and interactions that involve animal materials. Following this approach, the animals cooked in hearth four were unlikely to have been understood only as an economic resource rich in calorific value. Knowledge of the particular species, their behaviour, histories, identities and, their role in cosmologies will have affected interactions with these beings and how the activities in hearth four were understood.

The transformation of the animal corpse by fire may have been conceptualised in a similar way to the transformation of human bodies through fire with the soul of a being released to return to other realms, places or bodies. Correct methods may have been necessary to successfully complete this process and the production of a suitable fire would be central to this transformation. The release of the animal soul and correct treatment of the corpse when enacted within a system based on reciprocity may have been vital to the success of future hunting activities. Unlike human cremation however, the transformation of a potent animal corpse to safely edible food may have been testament to the power of fire through its ability to complete these sensitive processes.

In contrast to the light and visible fires in hearths one and two, hearth four will have employed hot stones charged alongside the fire itself to slowly cook the meat within a covered pit feature. However, the proximity of hearths one, two and four suggests that the fires they held they may have been understood as sharing similar properties such as their warmth and connections to the living world. All three hearths also enabled activities and transformations and are likely to have encouraged sociality amongst those present. The third hearth however, was set at a distance and it is interesting to note that although refits amongst the lithic material are distributed around hearths one, two and four few extend towards the third hearth. Not only was physical distance created between these hearths but it would appear that little activity took place in the vicinity of hearth three.

Spikins (2002) suggests that hearth three was used to heat flint and the nature of this process may explain its isolation. When heated, the crystalline structure of flint is physically altered causing the material to fracture more cleanly when worked. Too much heat however, can cause cracks, fractures, breaks and, in some cases, explosions to occur, introducing an element of risk to the practice. A range of factors can affect the success of this process including; the size of flint pieces, the temperatures reached; the duration of the heating process; the rate of heating and the rate of cooling. Experimental studies have often concluded that a slow and steady approach would have been required to achieve the desired effect and to avoid thermal damage to the stone (*e.g.* Olausson and Larsson 1982; Domanski and Webb 1992). Careful preparation and constant monitoring of the process is required; the method is time consuming and labour intensive. Ahler (1983), for example, reported that it took 48 hours to heat the material sufficiently and a further 20 hours to safely cool the pieces.

I would argue that this narrative is not reflected in the evidence found at March Hill Carr. The shallow depth of hearth three, (*c.* 0.2m; Manzi and Spikins 2008, 89) would not be suitable for the slow and steady method and, although it is not clear if all hearths were in use at once, there is certainly a suggestion that multiple activities were occurring at the site. People seem to have been cooking food in hearth four, gathering around the light and warmth of hearths one and two while making tools, and carrying out tasks such as the collection of fuel and tending of fires. It seems unlikely that constant monitoring and tending of the fire in hearth three took place. However, the rapid heating strategies described by Griffiths *et al* (1987) require little preparation or maintenance to achieve the successful heating of small pieces of material such as cores or blanks (see also Lee 2001; Mercieca and Hiscock 2008; Coles 2009). During experiments only occasional tending of the fires was required and an improvement in the flaking behaviour of the flint was apparent after only thirty minutes (Mercieca and Hiscock 2008). If a rapid method was used in hearth three the fire would only need to be fuelled intermittently, other activities could be carried out elsewhere, and transformed flint would have been available more quickly to those working around hearths one and two.

A further dimension can be explored in relation to the material interactions in hearth three. Hearth three at March Hill Carr involves interaction with stone in an everyday context where connections to places and people are brought into a transformative process involving fire. The molecular structure of flint is not the only aspect that changes when the material is heated. The colour and texture of the stone alters and the visible effects of over-heating include cracks and fractures. As mentioned above exceptionally high temperatures can also damage the stones to the point that they explode. However, I would suggest that the transformation itself and the materials involved may have also required a remoteness from people and the living world. The risk of a failed transformation, which could materialise as a potentially dangerous action, may have led to the interaction between fire and flint being understood as particularly dangerous. Changes in the colour of flint may have particularly contributed to this perception of the practice. Heated flint often becomes white in colour and alongside a cracked appearance; the stones may have been comparable to cremated bone. The process of heating flint may have been perceived as transformation as powerful as that of bodies in fire.

The fifth hearth excavated by Spikins (2002) was found uphill from the four features discussed so far and was of a later date (*c.* 4200-3800 cal. BC). The hearth was in an exposed position and the specificities of the location along with the use of a distinctive fuel would have produced a fire that created little heat but a large amount of light suggesting that the visible attributes of fire were being called upon (Manzi and Spikins 2008, 93). A large number of burnt stones and a few lithics were found in the vicinity and while the presence of flint flakes and unfinished tools attest to some activities the intensity of action seen around hearths one and two is not replicated. These might indicate a single person working flint or the deposition of token representations of the activities occurring elsewhere. Stone may have been understood to materialise places, people and identities and the deposition of worked stone at this hearth may have drawn on these properties to create landscapes through these connections.

The highly visible location of the hearth and the particularly bright fire that was created led Manzi and Spikins (2008, 94) to suggest that the feature acted as a communicative device. This may have involved specific groups within the landscape or more generally communicated to a broad area. In the same way that smoke travels and carries events to those not in close proximity to the fire, this fifth hearth may have similarly conveyed movements, activities and events to others. This should not be limited to people but may have included other beings that dwell in the lived world. The actions of the group on March Hill were extended both physically and visually through this hearth and, through communication, may have extended the sociality brought about by the four hearths downhill.

Described as five hearth features and accompanied by lithic and charcoal reports, the sites at March Hill could easily fall victim to the functional interpretations that have been dominant in Mesolithic narratives. A more social consideration of the hearths as presented by Manzi and Spikins (2008), highlights movement, structured activities and social interactions. This can be developed; fire may have been seen to hold life-sustaining properties embodied in warmth and light, bringing forth sociality and acting to (re)make the group through its role in everyday practices that reaffirmed these shared understandings. However, while this interpretation may be valid for hearths one and two its application across all uses of fire at this site would ignore the subtleties of the different practices seen at March Hill. This is where a detailed consideration of the properties of fire can contribute.

By considering the different properties of the fires and the material interactions within this narrative, it is possible to think about the complex way fire may have been understood. The range of activities seen at March Hill operate at a range of temporalities from the slow cooking of food in hearth four to the quick burning fires in hearths one and two. These temporalities carry into the tending and fuelling each fire would require with the different activities part of rhythms of movement at the site. Actions and materials connect to other people, materials, tasks and places, all of which, through movement and practice, create the landscape beyond the hearth site. The spatial patterns of hearths and lithics at March Hill perhaps suggest something of how the variability of fire was understood by those in the late Mesolithic. The three hearths involved in the production of food, light and warmth were in close proximity to one another and formed a focus for human activity and sociality. In contrast the fire that carried out a dangerous transformation was set apart away from the lived, social world.

Conclusions

Sørensen and Bille (2008) have suggested that archaeologists should think about what fire does rather than what it is; they argue that a study of the transformations fire brings about, rather than discussions of its nature, can tell us more of how fire was understood. Rather than a focus on the nature of fire or transformation by fire this paper has used the approach outlined by Conneller (2011) to demonstrate that a focus on active properties and cultural concepts can offer us new possibilities for our interpretations. In particular, this has involved considering the materials, transformations, combinations and interactions involved alongside the properties that emerged in the processes and activities evidenced by the hearths at March Hill.

As Edsman (1987) highlights, the ability to transform is only one aspect of fire; instead Edsman suggests that fire is a multifaceted phenomenon that can be discussed in terms of transformations, communication, metamorphosis and as a powerful symbol of life and the home; providing heat, light, warmth, and fuel for cooking. The hearth fires at March Hill involved interactions between people and fire as part of everyday activities that enabled human practice, fostered sociality and carried out powerful transformations. As people interacted with the different fires a range of properties and specific characteristics would have emerged and I suggest that sociable, enabling

and transformative characteristics might be thought of as an aspect of fire as much as temperature or light. Where the piece of quartz for the Cuebo Indians was understood as a powerfully transformative stone, the fires at March Hill combined mechanical properties with ideas drawn from cosmological schemes and worldviews. Two hearths were well oxygenated providing light and warmth but also enabled activities and encouraged social interaction. Another shared the brightness of these, perhaps a beacon of communication, but lacked their warmth whilst two more concealed, powerful fires that enacted dangerous transformations of other beings.

The properties of these fires changed with the context of their appearance as did the interactions and relationships they held with people. Rather than a single concept of fire it may be that it was understood to be powerful and variable demanding reconceptualization in different contexts. Broad understandings of fire may have been bound up with its mutability and the very range of properties that could be called to the fore, and practices in which fire played a role, may have been central to how it was understood.

Note

Portions of this paper were presented in my doctoral thesis while in receipt of an AHRC Doctoral Award.

Bibliography

Ahler, S. A. 1983. Heat treatment of Knife River flint. *Lithic Technology*, 12, 1–8.

Alberti, B., Jones, A. M. and Pollard, J. (eds.) 2013. *Archaeology After Interpretation:*

Returning Materials to Archaeological Theory. Walnut Creek, Left Coast Press.

Barth, F. 1993. *Balinese Worlds.* London, University of Chicago Press.

Bennett, K. D., Simonson, W. D. and Peglar, S. M. 1990. Fire and man in post-glacial woodlands of Eastern England. *Journal of Archaeological Science.* 17 (6), 635–642.

Boivin N. 2004. Mind over matter? Collapsing the mind-matter dichotomy in material culture studies. In E. De Marrais, C. Gosden, and C. Renfrew (eds.) *Rethinking Materiality: The Engagement of Mind with the Material World,* 63–71. Cambridge, McDonald Institute.

Borić, D. 2002. Apotropaism and the temporality of colours: colourful Mesolithic-Neolithic seasons in the Danube Gorges. In A. Jones and G. Macgregor (eds.), *Colouring the past: the significance of colour in archaeological research,* 23–43. Oxford: Berg.

Chard, C. S. 1963. The Nganasan: Wild Reindeer Hunters of the Taimyr Peninsula. *Arctic Anthropology*, 1 (2), 105-121.

Coles, D 2009 The Fire in The Flint: Arrowhead Production and Heat Treatment, *Internet Archaeology* 26.

Conneller, C. 2011. *An Archaeology of Materials. Substantial Transformation in Early Prehistoric Europe.* London, Routledge.

Cummings, V. 2012. What lies beneath: Thinking about the qualities and essences of stone and wood in the chambered tomb architecture of Neolithic Britain and Ireland. *Journal of Social Archaeology,* 12(1), 29-50.

Descola, P. 1994. *In the Society of Nature: A Native Ecology in Amazonia,* Cambridge, Cambridge University Press.

Domanski, M. And Webb, J. A. 1992. Effect of heat treatment on siliceous rocks used in prehistoric lithic technology. *Journal of Archaeological Science,* 19 (6), 601-614.

Dosedla, H. and Krauliz, A. 2009. The significance of fire within space concepts among *Mbowamb* and around *Motten*: parallels between prehistoric central Europe and contemporary archaic societies in New Guinea. In G. Nash and D. Gheorghiu (eds.), *The archaeology of people and territoriality,* 77–90. Budapest, Archaeolingua Alapítvány.

Downes, J. 1999. Cremation: a spectacle and a journey. In J. Downes and T. Pollard (eds.) *The Loved Body's Corruption: archaeological contribution to the study of human mortality,* pp 19-29. Glasgow, Cruithne Press.

Dussart. F. The Warlpiri. In R. B. Lee and R. Daly (eds.) *The Cambridge Encyclopedia of Hunters and Gatherers,* 363-366. Cambridge, Cambridge University Press.

Edsman, C. M. 1987. Fire. In M. Eliade (ed.) *The Encyclopedia of Religion* 5. 340 – 346. New York, MacMillan.

Edwards, K. J. 1990. Fire and the Scottish Mesolithic: Evidence from Microscopic Charcoal. In P. M. Vermeersch and P. Van Peer (eds.) *Contributions to the Mesolithic in Europe,* 71-79. Leuven, Leuven University Press.

Fowler. C. S. 2006. The Timbisha Shoshone of Death Valley. In R. B. Lee and R. Daly (eds.) *The Cambridge Encyclopedia of Hunters and Gatherers,* 66-70. Cambridge, Cambridge University Press.

Gheorghiu, D. And G Nash (eds.) 2007. *The archaeology of fire: understanding fire as material culture.* Budapest, Archaeolingua.

Godlier, M. 1986. *The Mental and the Material: thought, economy and society.* London, Blackwell Verso.

Gosden, C. 1999. *Anthropology and Archaeology: a changing relationship.* London. Routledge.

Graves-Brown, P. (ed.) 2000. *Matter, Materiality and Modern Culture,* London, Routledge.

Griffiths, D. R., Bergman, C. A., Clayton, C. J., Ohnuma, K., Robins,G. V. and Seele, N. J. 1987. Experimental investigations of the heat treatment of flint. In G. G. Sieveking, and

M.H. Newcomer (eds.) *The Human Uses of Flint and Chert,* 43-52. Cambridge, University Press.

Henare, A., Holbraad, M., and Wastell, S. 2007. Introduction: Thinking through things. In. A.

Henare, M. Holbraad and S. Wastell (eds.) *Thinking Through Things. Theorising Artifacts Ethnographically,* 1-31. London, Routledge.

Hutchings, A. 2007. Ritual Cleansing, Incense and the Tree of Life – Observations on Some Indigenous Plant Usage in Traditional Zulu and Xhosa Purification and Burial Rites. *Alternation. Interdisciplinary Journal for the Study of the Arts and Humanities in Southern Africa,* 14 (2), 189-218.

Ingold, T. 2000 Making culture and weaving the world. In P. M. Graves-Brown (ed.) *Matter, Materiality and Modern Culture,* 50-70. London, Routledge.

2007. Materials against materiality. *Archaeological Dialogues.* 14(1), 1-16.

2010. The textility of making. *Cambridge Journal of Economics,* 34, 91–102.

2012. Towards an Ecology of Materials. *Annual Review of Anthropology,* 41, 427-442.

Jones, A. M. 2012. *Prehistoric Materialities. Becoming Material in Prehistoric Britain and Ireland.* Oxford, Oxford University Press

Joiris, D. V. 1996. A comparable approach to hunting rituals among Baka. In S. Kent (ed.), *Cultural Diversity among 20th Century Foragers,* 245-275, Cambridge, Cambridge University Press.

Jordan, P. 2003. *Material Culture and Sacred Landscape.* Walnut Creek, Altamira Press.

Knappett C. 2005. *Thinking Through Material Culture: An Interdisciplinary Perspective.* Philadelphia, University of Pennsylvania Press.

Kroll-Lerner, A. M. 2007. Keep the yurt fires burning: ethnographic accounts and religious myths surrounding indigenous fire use in western Siberia. In D. Gheorghiu and G. Nash (eds.) *The archaeology of fire: understanding fire as material culture,* 183–200. Budapest, Archaeolingua.

Larsson, L. 2000. The passage of axes: fire transformation of flint objects in the Neolithic of southern Sweden. *Antiquity* 74, 602-610.

2002. Fire as a means of ritual transformation during the prehistory of southern Scandinavia. In. D. Gheorghiu (ed.) *Fire in Archaeology. British Archaeological Reports International Series 1089,* 35 - 45. Oxford, BAR Publishing.

Lee, K. 2001. Experimental heat-treatment of flint. *Lithics,* 22, 39-44.

Manzi, L and Spikins, P. A. (2008) El fuego en las altas latitudes: Los Selk'nam de Tuerre del Fuego como referente etnográfico para el Meolítico europeo, *Complutum*, 19(1), 79-96.

Mercieca, A. and Hiscock, P. (2008). Experimental insights into alternative strategies of lithic heat treatment, *Journal of Archaeological Science*, 35(9), 2634–2639.

Miller, D. 2005. Materiality: An Introduction. In. D. Miller (ed.) *Materiality*, 1-50, London: Duke University Press.

Morris, B. 1992. *Death ritual and social structure in classical antiquity*. Cambridge, Cambridge University Press.

Newland, L. 2004. Turning the Spirits into Witchcraft: Pentecostalism in Fijian Villages. *Oceania* 75 (1), 1 – 18.

Oestigaard, T. 2011. Water. In T. Insoll (ed.) *The Oxford Handbook of the Archaeology of Ritual and Religion*, 38 – 51. Oxford, Oxford University Press.

Olausson, D. B and Larsson, L. 1982. Testing for the presence of thermal pre-treatment of flint in the Mesolithic and Neolithic of Sweden. *Journal of Archaeological Science*, 9. 275–285

Olsen, B. 2003. Material Culture after Text: re-remembering things. *Norwegian Archaeological Review*, 36 (2), 87-104.

Pearson, J. L. 2002. *Shamanism and the ancient mind: a cognitive approach to archaeology*. New York, Altamira Press.

Reynolds, Ff. 2010. *Ways of seeing, being, doing: Reconstructing worldviews in the Early Neolithic of southern Britain*. Unpublished PhD thesis, University of Cardiff.

Rowlands, M. 2005. *A Materialist Approach to Materiality*. In D Miller (ed.) *Materiality*, 72-87. London: Duke University Press.

Sergant, J., Crombé, P. and Perdaen, Y. 2006. The 'invisible' hearths: a contribution to the discernment of Mesolithic non-structured surface hearths, *Journal of Archaeological Science*, 33 (7), 999-1007.

Smith, R. J. 1974. Ancestor Worship in Contemporary Japan. Stanford: Stanford University Press.

Sørensen, T. F. and Bille, M. 2008. Flames of transformation: the role of fire in cremation practices, *World Archaeology*, 40 (2), 253-267.

Spikins, P. 1999. *West Yorkshire Mesolithic Project Final (1996) Site Report*. Wakefield: West Yorkshire Archaeology Service and English Heritage.

2002. *Prehistoric People of the Pennines: Reconstructing the lifestyles of Mesolithic hunter-gatherers on Marsden Moor*. Wakefield: West Yorkshire Archaeology Service.

2010. *An Archaeological Research Agenda for West Yorkshire. Palaeolithic and Mesolithic West Yorkshire*. Wakefield: West Yorkshire Archaeology Service.

Spikins, P., Conneller, C., Auestaran, H. and Scaife, B. 2002 GIS Based Interpolation Applied to Distinguishing Occupation Phases of Early Prehistoric Sites, *Journal of Archaeological Science*, 29 (11), 1235-1245.

Stevenson, A. and White, N. C. C. (eds.) 2007. *The Materiality of Burial Practices*. Cambridge: University of Cambridge.

Strassburg, J. 2000. *Shamanic Shadows: One hundred generations , of undead subversions in southern Scandinavia. Stockholm Studies in Archaeology 20*. Stockholm: Stockholm Universitet.

Tilley, C. 2007. Materiality in Materials. *Archaeological Dialogues,* 14(1), 16-20.

Tringham, R. 2005. Weaving house life and death into places: a blueprint for a hypermedia narrative. In D. Bailey, A. Whittle and V. Cummings (eds.), *Unsettling the Neolithic*, 98–111. Oxford: Oxbow.

Utagawa, H. 1992. The "Sending-Back" Rite in Ainu Culture. *Japanese Journal of Religious Studies*, 19, (2/3), 255-270.

Viveiros de Castro, E. 1998. Cosmological deixis and Amerindian perspectivism. *Journal of the Royal Anthropological Institute* 4, 469-88.

Wiget, A. and Balalaeva, O. 2011. *Khanty. People of the Taiga: Surviving the 20*th *Century.* Fairbanks: University of Alaska Press.

Williams, E. And A. Costall. 2000. Taking things more seriously. Psychological theories of autism and the material-social divide. In P. M. Graves-Brown (ed.) *Matter, Materiality and Modern Culture*, 97-111. London, Routledge.

Chapter 7

Pots in Context: Aspects on Pottery Production and Use in the Early Neolithic Funnel Beaker (TRB) Culture on Öland, SE Sweden

Ludvig Papmehl-Dufay[1],*, Ole Stilborg[2], Anders Lindahl[3] and Sven Isaksson[4]

[1]Kalmar County Museum, Box 104, SE-39121 Kalmar, Sweden
[2]SKEA Stilborg Ceramic Analysis, Linköping, Sweden
[3]Laboratory for Ceramic Research, Lund University, Sweden
[4]Archaeological Research Laboratory, Stockholm University, Sweden

This paper discusses contextual aspects of pottery from the two early Neolithic Funnel Beaker (TRB) sites Resmo and Runsbäck, on the island of Öland, SE Sweden. The sites are situated 15km apart on the west side of the island and the C14 dates place the activities at the sites at c. 3900–3600 BC and 3600–3100 BC respectively, possibly with some overlap. The pottery has been analysed regarding its design, raw material use, technology and vessel use. While overall similarities in the ceramic craft at the two sites are obvious, some articulated differences were noted in the design as well as in the wares, while vessel use patterns are strikingly similar between the two assemblages. The Resmo assemblage is characterised by an exceptional degree of homogeneity while the Runsbäck pottery displays more variation. The observed differences are viewed against the contexts in which the pottery was recovered, and the different patterns of pottery production and use are suggested to reflect differences in function and duration between the sites. The Runsbäck pottery seems to be associated with everyday activities of mainly domestic character, whereas the Resmo pottery is suggested to reflect some form of special occasion possibly connected to ritual activities performed in a monumental landscape setting. This in turn can be related to later events in the area, which includes the construction of megalithic tombs only a few centuries later.

Keywords: Neolithic pottery, pottery technology, vessel function, vessel design, TRB (Funnel Beaker) culture

Introduction

This paper presents the results from a detailed multi-analytical study of Neolithic TRB pottery from two sites on the island of Öland, SE Sweden. Until recently early Neolithic settlement sites were known in the area mainly from flint scatters identified through field surveys (Alexandersson et al. 1996). In 2008 the excavation by Kalmar County Museum of two sites changed that situation, and the pottery from these sites form the focus of this paper. In both cases a wealth of TRB pottery was found together with flint debris and some burned bones, but the archaeological contexts differ. The analysis presented in the following targets ceramic technology, pottery design and vessel use in an attempt to understand how these differences were expressed in terms of pottery production and use. Apart from a general recording of stylistic parameters, analyses include thin sections, XRF and lipid residue analysis of selected wares and a clay sample. While previous studies on Swedish materials have used a similar multi-analytical approach (e.g. Papmehl-Dufay 2006; Brorsson et al. 2007), in the case of Resmo and Runsbäck we have consistently used the same sample sherds for all the different types of analyses. In this way, comparisons between various aspects of the two sites are enhanced.

Early Neolithic pottery in southern Sweden

Early farming in southern Scandinavia is generally attributed to the Funnel Beaker (TRB) culture, dating to c. 4000–2800 BC (Larsson 1992; Midgley 1992). Associated traits include polished flint axes, elaborate pottery, megalithic burial traditions, permanent settlements and ritual enclosures as well as cereal agriculture and domesticated animals (Andersen 1997; Malmer 2002). Hunting and fishing continued to be of major importance alongside domestication, and in many areas people did not fully depend on agriculture until the late Neolithic (Eriksson et al. 2008).

The origin of the Funnel Beaker Culture in Northern Europe is a long-standing discussion primarily centred around the

* Corresponding author. Email: lpd@kalmarlansmuseum.se

pottery (Koch 1998:26ff; Müller 2011:294f). Observations in southern Scandinavia point towards an internal gradual development of the late Mesolithic Ertebölle pottery craft (Andersen 2011:199ff; Stilborg & Bergenstråhle 2001:31), and there are reasons to believe that the TRB pottery craft reaching Öland in the Early Neolithic owes most of its existence to developments in the Late Mesolithic societies in Eastern Denmark and Scania. The TRB potters in southern Sweden generally seem to have accepted a variation from fine to medium coarse clays, in most cases avoiding the really coarse and often unsorted clays (Andersen 2011:199ff; Stilborg & Bergenstråhle 2001:31). They preferred granite or quartzite as a temper and started relating the coarseness of the tempering to the size of the vessel.

This general picture of the TRB pottery handicraft, which is based on analyses of pottery primarily from Scanian sites (Hulthén 1977; Stilborg 2002:59ff), will be used as one of the baselines for the technological interpretations presented in this study. The other baseline is the especially difficult natural conditions for pottery production offered by the geology of Öland (see below). Most of the clays accessible in the top soils are calciferous to calcium rich, something that any Neolithic potter in her/his right mind would always try to avoid due to the risks of lime blowing. From previous analyses of clay samples from the southern and central parts of the island, together with pottery samples from the TRB site at Alby and the Pitted Ware (PWC) sites at Köpingsvik and Ottenby, also on Öland, it is clear that non-calciferous clay beds were indeed preferred but that they are few, scattered, generally small and often coarse and unsorted (Stilborg 2006:319f). This raw material scarcity logically results in a marked diversity in the clays used for pottery even within each settlement, and in that the Öland potters fairly often used clays that would not have been regarded suitable for pottery making on the mainland.

Food remains found adhering onto and absorbed into ceramic vessels are today recognised as valuable source materials in archaeology (Evershed et al. 2001, Evershed 2008a). Even though the analysis of food lipid residues has become a fairly integrated tool in Swedish archaeology (Isaksson 2009), there are to date only a few studies published on materials from Öland (e.g. Papmehl-Dufay 2006).

Sites analysed

The island of Öland is situated off the Swedish east coast in the Baltic Sea (Figure 1). The island measures 130 km in length and c. 20km in width. The bedrock consists of Ordovician limestone and, below the western slopes, Cambrian shales, resulting in a level topography. On the southern part of the island, the Neolithic coastline is located some 8–12m above that of today. Neolithic stray finds are numerous all over the island, indicating a relatively dense settlement in the central and especially western parts of the

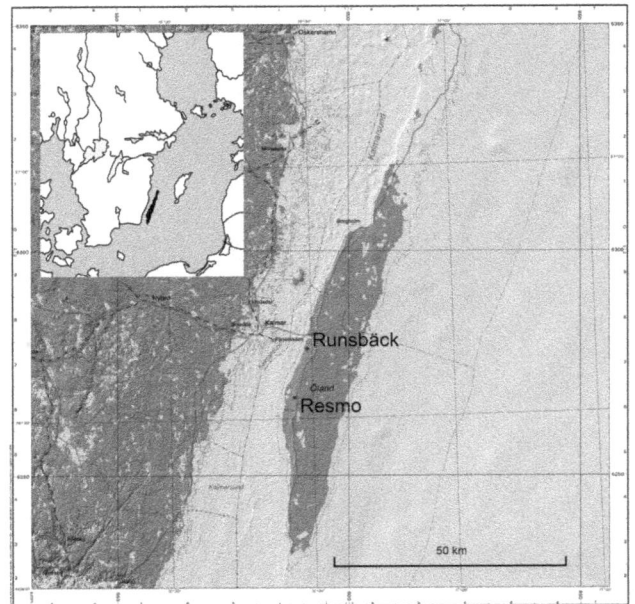

Figure 1. The island of Öland in the Baltic Sea, with the coastline c. 4050 cal BC and the location of the analysed sites indicated. © Sveriges Geologiska Undersökning (Geological Survey of Sweden).

island during the early and middle Neolithic (Åberg 1923; Gurstad-Nilsson 2001).

Resmo

The TRB site at Resmo was discovered and excavated in spring 2008 (Papmehl-Dufay 2009, Papmehl-Dufay 2012a). Situated on the western escarpment at elevations around 40–41m above the present sea level, it occupies a monumental location with vast views towards the west. A megalithic tomb (dolmen) is situated only some 300m to the SE, and three passage graves are located at Mysinge another c. 2.5km to the south (Arne 1909; Papmehl-Dufay 2006). The most dominant feature at the site is a cultural layer rich in finds of pottery, flint and burned bone. No built structures were identified during excavation, and the origin of the cultural layer remains to be fully understood. The layer covered some 150m² in the NE corner of the excavated area, and during a complementary trial excavation in 2012 its full extent was estimated at c. 1000–1200m², mainly extending to the north and east of the excavated area (Papmehl-Dufay 2012b). In 2008 only some 12% of the uncovered part of the layer was excavated (18 m²), yielding finds of c. 6 kg pottery, 300g flint and 130g burned bone. The complementary excavation of the outer parts of the layer yielded a similar frequency of finds. These figures suggest that the part of the cultural layer that was uncovered during the excavation probably contained something around 50kg of pottery and 2.5kg of flint. Furthermore, if this is extrapolated against the estimated full extent of the cultural layer, we are faced with a possible c. 400kg of pottery and 20kg of flint deposited within an area of c. 25 x 50m. Regardless of the exact figures, clearly this must represent some form of major activity and/or an extremely lengthy period of occupation. Typological traits as well as radiocarbon dates of burned bones place the formation of the cultural layer mainly in the earliest Neolithic at around 3900–3600 cal BC, which is a few centuries before the assumed date for the construction of the megalithic tomb a short distance to the SE.

Runsbäck

The TRB site at Runsbäck is located some 15km to the north of Resmo, in the SW part of Färjestaden, Öland. It was found in 2007 and excavated the following year (Alexandersson & Papmehl-Dufay 2009; Papmehl-Dufay 2012a). The most striking feature at this site was a dense concentration of finds and soil features covering an area of c. 20 x 30m on the western slopes of an ancient beach ridge, at around 14 metres above sea level. The collected finds from this area include c. 4kg pottery, c. 1kg flint and other lithic materials, as well as a few fragments of burned bone. Due to necessary prioritizations not all features were fully excavated, but most probably the collected finds constitute the majority of the material deposited and preserved at the site. The chronology of the finds span a period of 5000 years from the early Mesolithic at around 7000 BC to the late Neolithic c. 2000 BC, although the majority of the finds and most of the pottery can be attributed to the early Neolithic TRB culture at around 3600–3300 BC. This date is further strengthened by two radiocarbon dates of hazelnut shells contextually associated with TRB pottery.

Among the many features within the dense activity area at Runsbäck, three large post-holes were identified as the roof bearing construction of a two-aisled long house dating to the second half of the Early Neolithic. Measuring c. 12 x 5m, the house corresponds well in shape, size and orientation to Early Neolithic houses of the so-called Mossby type that have been found in parts of southern and central Sweden (Larsson 1992:66ff; Apel 1996; Artursson et al. 2003:64ff). The pottery and flint surrounding the house fit this interpretation well. The Runsbäck site represents an EN TRB dwelling site with the remains of a house and material traces of various domestic activities, mainly distributed within and around/in front of the house, which was located in a coastal setting a few hundred metres from, and facing, the sea.

Material, methods and limitations

The ceramic assemblages from the two sites form the basis of a comparative study in which technological, functional and stylistic aspects of the pottery are analysed. The main objective is to identify and explain any differences in ceramic craft and pottery use between the two sites. From the general recording of the complete assemblages, sample sherds were selected to capture the variation and general characteristics of the wares at the sites. The same ten sherds from each site have been subjected to thin section, XRF and lipid residue analysis, with the addition of another two sherds and a fired sample of local clay from Resmo being included in the thin section analysis. The selected sample sherds are shown in Figure 2.

Analysis of pottery design

Stylistic aspects were analysed based on macroscopic observations and detailed recording of relevant parameters of the complete assemblages from both sites (for details see Papmehl-Dufay 2006:156ff). The parameters used in the discussion below include vessel part (and indirectly vessel type), decoration (present or not present) and wall thickness. The composition of the decoration on individual vessels has not been analysed in detail.

Petrographic microscopy

Thin sections of 0.03mm thickness were prepared. The coarseness of the paste (the amount of silt, fine sand and sand) was estimated under a polarising microscope at magnifications from 25 to 1000 X, as was the presence of iron oxide, ore, mica, calcium carbonate and organic material. The mineralogy of the sand fraction was determined through standard petrographic procedures. Diatoms and other fossils were detected at the highest magnifications. Finally, the type, amount and maximum grain size was measured for any added temper. The material encompassed in the thin section analysis consists of 22 sherds: 12 from Resmo (no:s 1-10 and no:s 22-23) and 10 from Runsbäck (no:s 12-21), as well as a clay sample from Resmo (no 24).

XRF-analysis with portable equipment

X-ray fluorescence analysis (XRF) is a non-destructive method for chemical and elemental analysis. In the present study a Thermo Scientific portable (handheld) XRF analyzer (h-XRF), Niton XL3t 970 GOLDD+ has been used (Helfert & Böhme 2010). This apparatus is highly accurate in determining the presence of major elements. A limitation with this equipment is that elements in the range from Sodium (Na) and lighter cannot be detected. The elements that were analysed in this investigation were: Mg, Al, Si, P, S, Cl, K, Ca, Ti, V, Cr, Mn, Fe, Co, Ni, Cu, Zn, As, Se, Rb, Sr, Zr, Nb, Mo, Pd, Ag, Cd, Sn, Sb, Ba, W, Au, Pb and Bi. Analysis was performed on polished breakages of the sample sherds, and measuring time was set to 6 minutes on an 8mm radius spot to be analysed. The material encompassed in the h-XRF analysis consists of 20 sherds: 10 from Resmo (no:s 1-10) and 10 from Runsbäck (no:s 12-21). These are the same sherds that were analysed in the thin-section and lipid residue analyses. Two additional samples from Resmo were not included in the XRF analysis.

Lipid analysis

Lipids were extracted by means of ultrasonic aided solvent wash (Heron et al. 1994; Dudd and Evershed 1998; Isaksson 2000; Evershed et al. 2002; Copley et al. 2003, 2005; Craig et al. 2005, 2007; Spangenberg et al. 2006; Mirabaud et al. 2007; Mukherjee et al. 2007). The outer millimetre of the potsherd's sampled area was removed in order to reduce contamination. The sample was ground down using a low-

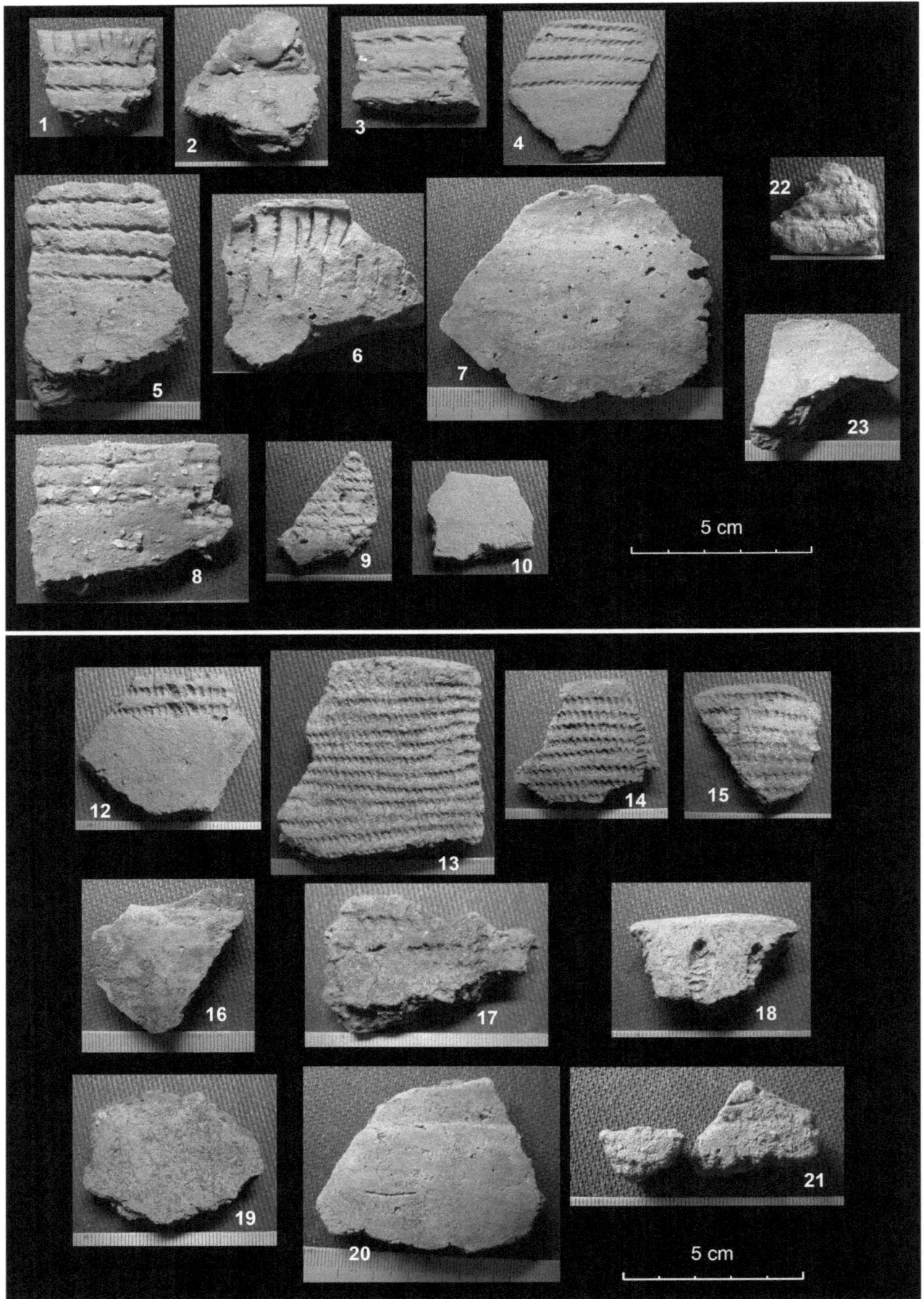

Figure 2. The sample sherds from Resmo (above) and Runsbäck (below). Photo by Ole Stilborg.

speed pottery grinder, transferred to an extraction vessel and an internal standard (n-hexatriacontane, 20 mg) was added. A mixture of chloroform and methanol (2:1, v:v) was used for the extraction and the lipid residues were analysed as trimethylsilyl derivatives. The analysis was performed on a HP 6890 Gas Chromatograph equipped with a SGE BPX5 capillary column using helium as carrier gas. The injection was done by pulsed splitless technique using an Agilent 7683B Autoinjector. The GC was connected to a HP 5973 Mass Selective Detector. The fragmentation of separated compounds was done by electronic ionisation at 70 eV. Using the *extract ion-chromatogram* tool in MSD ChemStation samples were screened for specific ions within the retention time windows (c. ±0.05 minutes chromatographic reproducibility) of authentic trimethylsilyl derivatives of a range of lipid biomarkers in the chromatographic system used. The detection limits of each specific lipid compound vary, primarily due to different fragmentations patterns in the ion source of the mass selective detector, but are in the range of 10s of ng/g. All solvents used were of *Pro Analysi*-grade, all glassware was thoroughly cleaned prior to use and experimental blanks were run in parallel with the samples. Exact analytical conditions have been published elsewhere (Papmehl-Dufay 2006:164). The material encompassed in the lipid residue analysis consists of 20 sherds: 10 from Resmo (no:s 1-10) and 10 from Runsbäck (no:s 12-21). These are the same sherds that were analysed in the thin-section and XRF residue analyses. The two additional samples from Resmo were not included in the lipid residue analysis.

Limitations

The laboratory analyses presented in this study were all carried out on small samples of large pottery assemblages. The issue of representativeness is therefore important to address. In principle, all archaeological assemblages are samples of what was once present, and furthermore, most excavations are governed by prioritizations and restrictions concerning what is to be investigated and collected and what is not. In most cases, the area to be investigated is designated by interests other than archaeology, and thus the excavated material in many cases represents a sample of a site of unknown extent. At Runsbäck, the distribution of finds and features suggests that the 'whole' site is present within the excavated area. On the other hand, not all features were fully excavated. At Resmo, the cultural layer covered the NE corner of the investigated area. It is clear that the excavated sample here constitutes a small fraction of what was present at the site. The analysed sherds were selected in order to grasp the variation in ware and design present in the available assemblages, and every sample was selected to represent individual and different vessels. At Runsbäck, there is no reason to believe that the selected sample does not mirror the variation in the assemblage at large. At Resmo, two sherds from a complementary excavation to the east and north of the area excavated in 2008 were added to the initial sample. While the possibility of spatial differences in pottery use and deposition within the site cannot be altogether ruled out (Dimc 2011), the

extra two sherds present a possibility to evaluate this to some extent.

Results

Analysis of pottery design

The only vessel type that has been identified in the Resmo assemblage is the funnel beaker. Rim diameters have not been analysed in detail, but vessels c. 15–30cm in diameter seem to be dominating. The vessels have been decorated mainly on the uppermost part of the neck and in some cases on the edge of the rim. The dominating decoration technique at Resmo is impressions of twisted cord, which has been applied on most vessels either in horizontal rows or check board patterns.

Funnel beakers are the dominating vessel type at Runsbäck as well, although somewhat smaller in size with rim diameters of c. 10–20cm. Decoration generally covers the upper part of the vessel, while some sherds appear to represent undecorated funnel beakers. Impressions of whipped cord are by far the most common decoration, which was again applied in various fashions including horizontal lines and check board pattern.

The amount of collected pottery is much greater at Resmo (2250 sherds and fragments, as compared to 767 at Runsbäck), despite the fact that only 18 m² of the extensive cultural layer were excavated. Furthermore, the Resmo pottery is generally more thin-walled (mean 8.2mm) than the Runsbäck pottery (mean 9.8mm). In combination with the larger vessel size at Resmo, this addresses the question of quality: does the thin-walled Resmo pottery represent a more skilled production than the Runsbäck pottery, and what would such an observation imply? The degree of decoration for the different vessel parts give an idea of the designs present in the assemblage; at Resmo a great majority of the rim sherds (80%) display decoration, while the corresponding figure at Runsbäck is c. 48%. Given the fact that decoration in both cases seems to be concentrated to the upper part of vessels, these figures clearly suggest that undecorated vessels occur in the Runsbäck assemblage but not to any great extent at Resmo. Still, seen on the whole assemblage, the degree of decoration is higher at Runsbäck (13%) than at Resmo (8%), which in turn reflects the fact that decoration is more widely distributed on the vessel bodies at Runsbäck.

Petrographic analysis of clays and wares

For the ten Runsbäck pots analysed, at least three different clays have been used: one medium coarse clay of a well sorted quality (four samples), one poorly sorted, medium coarse clay with iron oxide rich pellets (four samples; Stilborg 2006:301) and one unsorted, medium coarse clay with sponge spicula needles (one sample). All of the wares are tempered with crushed granite or granitoid rock in qualities varying from 12% volume and 2.2mm maximum, to 20% volume and 3.6mm maximum (Figure

3). Although conditions for pottery making are difficult on Öland, the Runsbäck potters managed to locate at least one good, well sorted clay. In addition to this, however, less optimal clays had to be used as well. In their choice of tempering the wares with crushed granite, the Runsbäck potters meet the expectations for the traditional TRB craft (Hulthén 1977:52ff; Stilborg 2003:220ff). The tradition involves the granite being coarsely crushed with a clear, positive correlation between temper amount and maximum grain size – the latter most clearly related to vessel wall thickness.

The twelve Resmo samples, on the other hand, were all made from practically identical clays: medium coarse, well sorted, silt rich with some mica. The variation in iron oxide content and in the mineralogy of the relatively few accessory minerals is well within the variation to be expected from a single clay bed. In accordance with

Runsbäck, all wares at Resmo were tempered with crushed granite or granitoid rock and the range of temper qualities is also the same (Figure 3).

XRF analysis

Several of the elements included in the analysis were missing or present in amounts below the detection limit. For the elements detected, bivariate scatterplots were used to compare the composition of the analysed samples from the two sites. For most of these, the Resmo samples formed a discrete cluster while the Runsbäck samples were more disperse. This is comprehensively illustrated through a Principal Component Analysis (SPSS ver. 19), where more than 80% of the analysis was explained in the three first factor scores (Figure 4). In the three-dimensional plot, all the Resmo sherds form a very neat cluster, whereas the Runsbäck sherds form two groups and one isolated sample

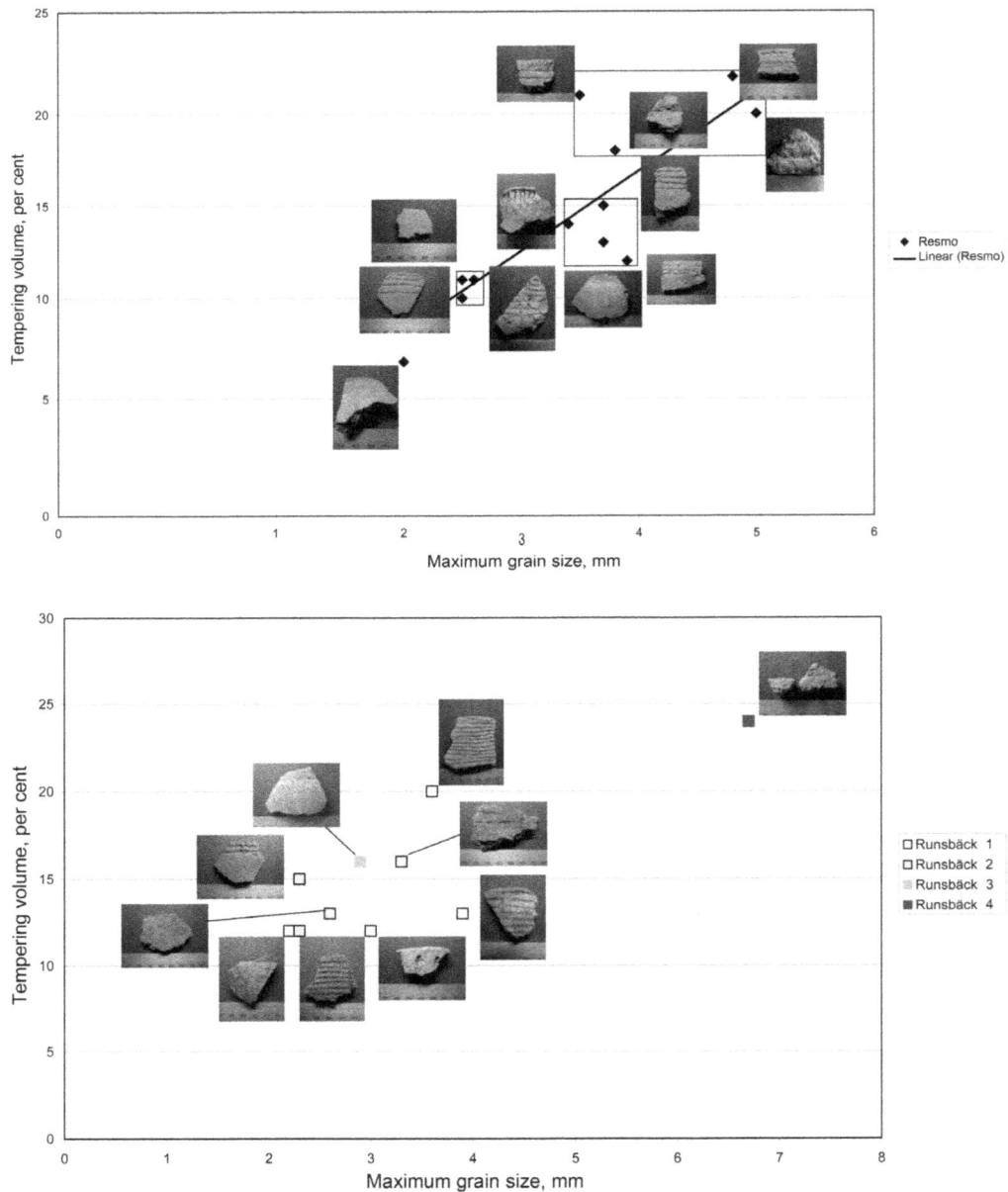

Figure 3. Variation in temper quality of the analysed sherds: Resmo at the top, Runsbäck below.

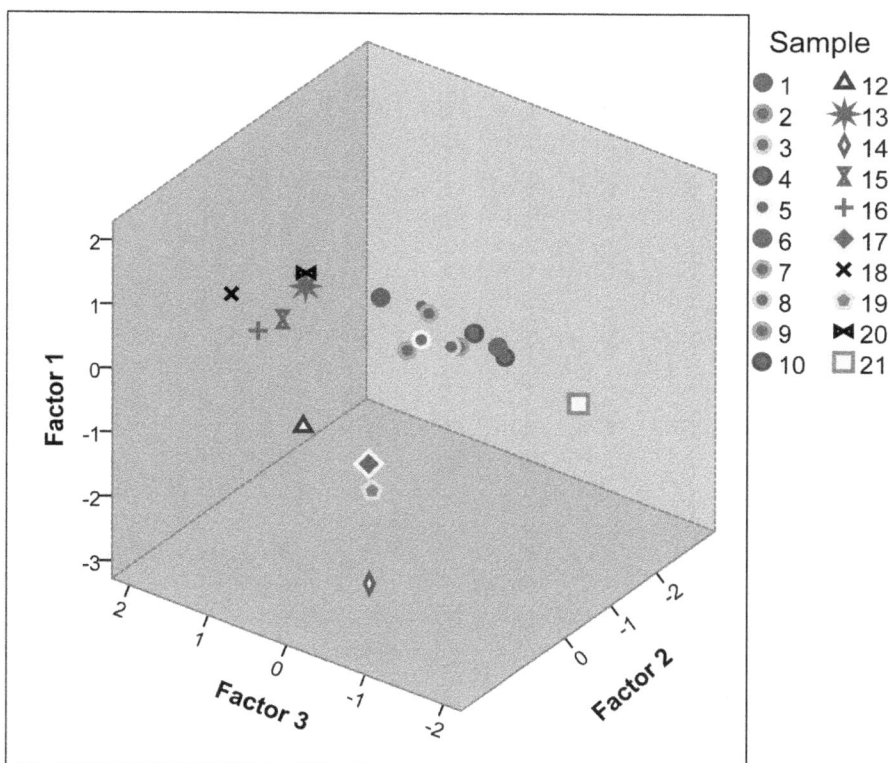

Figure 4. Three-dimensional scatterplot between the three first factors of a Principal Component Analysis (PCA). The used elements are Al, Si, P, S, K, Ca, Ti, V, Cr, Mn, Fe, Cu, Zn, Rb, Sr, Zr, Nb, Pb and Bi. Samples 1-10 represent Resmo and samples 12-21 represent Runsbäck.

(no 21). The XRF-results thus matches and confirms the mineralogical findings from the thin section analysis. The most important result was the great homogeneity of the Resmo pottery and the fact that the clay 1-group at Runsbäck is clearly separated from the Resmo clay despite some similarity in the coarseness and sorting of the clay.

Lipid residue analysis

With the molecular analysis applied in this study it is possible to identify lipids from terrestrial animals (T), aquatic animals (A) and vegetables (V), and mixtures thereof (e.g. Charters et al. 1997; Hansel et al. 2004; Isaksson et al. 2005; Olsson & Isaksson 2008; Hansel & Evershed 2009). The results of the lipid residue analyses of the 20 sample sherds, as expressed in vessel use classes, are shown in Figure 5. As seen here, vessel use at the two sites are very similar and the only significant difference (c^2=6,67, df=1, Fishers exact p, two-tailed, p = 0.0325) between the two is in the number of samples with traces of diterpenes, which may enter the vessel walls as sooth and smoke. Five of the Resmo samples contained diterpenes, while this was not at all detected in the samples from Runsbäck. Furthermore, a slightly higher diversity was noted in the lipid residues from Runsbäck as compared to Resmo. This is seen both in the width in distribution of lipid residue amounts and in the distribution of C18:0/C16:0 ratios. It is also seen in the distribution of pottery use classifications; the diversity index (= $1/\sqrt{[(S\ P_i/100)^2]}$, P_i is each pottery use class in %) of these distributions is 1.54 for the Resmo pots and 1.96 for the Runsbäck pots.

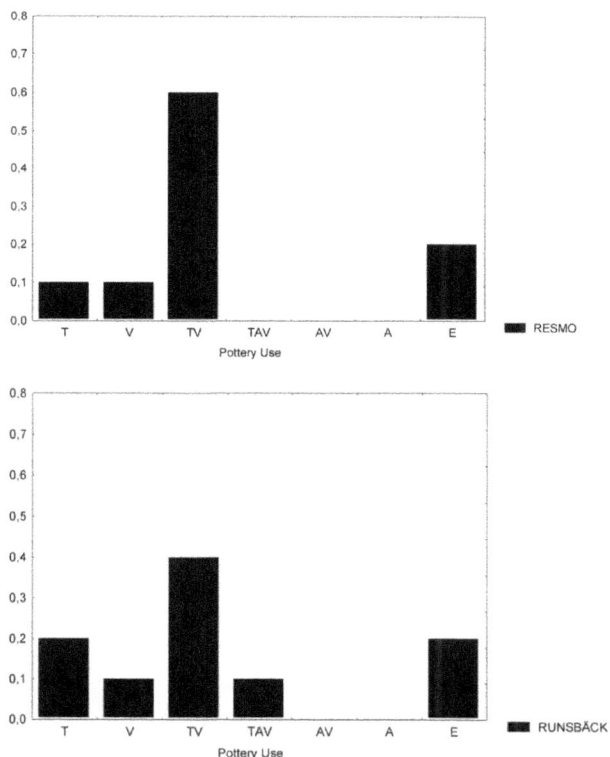

Figure 5. Distribution of pottery use classes (per no. of samples) in the sample from Resmo (at the top) and Runsbäck (below), based on the molecular distribution of lipid residues. T = terrestrial animals, A = aquatic animals, V = vegetables, E = empty.

In order to illustrate the similarity of the two sites, the vessel use results can be compared with those from Köpingsvik, a previously analysed PWC site on Öland dating to MNA at around 3000 BC (Papmehl-Dufay 2006:214ff). Here the pottery use is much more homogenous (diversity index = 1.35), with aquatic animal residues dominating, a trait typical of PWC pottery use in eastern Sweden (e.g. Brorsson et al. 2007; Dimc 2011). The two Funnel Beaker assemblages have much more similar distributions of pottery use classes compared to the sample of PWC pots from Köpingsvik. Ottenby is another excavated and analysed PWC site on the island, but with a pottery use that is actually more similar to that of Runsbäck than to the Köpingsvik results (Papmehl-Dufay 2006:220ff).

Discussion

The pottery assemblages from Runsbäck and Resmo both adhere to the same overall archaeologically defined tradition, i.e. Funnel Beaker pottery, and they most probably overlap chronologically or follow closely one after the other during the course of the Early Neolithic. Stylistically the assemblages display great overall similarities while at the same time some distinct differences could be identified. This observation initiated the present set of analyses, which seeks to penetrate the relation of these ornamental differences to other aspects of the pottery craft and use at the sites.

Apart from details in the design, the degree of diversity in the clay choices separates the two materials of which the Resmo pots display a remarkable homogeneity. At Runsbäck, the potters used the same quality of clay for some of their pots that the Resmo potters used for all of theirs. Also, they seem to have agreed on both type of temper and appropriate temper qualities, with figures in line with what is generally expected for Funnel Beaker pottery in southern Sweden. Concerning lipid residues, the striking impression is the similarity between the two sites in the distribution of pottery use classes, with only a slight difference in diversity where Resmo stands out as the more homogeneous of the two.

The homogeneity in clay raw material and tempering technology represented at Resmo is remarkable, not only in relation to the specific Öland conditions but also in relation to previously analysed TRB pottery from the Swedish mainland (Hulthén 1977:52ff; Stilborg 2003:220ff). Besides the raw material preconditions in the resource area for a pottery production, the number of potters involved and the duration of the production over generations constitute the main 'mechanical' factors behind the degree of homogeneity in any given prehistoric pottery material. Cultural rules restraining the options for pottery making or socially induced changes in pottery design may override or change these mechanical factors towards more or less homogeneity (e.g. Sillar 1997:11). With the limitations of the present study in mind, some possible alternative explanations for the remarkable homogeneity observed in the Resmo material can be formulated:

- The Resmo potters utilised a large homogenous clay bed, and they used it for a long time.
- The Resmo pottery was made over a short period of time and by one or a couple of potters working closely together.
- The Resmo pottery manufacture was controlled by rigid restrictions as to the choice of clay.

As for the first suggestion, perhaps the simplest explanation would be that the Resmo pottery was not made on Öland but on the mainland where the chances of finding large, homogenous clay beds are much better. From analyses of PWC pottery from Ottenby Royal Manor (Öland) and Kalmar (mainland), we know that pottery was actually being transported across the Kalmar Strait in the Neolithic (Papmehl-Dufay 2006:204ff; Stilborg 2012). However, the homogeneity among the Resmo samples is still greater than any observed even on the mainland and, more importantly, a fairly similar clay (albeit more varied) was used for four of the pots analysed from Runsbäck which indicates that this quality of clay could be found on Öland.

We can neither exclude the possibility nor confirm the existence of strong cultural rules guiding raw material choice, but there is nothing to indicate such strong rules in the TRB culture at large and certainly they were not in action at Runsbäck. Following these arguments, we are left with the alternative that the Resmo pottery may represent a short-lived, concentrated pottery production activity. Runsbäck, on the other hand, can be interpreted as a settlement site with a pottery production and use that was carried on for some time and distributed over a number of potters and pottery users. This interpretation is in good accordance with observations during excavation, with the identification of house remains at Runsbäck and the lack of such structures at Resmo (Alexandersson & Papmehl-Dufay 2009; Papmehl-Dufay 2009). Possibly, the activities at Resmo in some way involved extensive burning that would have introduced diterpenoids from sooth or smoke into the vessels from Resmo, which is missing in the analysed vessels from Runsbäck.

The patterns of vessel use are similar at both sites, with a clear dominance for terrestrial and/or vegetable origin of the lipids detected. This is an interesting observation, considering the attribution of both sites to the TRB culture and the general association of this tradition to early agriculture. The PWC, on the other hand, is generally associated with marine hunting and fishing, as seen in the pottery use at Köpingsvik, which was completely dominated by lipids of aquatic and/or vegetable origin. While the present data does not allow the separation of domestic and wild species, the Resmo and Runsbäck results could well reflect an economy with a certain input of domesticated animals and/or cereal agriculture. It should be noted that at both sites, impressions in the pottery of cereal grains have been identified (Mats Regnell personal comment) and that at Resmo, four cow teeth were found during excavation (Papmehl-Dufay 2009).

The ware variation of the two TRB materials was compared to that of the previously analysed PWC-pottery from the island (Papmehl-Dufay 2006; Stilborg 2006). The Runsbäck potters not only used a broader selection of clays more in line with the ware variation at the PWC-sites, they also used the same type of poorly sorted clay with pellets which was dominating in the PWC-production at Ottenby (Stilborg 2006:310). This raises the question whether the Runsbäck production is culturally closer to the PWC handicraft than the Resmo production. The same pattern is seen in the categories of pottery use, where Runsbäck is more similar to Ottenby than it is to Resmo. Both productions analysed here are clearly separated from the PWC pottery productions through the exclusive tempering with crushed granite, which was used only sporadically for PWC pots. A small EN TRB pottery assemblage from Solberga, Köpingsvik, may shed some light on this issue (Stilborg 2011). These pots were decorated with twisted cord in a way similar to, and are probably contemporary to, the Resmo pots, but the variation in clay choice was more akin to the situation at Runsbäck. All the Solberga wares were tempered with granite. However four out of six samples displayed temper volumes below 10%. In conjunction with a relatively large maximum grain size this represents a suboptimal temper quality (relation between temper amount and maximum grain size) that has no parallels in either Resmo or Runsbäck. Instead we find the parallels among sandstone tempered PWC-wares locally in Köpingsvik (Stilborg 2006). Does this mean that we see a gradual development away from the TRB culture pottery traditions characterized by a limited clay variation and stereotypic granite tempering? A new trend seems to lead towards greater diversity of clays followed by increased variation in the temper qualities before, finally, the culturally redefining changes of temper type and vessel design are realized? Furthermore, is a similar journey visible in the pottery use, with a mainly terrestrial and vegetable vessel use in the EN TRB pottery and gradually moving towards the typically highly aquatic pottery use of the MNA PWC?

Of potential significance in the context of the Resmo pottery is the group of four Neolithic megalithic tombs located in the area (Papmehl-Dufay 2006, 2011). One is a dolmen situated north of Resmo Church only some 300m to the east of the excavated site, and the other three are passage graves located a few hundred metres apart in the village of Mysinge c. 2.5km to the south. The southernmost of the graves was excavated in 1908 (Arne 1909), while the other three remain unexcavated. Seen in relation to the distribution of megalithic monuments in Northern Europe, the Öland tombs are located in the eastern periphery some 150 km as the bird flies to the east of the nearest concentration of megaliths on the Swedish mainland (see Papmehl-Dufay 2011:132). This seemingly peculiar occurrence indicates that the Resmo area was attributed with some form of quality apparently lacking in other neighbouring and more distant areas in which megaliths were not built (Papmehl-Dufay 2012c). This quality would have been associated with the meaning of

place, probably connected in some way to the physical appearance/objective morphology of the area, to activities by and interactions between people in the area, and/or to meanings and histories related to collective memory of the place (Relph 1976; Castello 2010).

Often it has been argued that megalithic monuments refer to existing architectural or natural features (see Thomas 1996:90; Richards 1996). At Resmo, the monumental and dramatic landscape setting on the crest of the western escarpment may be one such aspect of physical appearance, as could the rich spring located c. 500m to the W of the dolmen at Resmo. However, in an objective sense none of these features are unique to this specific locality. Instead, while not excluding aspects of physical appearance altogether, memory and human interaction are more likely to be responsible in this case. The rich cultural layer and large amounts of high quality early Neolithic pottery at Resmo is quite interesting in this respect. The striking homogeneity revealed by the analyses presented above fits well with the impression that this was a special place. The site and the results provide undisputable evidence of intense activities in the immediate area preceding the construction of the dolmen a few generations later. Thus at the time of monument construction, the place of this megalith already had a long history of human–environment interaction, memory and meaning.

Acknowledgements

The analyses were made possible due to generous financial support from the Berit Wallenberg foundation.

Bibliography

Åberg, N. 1923. Kalmar läns förhistoria. *Södra Kalmar län*. Volume 1.

Alexandersson, K., Gurstad-Nilsson, H., & Källström, M. 1996. Stenålder i järnåldersland. Om den pågående specialinventeringen på Öland. *Bulletin för arkeologisk forskning i Sydsverige nr 2–3 1996*: 4–17.

Alexandersson, K. & Papmehl-Dufay, L. 2009. Två stenåldersboplatser i Runsbäck. Särskild arkeologisk undersökning 2008, Runsbäck 5:2, 5:66 och 7:9, Torslunda socken, Mörbylånga kommun, Öland. Unpublished excavation report, Kalmar county museum, Arkeologisk rapport 2009:49.

Andersen, N. H. 1997. *Sarup vol 1. The Sarup enclosures. The Funnel Beaker culture of the Sarup site including two causewayed camps compared to the contemporary settlements in the area and other European enclosures.* Højbjerg: Jutland Archaeological Society.

Andersen, S. H. 2011. Kitchen middens and the early pottery of Denmark. In: Hartz, S., Lüth, F. & Terberger, T. (eds.) *Early Pottery in the Baltic –Dating, Origin and Social Context.* RGK band 89. 2008: 193-216. Frankfurt.

Apel, J. (ed.) 1996. *Skumparberget 1 och 2. En mesolitisk aktivitetsyta och tidigneolitiska trattbägarlokaler vid Skumparberget i Glanshammars sn, Örebro län, Närke.* Unpublished excavation report, Arkeologikonsult AB.

Arne, T. J. 1909. Stenåldersundersökningar II. En Öländsk gånggrift. *Fornvännen*: 86–95.

Artursson, M., Linderoth, T., Nilsson, M. L. & Svensson, M. 2003. Byggnadskultur i södra och mellersta Sverige. In: Svensson, M. (ed.) *I det neolitiska rummet.* Skånska spår – arkeologi längs Västkustbanan, 41–171. Lund: Riksantikvarieämbetet.

Brorsson, T., Isaksson, S. & Stenbäck, N. 2007. Stil, gods och kärlanvändning - neolitisk keramik från E4:an undersökningarna i norra Uppland. *Stenålder i Uppland. Uppdragsarkeologi och eftertanke.* Arkeologi E4 Uppland - Studier. Volym 1. 409-438. Uppsala: Societas Archaeologica Upsaliensis.

Castello, L. 2010. *Rethinking the meaning of place: conceiving place in architecture-urbanism.* Farnham: Ashgate.

Charters, S., Evershed, R. P., Quye, A., Blinkhorn, P. W. & Reeves, V. 1997. Simulation experiments for determining the use of ancient pottery vessels: the behaviour of epicuticular leaf wax during boiling of leafy vegetable. *Journal of Archaeological Science* 24(1):1–7.

Copley, M. S., Bertan, R., Dudd, S. N., Docherty, G., Mukherjee, A. J., Straker, V., Payne, S., and Evershed, R. P., 2003, Direct chemical evidence for widespread dairying in prehistoric Britain. *Proceedings of the National Academy of Sciences*, USA, 100(4), 1524–9.

Copley, M. S., Berstan, R., Dudd, S. N., Straker, V., Payne, S., and Evershed, R. P., 2005, Dairying in antiquity. III. Evidence from absorbed lipid residues dating to the British Neolithic. *Journal of Archaeological Science*, 32(4), 523–46.

Craig, O. E., Chapman, J., and Heron, C., 2005, Did the first farmers of central and eastern Europe produce dairy foods? *Antiquity*, 79 (306), 882–94.

Craig, O. E., Forster, M., Andersen, S. H., Koch, E., Crombé, P., Milner, N. J., Stern, B., Bailey, G., Heron, C. P., 2007. Molecular and isotopic demonstration of the processing of aquatic products in Northern European prehistoric pottery. *Archaeometry* 49(1), 135–152.

Dimc, N. 2011. *Pits, Pots and Prehistoric Fats. A Lipid Food Residue Analysis of Pottery from the Funnel Beaker Culture at Stensborg, and the Pitted Ware Culture from Korsnäs.* Unpublished Master Thesis in Archaeological Science. Archaeological Research Laboratory, Stockholm University.

Dudd, S. N., & Evershed, R. P., 1998, Direct demonstration of milk as an element of archaeological economies. *Science*, 282, 1478–81.

Eriksson, G., Linderholm, A., Fornander, E., Kanstrup, M., Schoultz, P., Olofsson, H. & Lidén, K. 2008. Same island, different diet: Cultural evolution of food practice on Öland, Sweden, from the Mesolithic to the Roman Period. *Journal of Anthropological Archaeology* 27: 520–543.

Evershed, R. P. 2008a. Organic residue analysis in archaeology: the archaeological biomarker revolution. *Archaeometry* 50: 895–924

Evershed, R. P. 2008b. Experimental approaches to the interpretation of absorbed organic residues in archaeological ceramics. *World Archaeology* 40.

Evershed, R. P., Stott, A. W., Raven, A., Dudd, A. N., Charters, S. & Leyden, A .1995. Formation of Loch-Chain Ketones in Ancient Pottery Vessles By Pyrolysis of Acyl Lipids. *Tetrahedron Letters* 36:8875–8878.

Evershed, R. P., Dudd, S. N., Lockhart, M. J. & Jim, S. 2001. Lipids in archaeology. In: Brothwell, D. R. & Pollard, A. M. (eds.) *Handbook of Archaeological Science.* Chichester.

Evershed, R. P., Dudd, S. N., Copley, M. S., and Mukherjee, A., 2002. Identification of animal fats via compound specific $d^{13}C$ values of individual fatty acids: assessments of results for reference fats and lipid extracts of archaeological pottery vessels. *Documenta Praehistorica*, XXIX, 73–96.

Gurstad-Nilsson, H. 2001. En neolitisering – två förlopp. Tankar kring jordbrukets etablering i Kalmarsundsområdet. In: Magnusson, G. (ed.) *Möre. Historien om ett småland. E22-projektet.* 129–164. Kalmar: Kalmar läns museum.

Hansel, F. A., Copley, M. S., Madureira, L. A. S. & Evershed, R. P. 2004. Thermally produced w-(*o*-alkylphenyl)alkanoic acids provide evidence for the processing of marine products in archaeological pottery vessels. *Tetrahedron Letters* 45(14):2999–3002.

Hansel, F. A. & Evershed, R. P. 2009. Formation of dihydroxy acids from Z-mon-unsaturated alkenoic acids and their use as markers for processing of marine commodities in archaeological vessels. *Tetrahedron Letters* 50, 5562–3.

Helfert, M., Böhme, D. 2010. Herkunftbestimmung von römischer keramik mittels protabler energiedispersiver röntgenfluoreszenzanalyse (P-ED-RFA) – Erste ergebnisse einer anwendungsbezogenen teststudie. In: Ramminger, B. & Stilborg, O. (eds.) *Naturwissenschaftliche Analysen vor- und frühgeschichtlicher Keramik I.* Universitätsforschungen zur prähistorischen archäologie Band 176. Bonn: Habelt.

Heron, C. P., Nemcek, N., Bonfield, K. M., Dixon, D., and Ottaway, B. S., 1994. The chemistry of Neolithic beeswax. *Naturwissenschaften*, 81(6), 266–9.

Hjulström, B. Isaksson, S. & Karlsson, C. 2008. Prominent Migration Period Building. Lipid and elemental analyses from an excavation at Alby, Botkyrka, Södermanland, Sweden. *Acta Archaeologica* 79:62–78.

Hulthén, B. 1977. *On Ceramic Technology during the Scandinavian Neolithic and Bronze Age.* Theses and Papers in North-European Archaeology 6. Stockholm: Stockholm University.

Isaksson, S. 2000. *Food and Rank in Early Medieval Time.* Theses and Papers in Scientific Archaeology 3. Stockholm: Stockholm University.

Isaksson, S. 2009. Vessels of change. A long-term perspective on prehistoric pottery use in southern and eastern middle Sweden based on lipid residue analyses. *Current Swedish Archaeology* 17: 131–149.

Isaksson, S., Olsson, M. & Hjulström, B. 2005. De smorde sina kräs. Spår av vegetabilisk olja i keramik från yngre järnålder. *Fornvännen* 100: 179–191.

Isaksson, S., Karlsson, C. & Eriksson, T. 2010. Ergosterol (5, 7, 22-ergostatrien-3b-ol) as a potential biomarker for alcohol fermentation in lipid residues from prehistoric pottery. *Journal of Archaeological Science* 37: 3263–8.

Koch, E. 1998. *Neolithic Bog Pots from Zealand, Mön, Lolland and Falster.* Nordiske Fortidsminder Ser B. 16. København: Det Konglige Nordiske Oldskriftselskab.

Larsson, M. 1992. The early and middle Neolithic Funnel Beaker culture in the Ystad area (southern Scania). Economic and social change, 3100–2300 BC. In: Larsson, L., Callmer, J. & Stjernquist, B. (eds) *The archaeology of the cultural landscape. Field work and research in a South Swedish rural region.* Acta Archaeologica Lundensia Series in 4 N 19: 17–90. Lund: Lund University.

Malmer, M. P. 2002. *The Neolithic of South Sweden. TRB, GRK and STR.* Stockholm: Royal Swedish Academy of Letters, History and Antiquities.

Midgley, M. 1992. *TRB culture. The first farmers of the North European plain.* Edinburgh: Edinburgh University Press.

Mirabaud, S., Christian, R. & Regert, M., 2007. Molecular criteria for discriminating adipose fat and milk from different species by NanoESI MS and MS/MS of their triacylglycerols: application to archaeological remains. *Analytical Chemistry*, 79, 6182–92.

Mukherjee, A. J., Berstan, R., Copley, M. S., Gibson, A. M., and Evershed, R. P. 2007. Compound-specific stable carbon isotopic detection of pig product processing in British late Neolithic pottery. *Antiquity*, 81(313), 743–54.

Müller, J. 2011. Early Pottery in the North – a southern perspective. In: Hartz, S., Lüth, F. & Terberger, T. (eds.) *Early Pottery in the Baltic –Dating, Origin and Social Context.* RGK band 89. 2008:287–300. Frankfurt.

Olsson, M. & Isaksson, S. 2008. Molecular and isotopic traces of cooking and consumption of fish at an Early Medieval manor site in eastern middle Sweden. *Journal of Archaeological Science*, 35(3):773–780.

Papmehl-Dufay, L. 2006. *Shaping an identity. Pitted Ware pottery and potters in southeast Sweden.* Theses and papers in scientific archaeology 7. Stockholm: Stockholm University.

Papmehl-Dufay, L. 2009. *En trattbägarlokal i Resmo. Arkeologisk förundersökning och särskild arkeologisk undersökning 2008, Resmo 1:13, 1:14, 1:15 och 1:16, Resmo socken, Mörbylånga kommun, Öland.* Unpublished excavation report, Kalmar county museum, Arkeologisk rapport 2009:29.

Papmehl-Dufay, L. 2011. The passage grave at Mysinge, Öland, SE Sweden in a long-term perspective. *Archaeologia Lituana* 12:131–141.

Papmehl-Dufay, L. 2012a. Trattbägarkulturen på Öland, i ljuset av äldre och nyare undersökningar. *Fornvännen* 107:153–156.

Papmehl-Dufay, L. 2012b. *Åter i Resmo backe. Efterundersökning i mars 2012 av RAÄ 159 i Resmo sn, Mörbylånga kommun, Öland.* Unpublished excavation report, Linnaeus University, Kalmar.

Papmehl-Dufay, L. 2012c. Places that matter. Megalithic monuments from a biographical perspective. Accepted for: Kolens et al. (eds.) *Landscape biographies. Geographical, historical and archaeological perspectives on the production and transmission of landscapes.* Amsterdam: Amsterdam University Press.

Relph, E. 1976. *Place and placelessness.* London: Pion Limited.

Richards, C. 1996. Monuments as landscapes: creating the centre of the world in late Neolithic Orkney. *World Archaeology* 28(2): 190–208.

Sillar, B. 1997. Reputable pots and disreputable potters: Individual and community choice in present-day production and exchange in the Andes. In: Cumberpatch, C. G. & Blinkhorn, P.W. (eds.) *Not so much a pot, more a way of life.* Oxbow Monograph 83:1-20. Oxford: Oxbow.

Spangenberg, J. E., Jacomet, S. & Schibler, J., 2006. Chemical analyses of organic residues in archaeological pottery from Arbon Bleiche 3, Switzerland— evidence for dairying in the late Neolithic. *Journal of Archaeological Science*, 33(1), 1–13.

Steele, V., Stern, B. & Stott, A. W. 2010. Olive oil or lard? Distinguishing plant oils from animal fats in the archaeological record of the eastern Mediterranean using gas chromatography/combustion/ isotope ratio mass spectrometry. *Rapid Communications in Mass Spectrometry* 24:3478–3484

Stilborg, O. 2002. Tidigneolitikum 4000-3300 f.Kr. In: Lindahl, A., Olausson, D. & Carlie, A. (eds.) *Keramik i*

Sydsverige. En handbok för arkeologer. Monographs on Ceramics 1. Lund: Lund University.

Stilborg, O. 2003. Neolitiskt keramikhantverk i Välabäcksdalen – lokalt och regionalt. In: Svensson, M. (ed.) *I det neolitiska rummet. Skånska spår - arkeologi längs Västkustbanan.* Skånska spår, 214–233. Lund: Riksantikvarieämbetet.

Stilborg, O. 2006. Clays and tempering in wares from Köpingsvik and Ottenby. Appendix 4 in: Papmehl-Dufay, L. 2006. *Shaping an identity. Pitted Ware pottery and potters in southeast Sweden.* Theses and papers in scientific archaeology 7. Stockholm: Stockholm University.

Stilborg, O. 2011. *Solberga – en tidigneolitisk boplats.* Unpublished analysis report, SKEA ceramic analysis.

Stilborg, O. 2012. On the other side. In: Ramminger, B. & Stilborg, O. (eds.) *Naturwissenschaftliche Analysen vor- und frühgeschichtlicher Keramik II: Methoden, Anwendungsbereiche, Auswertungsmöglichkeiten.* Universitätsforschungen zur Prähistorischen Archäologie Band 176. Bonn: Habelt.

Stilborg, O. & Bergenstråhle, I. 2001. Traditions in Transition: A Comparative Study of the Patterns of Ertebölle Lithic and Pottery Changes in the Late Mesolithic Ceramic Phase at Skateholm I, III and Soldattorpet in Scania, Sweden. *Lund Archaeological Review* vol. 6. 2000: 23–42.

Thomas, J. 1996. *Time, culture and identity. An interpretive archaeology.* London/New York: Routledge.

Section 4

The Transition

Chapter 8

Timing and Process in the Fifth and Early Fourth Millennium cal BC

Frances Healy

Cardiff University, UK

The chronology of the Mesolithic/Neolithic transition in Britain and its implications for the nature of that process are examined in one region. The basis of a previous analysis of the chronology of the process at an insular level is questioned. Further possibilities are considered.

Keywords: Bayesian analysis, Britain, chronology, radiocarbon, time, transition

Background

The *Gathering Time* project (Whittle *et al.* 2011) set out to date the early Neolithic enclosures of southern Britain by applying Bayesian modelling to radiocarbon dates measured on stringently selected samples and to pre-existing dates assessed by the same criteria as samples selected for dating in the course of the project. To place the enclosures in context, it also assessed and modelled pre-existing dates for other early Neolithic activity in the regions where enclosures were dated and in other selected areas. This was undertaken without commissioning any new determinations, since this would have been beyond the remit of the project, and was thus dependent on the availability and the quality of dates obtained by other researchers for other purposes. It is this aspect of the exercise that figures in this paper, since the English enclosures themselves began to be built some time after the start of the insular Neolithic (Whittle *et al.* 2011, fig. 14.179). While this paper draws heavily on the project, the opinions expressed are entirely the author's.

Bayesian analysis

The methods employed have been described in detail elsewhere (Bayliss *et al.* 2011 and references therein). Some essential points will be recapitulated here. The essence of Bayesian analysis is to combine numerical information ('standardised likelihoods') with other information ('prior beliefs'). When it comes to dating an archaeological site, the 'standardised likelihoods' component of the chronological model is formed by radiocarbon or other scientific dates and the 'prior beliefs' component by the understanding of the site, the taphonomy of the dated samples, and the stratigraphic relationships of the deposits from which they were recovered. Together, these strands of evidence make it possible to suggest dates for when the site was in use. These are the 'posterior beliefs' that are the outputs of the model. Another commonly employed form of prior information is the assumption that the events concerned

occurred within a more-or-less continuous bounded phase, in other words that they started, continued fairly uniformly, and ended, and that the samples are randomly distributed throughout that phase. The boundaries of such a phase counteract the scatter derived from the errors attached to radiocarbon dates, an effect of which is that, within any group of dates relating to a period of activity, a proportion of the probability distributions will fall earlier or later than its actual span, making it appear to start earlier and finish later than it actually did (Steier and Rom 2000; Bronk Ramsey 2000). This form of constraint is particularly significant when examining dates from contexts without physical relation but linked by, for example, association with a single cultural or artefactual horizon. The resulting posterior density estimates vary with the information incorporated into the model and are conventionally cited *in italics* to distinguish them from dates based on independent scientific information alone, which are shown in regular type. Results quoted here from the *Gathering Time* project were calculated by Alex Bayliss using OxCal v3.10 (Bronk Ramsey 2001 and references therein) and the IntCal04 dataset (Reimer *et al.* 2004). The model the results of which are shown in Figures 1–4 and the simple calibrations of individual dates quoted in the test were calculated by the author using OxCal v4.2 (Bronk Ramsey 2009) and the Intcal09 dataset (Reimer *et al.* 2009).

Samples and their contexts

This approach would not work unless the samples dated were contemporary with their contexts. Accurate assessment of the taphonomy of each sample, and hence its relation to the context it is intended to date, is essential. Desirable samples include articulated bone, because it must still have been connected by soft tissue and hence not long dead when it reached its context (Mant 1987); objects of short-lived material in direct functional relation to their contexts, such as — by no means exclusively — antler picks from the bases of earthwork ditches; or single charred grains or nuts or single fragments of charcoal from short-lived taxa, since they represent a year or a few years' growth. In this last case the risk of redeposition or intrusion is reduced by selecting them from coherent, single-event, deposits like hearths or dumps of charred material, and by dating multiple single-entity sample from a single context: the single fragments eliminate the risk of combining material of different ages in the same sample (Ashmore 1999), and the dating of more than one sample from the same context makes it possible to check against the inclusion of stray fragments of older and/or younger material using a χ^2 test (Ward and Wilson 1978). Many legacy dates, some going back to the late 1950s or the 1960s, were measured on bulk samples, made up of several charcoal fragments or several disarticulated bone fragments, which may have been of different ages, making the result potentially a mean of all and the age of none. Many of these samples also included or consisted of charcoal from mature wood, especially oak, and are thus capable of having been much older, even centuries older, than their contexts. Such results can be modelled only as *termini post quos* for their contexts unless there are solid grounds for believing otherwise.

Assessing the then available pre-existing early Neolithic dates by these criteria, and modelling them accordingly, the *Gathering Time* project estimated that Neolithic traditions and practices first appeared in south-east England in *4075–3975 cal BC (95% probability)*, probably in *4035–3990 cal BC* (*68% probability*; Whittle *et al.* 2011, fig. 14.57: *start SE Neolithic*), spreading across the island over the ensuing centuries (Whittle *et al.* 2011, fig. 14.176).

Seeing the Latest Mesolithic

In these circumstances, any consideration of the transition necessitates examining insular activity in the late 5th millennium cal. BC. Not very long ago the second half of the fifth millennium appeared empty, compared with earlier stages of the Mesolithic (cf Pryor 2003, 122). It no longer does. An accumulation of radiocarbon dates documents a fair scattering of human activity, sometimes in inconspicuous contexts undatable or only very approximately dateable by their contained artefacts alone, such as a burnt-out treethrow hole on Irthlingborough island at Raunds, Northamptonshire, which contained typologically Mesolithic lithics and a single radiocarbon date measured on short-life charcoal of 4360–3990 cal BC (95% confidence; OxA-3057; 5730±80 BP; Harding and Healy 2007, 51–53). There are also larger living sites, where diagnostic artefacts, a hunter-gather subsistence base and series of dates on short-life charcoal from secure contexts demonstrate the continuation of what is customarily seen as a Mesolithic way of life to the end of the fifth millennium. The best known is part of the March Hill complex on the Pennines (Spikins 2002); others are considered by Griffiths (forthcoming).

Some, like March Hill, are in locations which would have been marginal to areas of early Neolithic settlement and could conceivably reflect the survival of old ways alongside innovation. One site is of particular interest because it

preserves *in situ* late Mesolithic artefacts for which fairly precise dating can be achieved, in an area of both late Mesolithic and early Neolithic activity, in at least parts of which a relatively open grassland/woodland mosaic vegetation on rendzina soils had developed in the course of the Mesolithic (French *et al.* 2007, 210–221, 225–226).

The Fir Tree Field shaft

This natural solution feature lies on the Wessex Chalk in Cranborne Chase, Dorset, and was excavated to a depth of over 13 m, augering suggesting that it continued for about another 12 m. Most of the excavated fills had accumulated in the course of the fifth and fourth millennia cal BC, incorporating material from the surrounding surface (Allen and Green 1998; Green 2000, 27–8; Allen 2000, 40–3; Green 2007a).

The radiocarbon dates and samples from the sequence are listed by Allen and Green (1998, table 1) and by Whittle *et al.* (2001, table 4.6). They have been modelled in whole or part by Derek Hamilton (in Whittle 2007, fig. 4), Alex Bayliss (Whittle *et al.* 2011, fig. 4.21), Seren Griffiths (forthcoming) and Alistair Barclay (forthcoming). A further version is offered here (Fig. 1). All agree on the lower part of the sequence, up to and including layer 6b, which can be summarised as follows. Most of the shaft was filled with chalk rubble, punctuated by soil lenses. The lowest of these contained pine charcoal dated to 6480–6230 cal BC (7530±70 BP; OxA-8907), a date which is not included in the model shown in Figure 1. The overlying samples from the chalk rubble all dated from the fifth millennium cal BC, including two articulated roe deer skeletons, one nearly 2 m above the other, which seem to have fallen into the shaft (French *et al.* 2007, fig. A4.8; Fig. 1: *OxA-7991, -7990*) and three patches of hazel charcoal (Fig. 1: *OxA-8013, -8012, -8011*). A human presence in the surrounding area is evidenced not only by the charcoal, but by scattered Mesolithic lithics between 9 m and 3.4 m and by cut marks on one of two disarticulated red deer bones, both modelled as *termini post quos* (Fig. 1: *OxA-7989, -7988*).

The sample for *OxA-8011* came from the last rubble layer (L8). Above this, more slowly deposited earthy deposits filled the weathering cone at the top of the shaft. *Termini post quos* for the first of these, L7, are provided by dates for two disarticulated animal bones (Fig. 1: *OxA-7987, -8000*). These, like the rest of the identifiable fauna from the layer, were wild (red deer, aurochs) or of indeterminate status because of their immaturity (Maltby 2007, 297). The lithics, more abundant than previously, were of Mesolithic character, over 400 pieces including 8 microliths, a notched bladelet and a tranchet adze sharpening flake. Seven of the microliths, all rod forms (Green 2007b, fig. A4.3), were found clustered together at the base of the layer, indicating that they had entered the weathering cone hafted in the head of a spear, or similar weapon. They would, in other words, have been deposited there while such weapons were still in use. Above this, the model varies from those of Hamilton and Bayliss because, while the relation between

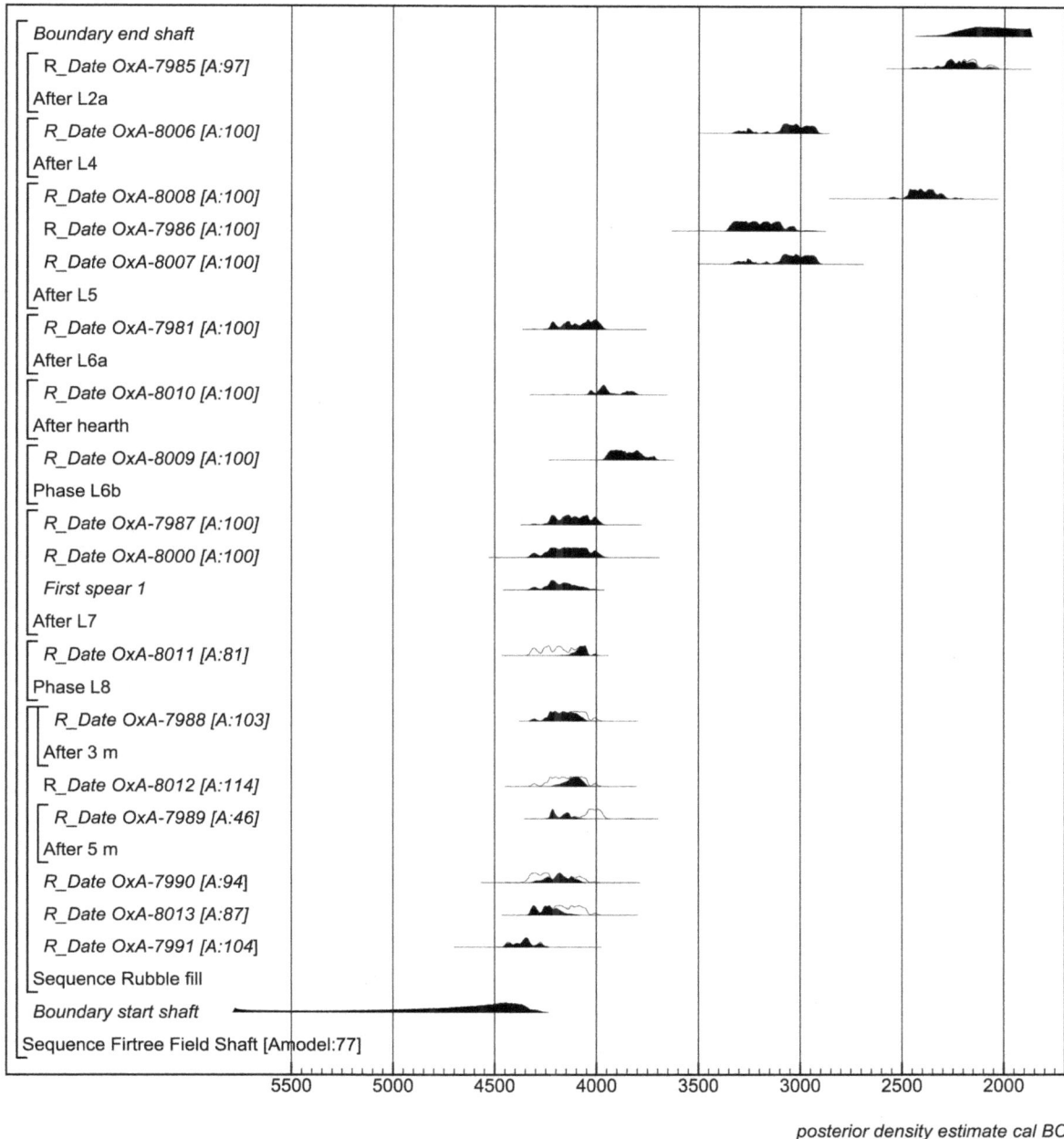

Figure 1. Probability distributions of dates from the Fir Tree Field shaft. Each distribution represents the relative probability that an event occurred at a particular time. For each date, the distribution in outline is the result produced by the radiocarbon measurement alone and the distribution in solid black is based on the chronological model used. The other distributions correspond to aspects of the model. For example, the distribution 'spear 1' is the estimated date for the deposition of a projectile fitted with microliths. The structure of the model is defined by the brackets down the left hand side of the diagram. 'After' denotes that a date has been modelled as a *terminus post quem*. Two further models which are not shown are identical, except for the variations noted in Figure 4.

the overlying layers 6b, 6a and a hearth is not completely clear from the publications, in fact L6b directly overlay L7, the hearth was at the top of L6b, and was covered by L6a. This provides more sequence for the subsequent samples. Charred clematis roots from L6b provide a short-life sample post-dating the spear (Fig. 1: *OxA-8009*). The scant contents of layer 6b included only four identifiable animal bone fragments, one uncertainly of domesticated cattle, and one uncertainly of domesticated pig. (Maltby 2007). Whether or not these were from domesticated animals, *OxA-8009* serves to constrain the estimated date of the spear, which must be later than *OxA-8011* and earlier than

OxA-8009. Within these limits, its estimated age depends on the precise structure of the model. Options are shown in Figure 2 and listed in Figure 4. They are comparable with Bayliss' estimate of *4330–4285 cal BC* (*6% probability*) or *4270–4035 cal BC* (*89% probability*), probably *4240–4100 cal BC* (*68% probability*: Whittle *et al.* 2011, fig. 4.21: *microliths*).

The spear was not an isolated hunting loss. Not only was contemporary activity evidenced by further Mesolithic lithics and wild animal bone in the same layer, but a surface scatter 300 m to the north-west also contains rod microliths

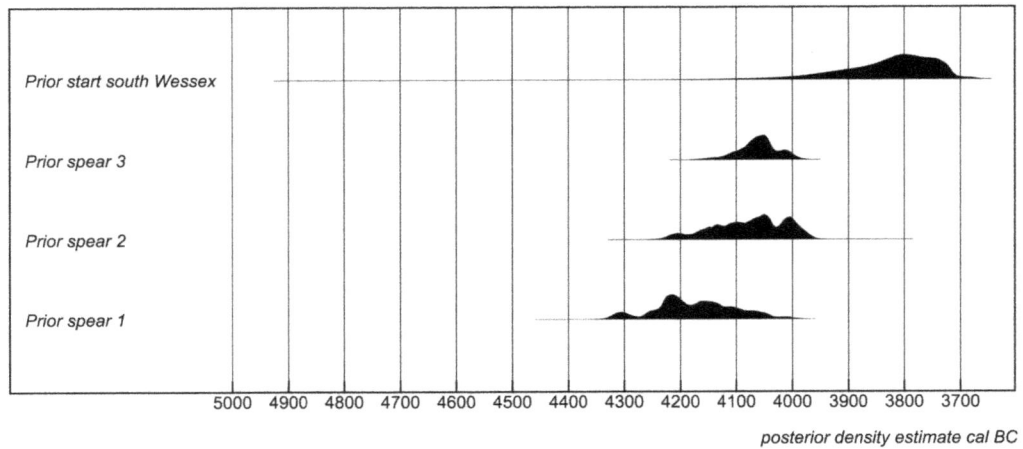

Figure 2. Three estimated dates for the projectile from the Fir Tree Field shaft, the first derived from the model shown in Figure 1, the second and third from models which vary as described in Figure 4, plotted with an estimated start for the Neolithic in south Wessex derived from the model shown by Whittle *et al.* (2010, fig. 14.53: *start south Wessex*).

occur in, suggesting possibly contemporary activity (Green 2000, 28). On the site of the Thickthorn Down long barrow, some 4 km to the south-west, a rod microlith was found beneath the mound (Drew and Piggott 1936, fig. 5: F59); this may also reflect contemporary activity, whether or not credence is placed in a radiocarbon date of 4050–3800 cal BC (95% confidence; 5160 ± 45 BP; BM-2355) for a red deer antler from the same surface, which may have been made inaccurately old by the incomplete removal of polyvinyl acetate from the sample (Ambers *et al.* 1987, 180). An even earlier human presence may be evidenced by a row of three irregular pits sealed by the turfline on which these finds lay. The pits contained only burnt flint and charcoal, which was, in the one case where it was identified, of pine — compatible with an early Holocene date Their plans might suggest that they were treeholes (Drew and Piggott 1936, 81, 94, pl. XVI). Their burning by human agency would accord with local human activity throughout the Mesolithic, evidenced by numerous artefact scatters (Arnold *et al.* 1988; Barrett *et al.* 1991, 29–30; Green 2000, 20–28). Hunter-gathers were living in the

area through the Holocene and up to the end of the fifth millennium cal BC.

It is above the hearth, in layer 6a, that unambiguously Neolithic fauna and cultural material appeared, notably a fragment of domesticated cattle bone, a fragment of possibly domesticated pig bone, Neolithic Bowl pottery and a fragmentary ground flint axe (Maltby 2007; Cleal 2007; Green 2007b). On the face of it, this should offer an opportunity to gauge the speed at which Neolithic innovations were taken up, within something like 0.25 m of accumulation. It does not, because from here upwards all the remaining dates can be modelled only as *termini post quos*. *OxA-8010*, from the hearth, was measured on charcoal of beech, which can be relatively long-lived. Four others (*OxA-7981, 7986, -8008, -8006*) were measured on disarticulated animal bones, one of them (*OxA-7981*) in addition being older than underlying samples, and another (*OxA-7986*) in addition being older than a sample from the same layer. Hazel charcoal dated by *OxA-8007* was probably made up of fragments of mixed ages, since

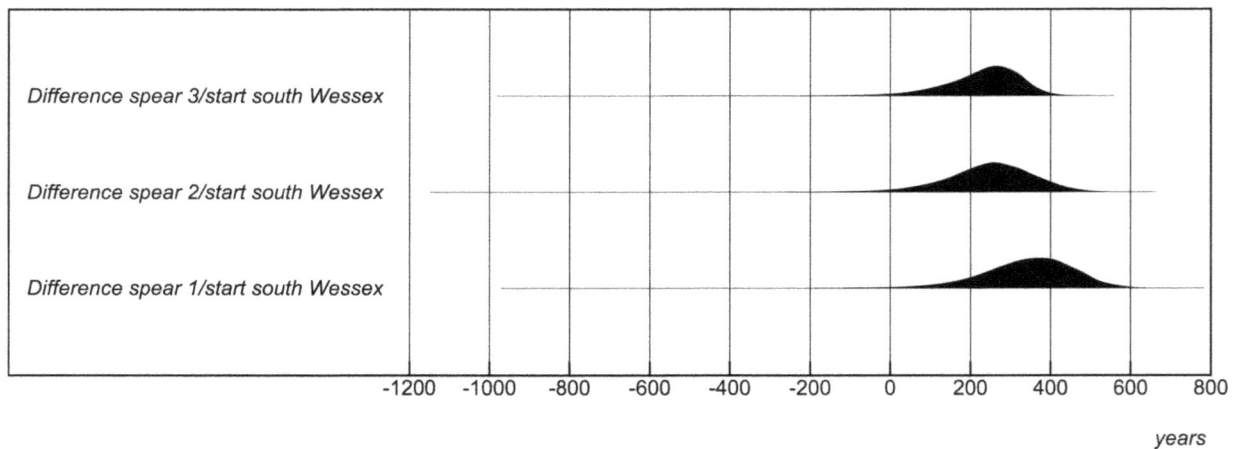

Figure 3. Estimated intervals between the deposition of the spear in the Fir Tree Field shaft, derived from the model shown in Figure 1 and two others described in Figure 4, and an estimated start for the Neolithic in south Wessex derived from the model shown by Whittle *et al.* (2010, fig. 14.53: *start south Wessex*).

Figure 4. Estimated dates for the Fir Tree Field shaft spear (Fig. 2) and estimated intervals (Fig. 3) between it and the start of the Neolithic in South Wessex (Whittle *et al.* 2011, fig. 14.53: *start south Wessex***)**

Model	Parameter name	Posterior density estimate cal BC (95% probability)	Posterior density estimate cal BC (68% probability)	Number of years between spear and start South Wessex (95% probability)	Number of years between spear and start South Wessex (68% probability)
Deposition of spear treated as first event in L7 because near base. Dates for bone samples treated as *termini post quos* (Fig. 1)	spear 1	4330–4280 (7%), 4270–4035 (88%)	4245–4100	105–560	255–470
Deposition of spear treated as last event in L7 because disarticulated bone samples may pre-date layer. Dates for bone samples treated as *termini post quos*	spear 2	4220–3970	4145–4130 (4%), 4120–4035 (45%), 4025–3990 (19%)	20–465	160–365
Deposition of spear treated as first event in L7 because near base. 2 dates for disarticulated animal bone from L7 treated as contemporary with context because dates in good agreement with stratigraphic position and statistically consistent with each other (T'=0.1; T'(5%)=3.8; v=1)	spear 3	4140–3990	4100–4030 (65%), 4020–4010 (3%)	25–405	170–340

it consisted of small scraps scattered through the layer (Martin Green pers comm.); also, although short-lived, it was older than another sample from the same layer (Fig. 1: *OxA-8008*). The nature of the deposits contributes to the low information value of the dates. At this stage, the weathering cone was almost infilled (Green 2000, fig. 23), and virtually horizontal layers of deposit were accumulating slowly, incorporating some distinctly second-hand material; sherds of the Neolithic Bowl represented in layer 6a continued, for example, to enter the feature from the surface as subsequent deposits accumulated (Cleal 2007). Layer 5, in particular, was a buried soil in which material could have accumulated over some time.

With dates from layer 6b upwards modelled as *termini post quos*, it is possible to estimate only a very imprecise date for the transition from conventionally Mesolithic to conventionally Neolithic. There is, however, a more robust alternative in an estimate of *4065–3705 cal BC (95% probability)*, probably *3905–3735 cal BC (68% probability)* for the start of Neolithic things and practices in the surrounding south Wessex area, derived from the available dates for contexts other than causewayed enclosures (Whittle *et al.* 2011, 732–34, fig. 14.53: *start south Wessex*). It is shown with different estimates for the spear in Figure 2 and the estimated intervals between it and them are shown in Figure 3 and listed in Figure 4. Even with the latest of the estimates for the spear (*spear 3*), the interval between the two is *25–405 years (95% probability)*, probably *170–340 years (68% probability)* with the probability concentrated in the centre of each distribution (Fig. 3). An interval between the last visible hunter-gatherer presence and the first visible Neolithic presence of two or three centuries could encompass all manner of processes, rapid and gradual, leaving the nature of the transition as open to debate as ever. In an historical

perspective, it is equivalent to the period from Queen Anne or from William III to the present.

The Process of Transition

Moving from a regional to an insular level, this degree of uncertainty contrasts with the confidence of a paper by Collard *et al.* entitled 'Radiocarbon evidence indicates that migrants introduced farming to Britain', which concludes 'That a dramatic increase in the population of Britain began coincident with the earliest evidence of food production, and that the average annual growth rate during the period of population increase in question was 0.37%. The former finding is consistent with the migrant farmers hypothesis and the rapid indigenous adoption hypothesis but not with the slow indigenous adoption hypothesis, while the latter is in line with the migrant farmers hypothesis but not with the rapid indigenous adoption hypothesis.' (2010, 869).

Although this has provided welcome ammunition to some authors (e.g. French *et al.* 2012, 31), its validity can be questioned. The 0.37% annual growth rate was based on the hypothesis that '. . . because the number of site phases in a given time period can be expected to relate monotonically to population size, changes in summed probability distributions of calibrated ^{14}C dates derived from different site phases serve as a proxy for changes in population size. (Collard *et al.* 2010, 867). This premise might be valid if the intensity of archaeological investigation was constant across the 8000–4000 cal BP (c 7000–2500 cal BC) period of the study and if the character of the archaeological record remained constant across the same period.

Neither is true. Over the last century or so, many more researchers in Britain have concerned themselves with the Neolithic than with the Mesolithic. More researchers

Frances Healy

mean more collected material — hence more potential radiocarbon samples, and more motivation to obtain radiocarbon dates. This effect is multiplied by the different character of the archaeology of the two periods. Even excluding monuments, which Collard *et al.* separate from other kinds of site in their analysis, there is, from the start of the Neolithic, a major change in the kinds of context from which evidence for human activity is recovered, and hence in the supply of potential radiocarbon samples. All the previously generated kinds of context persist, among them artefact scatters, hearths and deposits in treethrow holes. But pits and post-built structures become far more frequent, and it is these, with their capacity for preserving charcoal, charred plant remains, bone, and other organic material, that have provided the bulk of the non-monument dates in Collard *et al.*'s analysis. When monuments, including barrows and cairns containing human burials and enclosures rich in cultural material, are taken into consideration, the capacity for obtaining and dating radiocarbon samples is vastly increased again. A salient feature of the early Neolithic is an increased tendency to dig holes in the ground and to put things in them. The increased frequency of radiocarbon dates may owes a lot to behavioural change. What is seen as an abrupt population decline after 5400 cal BC (*c* 3450 cal BC), when there is a drop in the frequency of dates from both monumental and non-monumental contexts, similarly corresponds to the time when the sample-rich barrows, cairns and enclosures of the first half of the fourth millennium begin to give way to other monument types, notably cursūs and other long enclosures, in which very little material of any kind was deposited, and when domestic structures become less frequent (Whittle *et al.* 2011, 846). *Some* of the shifting frequency of radiocarbon dates may be due to changing population size, but it is difficult to see how this factor can be isolated from others.

Beyond the basic premise

It is also possible to question other aspects of the Collard *et al.* analysis. There was no critical evaluation of the dates employed: 'Our approach to date selection was conservative.

The only dates not included in the dataset were ones deemed invalid by the originating laboratory. Dates claimed to be invalid on the basis of apparent stratigraphic inconsistency were included. We also included dates with large standard errors. This approach is

conservative because the inclusion of residual and imprecise dates can be expected to diminish any differences between the Mesolithic and Neolithic in terms of inferred population size.' (Collard *et al.* 2010, 867). The imprecision introduced by this procedure is significant because many of the dates will have been measured on mature or mixed charcoal samples, capable of being older than the human activity which they are treated as representing, especially as the dates used include those made available by the Archaeology Data Service, Department of Archaeology,

University of York, a dataset which goes back to the start of radiocarbon dating in Britain, when the need for large samples made for much use of mixed charcoal samples and mature timber, especially oak. The inherent level of imprecision is illustrated by the contrast between late fifth/early fourth millennium cal BC dates obtained in the 1950s on bulked, predominantly oak, charcoal, from the Hembury causewayed enclosure in Devon and mid fourth millennium dates obtained in the 2000s on single-entity short-life samples from the same and comparable contexts (Whittle *et al.* 2011, fig. 10.10). Such a level of imprecision in the dataset weakens inferences drawn from it.

There is similar imprecision in the dataset employed for the appearance of cultivated cereals, which is the collection of radiocarbon dates published by Brown (2007). The earliest of those dates were not measured directly on cereals but on samples taken to have been associated with cereals. Some of those samples, including the Hembury examples already noted, certainly or probably included wood which was already old when it was burnt and some, again including the Hembury ones, were associated only loosely with the cereals in question. Where conclusions are founded on chronology, that chronology needs to be as rigorous and as precise as possible.

A further problem is that, even if the dates used had been rigorously selected, summing their distributions, as has been done in this analysis, also sums the scatter inherent in radiocarbon dates, which makes phenomena appear to start earlier, continue longer and end later than in fact they did (Bayliss *et al* 2007, 9–11; Whittle *et al.* 2011, 914). 'This logical operation [summing] is sometimes used to provide an estimate for the distribution of different parameters — however, this distribution is folded together with the uncertainty in those parameters and so can give a misleading impression.' (Bronk Ramsey 2013).

State of play

The immigration/acculturation dichotomy is simplistic (cf Cummings and Harris 2011), since the combination of continuity and innovation shows that both must have been significant (cf Whittle *et al.* 2011, 861). A more realistic question is the role of each in the start of the Neolithic in Britain and, especially, how those roles played out. Alongside the self-evident innovations, the strongest elements of continuity are perhaps enduring use of particular landscapes and locations, suggesting a persistence of traditional routines, including the seasonal rhythms of movement developed by previous generations (cf Edmonds *et al* 1999, 74); and technological similarities in the debitage, although not in all of the finished implements, of 5th and 4th millennium flint assemblages in England (Healy and Jacobi 1984; Pitts and Jacobi 1979, 171–3). There is no British Ertebølle or Swifterbant, rather a transformation of old ways.

A great deal changed in a few centuries, but they were centuries. At a regional scale, an interval probably of

74

200–300 hundred years separated the last visible hunter-gather activity in south Wessex and the appearance of Neolithic practices there (Figs. 1–4). At an insular scale, the results of the *Gathering Time* project indicate that it took from the 41st or the 40th century cal BC to the 39th or the 38th century cal BC for Neolithic practices to spread across Britain, slowly at first, with innovations appearing successively, monument-building being among the later developments; but accelerating from the late 39th century, with the consolidation what could be seen as a 'package' (Whittle *et al.* 2011, 833–841, 860, fig. 14.179). This could be consistent with the perhaps small-scale establishment of new people and practices in the south-east, followed by the attainment of a critical mass, both by continued immigration flow and by acculturation, after which there was a more rapid spread (Whittle *et al.* 2011, 860–64).

From a personal view, the drivers of this transformation must have included a strong ideological element, in the sense of new beliefs and values embracing the whole spectrum of relation to the natural world, substance base, treatment of the dead and other ceremonial practice. Only a force such as, say, the conversion of pagan Anglo-Saxon England to Christianity, could bring about such a transformation of behaviour and its material expression. Its spread may well have been facilitated by pre-existing long distance communication networks with few nodes, of the kind posited by Ashmore (2003).

Acknowledgements

This paper springs from the *Gathering Time* project. I am profoundly grateful to Alasdair Whittle and Alex Bayliss for their invitation to participate in the enterprise. I am equally grateful to Julian Thomas, Mats Larsson and Jolene Debert for their invitation to take part in the original conference and to contribute to this volume.

Bibliography

Allen, M.J. 2000. Soils, pollen and lots of snails. In M. Green, *A Landscape Revealed: 10,000 Years on a Chalkland Farm*, 36–49. Stroud: Tempus.

Allen, M. J. and Green, M. 1998. The Fir Tree Field shaft; the date and archaeological and palaeo-environmental potential of a chalk swallowhole feature. *Proceedings of the Dorset Natural History and Archaeological Society* 120, 25–37.

Ambers, J., Matthews, K. and Bowman, S. 1987. British Museum natural radiocarbon measurements XX. *Radiocarbon* 29, 177–96.

Arnold, J., Green, M., Lewis, B., and Bradley, R. 1988. The Mesolithic of Cranborne Chase. *Proceedings of the Dorset Natural History and Archaeological Society* 110, 117–25.

Ashmore, P. 1999. Radiocarbon dating: avoiding errors by avoiding mixed samples. *Antiquity* 73, 124–30

Ashmore, P. 2003. Terminology, time and space: labels, radiocarbon chronologies and a 'Neolithic' of small worlds. In I. Armit, E. Murphy, E. Nelis and D. Simpson (eds), *Neolithic Settlement in Ireland and Western Britain*, 40–46. Oxford: Oxbow Books

Barclay, A. forthcoming. *Dating the Earliest Neolithic Ceramics of Wessex. Scientific Dating Report.* English Heritage Research Report series. Portsmouth: English Heritage.

Barrett, J.C., Bradley, R. and Green, M. 1991. *Landscape, Monuments and Society: the Prehistory of Cranborne Chase.* Cambridge: Cambridge University Press.

Bayliss, A., Bronk Ramsey, C., van der Plicht, J. and Whittle, A. 2007. Bradshaw and Bayes: towards a timetable for the Neolithic. *Cambridge Journal of Archaeology* 17.1, supplement, 1–28.

Bayliss, A., van der Plicht, J., Bronk Ramsey, C., McCormac, G., Healy, F. and Whittle, A. 2011. Chapter 2. Towards generational time-scales: the quantitative interpretation of archaeological chronologies. In Whittle, A., Healy, F. and Bayliss, A 2011. *Gathering Time: Dating the Early Neolithic Enclosures of Southern Britain and Ireland*, 16–60. Oxford: Oxbow Books.

Bronk Ramsey, C. 2000. Comment on 'The Use of Bayesian Statistics for ¹⁴C dates of chronologically ordered samples: a critical analysis', *Radiocarbon*, **42** (2) 199–202.

Bronk Ramsey, C. 2001. Development of the radiocarbon calibration program Oxcal. *Radiocarbon* 43, 355–363

Bronk Ramsey, C. 2013. *OxCal 4.2 Manual. http://c14. arch.ox.ac.uk/*

Brown, A. 2007. Dating the onset of cereal cultivation in Britain and Ireland: the evidence from charred cereal grains. *Antiquity* 81, 1042–1052.

Cleal, R. 2007. Pottery from the shaft. In C. French, H. Lewis, M. J. Allen, M. Green, R. Scaife and J. Gardiner, *Prehistoric Landscape Development and Human Impact in the Upper Allen Valley, Cranborne Chase, Dorset*, 290–295. Cambridge: McDonald Institute for Archaeological Research.

Collard, M., Edinborough, K., Shennan, S. and Thomas, M. G. 2010. Radiocarbon evidence indicates that migrants introduced farming to Britain. *Journal of Archaeological Science* 37(4), 866–70.

Cummings, V. and Harris, O. 2011. Animals, people and places: the continuity of hunting and gathering practices across the Mesolithic-Neolithic transition in Britain. *Journal of European Archaeology* 14(3), 361–382

Drew, C.D. and Piggott, S. 1936. The excavation of long barrow 163a on Thickthorn Down, Dorset. *Proceedings of the Prehistoric Society* 2, 77–96.

Edmonds, M., Evans, C. and Gibson, D. 1999. Assembly and collection — lithic complexes in the Cambridgeshire fenlands. *Proceedings of the Prehistoric Society* 65, 47–82.

French, C., Lewis, H., Allen, M.J., Green, M., Scaife, R. and Gardiner, J. 2007. *Prehistoric Landscape Development and Human Impact in the Upper Allen Valley, Cranborne Chase, Dorset*. Cambridge: McDonald Institute for Archaeological Research.

French, C., Scaife, R. and Allen, M. 2010. Durrington Walls to West Amesbury by way of Stonehenge; a major transformation of the Holocene landscape. *Antiquaries Journal* 92, 1–36.

Green, M. 2000. *A Landscape Revealed: 10,000 Years on a Chalkland Farm*. Stroud: Tempus.

Green, M. 2007a. Fir Tree Field shaft. In C. French, H. Lewis, M. J. Allen, M. Green, R. Scaife and J. Gardiner, *Prehistoric Landscape Development and Human Impact in the Upper Allen Valley, Cranborne Chase, Dorset*, 76–82. Cambridge: McDonald Institute for Archaeological Research.

Green, M. 2007b. Lithics from the shaft. In C. French, H. Lewis, M. Allen, M. Green, R. Scaife and J. Gardiner, *Prehistoric Landscape Development and Human Impact in the Upper Allen Valley, Cranborne Chase, Dorset*, 280–5. Cambridge: McDonald Institute for Archaeological Research

Griffiths, S. forthcoming. Points in time: the Mesolithic–Neolithic transition and the chronology of rod microliths in Britain

Harding, J. and Healy, F. 2007. *The Raunds Area project: a Neolithic and Bronze Age landscape in Northamptonshire*. Swindon: English Heritage.

Healy, F and Jacobi, R 1984, The beginnings?. In F. Healy, Farming and field monuments: the Neolithic in Norfolk. In C. Barringer (ed), *Aspects of East Anglian Prehistory (Twenty Years after Rainbird Clarke)*, 79–84. Norwich: Geo Books.

Maltby, M. 2007. Animal bone from the Fir Tree Field Shaft and associated pits. In C. French, H. Lewis, M.J. Allen, M. Green, R. Scaife and J. Gardiner, *Prehistoric landscape development and human impact in the upper Allen valley, Cranborne Chase, Dorset*, 295–9. Cambridge: McDonald Institute for Archaeological Research.

Mant, A.K., 1987. Knowledge acquired from post-War exhumations. In A. Boddington, A.N. Garland & R.C. Janaway (eds), *Death, Decay, and Reconstruction. Approaches to Archaeology and Forensic Science*, 65–80. Manchester: Manchester University Press

Pitts, M.W. and Jacobi, R.M. 1979. Some aspects of change in flaked stone industries of the Mesolithic and Neolithic in southern Britain. *Journal of Archaeological Science* 6, 163–177

Pryor, F. 2003. *Britain BC. Life in Britain and Ireland before the Romans*. London: HarperCollins.

Reimer, P.J., Baillie, M.G.L., Bard, E., Bayliss, A., Beck, J.W., Bertrand, C.J.H., Blackwell, P.G., Buck, C.E., Burr, G.S., Cutler, K.B., Damon, P.E., Edwards, R.L., Fairbanks, R.G., Friedrich, M., Guilderson, T.P., Hogg, A.G., Hughen, K.A., Kromer, B., McCormac, F.G., Manning, S., Bronk Ramsey, C., Reimer, R.W., Remmele, S., Southon, J.R., Stuiver, M., Talamo, S., Taylor, F.W., van der Plicht, J. and Weyhenmeyer, C.E. 2004. IntCal04 terrestrial radiocarbon age calibration, 0–26 cal kyr BP. *Radiocarbon* 46, 1029–1058.

Reimer, P.J., Baillie, M.G.L., Bard, E., Bayliss, A., Beck, J.W., Blackwell, P.G., Bronk Ramsey, C., Buck, C.E., Burr, G.S., Edwards, R.L., Friedrich, M., Grootes, P.M, Guilderson, T.P., Hajdas, I., Heaton, T.J., Hogg, A.G., Hughen, K.A., Kaiser, K.F., Kromer, B., McCormac, F.G., Manning, S.W., Reimer, R.W., Richards, D.A., Southon, J.R., Talamo, S., Turney, C.S.M., van der Plicht, J. and Weyhenmeyer, C.E. 2009. Intcal09 and marine09 radiocarbon age calibration curves, 0–50,000 years cal BP. *Radiocarbon,* 51(4), 1111–1150

Spikins, P A, 2002 *Prehistoric People of the Pennines. Reconstructing the Lifestyles of Mesolithic Hunter-gatherers on Marsden Moor*. Leeds: West Yorkshire Archaeology Service

Steier, P. and Rom, W. 2000. The use of Bayesian statistics for ^{14}C dates of chronologically ordered samples: a critical analysis. *Radiocarbon* 42(2), 183–198

Ward, G.K. and Wilson, S.R. 1978. Procedures for comparing and combining radiocarbon age determinations: a critique. *Archaeometry* 20, 19–31.

Whittle, A. 2007. The temporality of transformation: dating the early development of the southern British Neolithic. In A. Whittle and V. Cummings (eds), *Going Over: the Mesolithic-Neolithic Transition in North-West Europe*, 377–398. Oxford: Oxford University Press for the British Academy

Whittle, A., Healy, F. and Bayliss, A. 2011. *Gathering Time: Dating the Early Neolithic Enclosures of Southern Britain and Ireland*. Oxford: Oxbow Books

Chapter 9

Late Mesolithic-Early Neolithic in Southern Scandinavia: Tradition and Interaction

T. Douglas Price

Aarhus University, Denmark

A wide range of evidence regarding the transition from the late Mesolithic to the Early Neolithic in southern Scandinavia has appeared in the last few decades. Archaeological fieldwork, largely as a part of heritage mitigation projects, has produced important new information on material culture and settlement. Various studies involving isotopes and aDNA have added new dimensions to the study of this major time of change. Theoretical frameworks, however, have not expanded to incorporate these new insights. A summary of recent evidence, both from the larger arena of the origins of agriculture and from the transition from hunting to farming in southern Scandinavia will be presented and some new avenues for understanding this information will be suggested.

Keywords: S. Scandiavia, Early Neolithic, transition to farming, aDNA, isotopes

Over the last 30 years there has been a dramatic shift in our understanding of the transition from the Mesolithic to the Early Neolithic in southern Scandinavia. The basic parameters of the time and space distribution of these Stone Age cultures have generally remained in place, but very little of what was assumed prior to 1980 remains valid. These changes can be said to have begun with the seminal 1981 paper by Henrik Tauber, employing carbon isotopes to measure past diets and identify the dramatic contrast between marine oriented Mesolithic menus and the terrestrially based diet of the Early Neolithic. Stone Age archaeology in southern Scandinavia has been hugely impacted by the advent of AMS dating and the thousands of determinations that have been made over the last three decades (e.g., Persson 1999, Hinz et al. 2012, Sørensen and Karg 2012). The biggest factor in changing our understanding of these last hunters and first farmers, however, has come from the explosive growth of rescue or heritage archaeology in the face of new legislation and the development of infrastructure. My own impression is that new data, rather than new ideas, have been the primary engine responsible for this expansion of archaeological knowledge.

In the following pages I want to consider these changes in several ways. First I will review some of the problems and questions that are being addressed. Then I will consider some of the new discoveries and their implications for the transition to agriculture in southern Scandinavia. Finally I will suggest a non-answer to the difficulties involved in making sense of the transition to agriculture, but one that may, in fact, help us comprehend the nature of the problem.

The origins and transition to agriculture is one of those big, thorny problems in archaeology that have occupied many people for many decades without obvious solution. The question has been under investigation in Scandinavia for more than 150 years (Fischer 2002). This issue is multidimensional, involving environment, people, society, plants and animals. A huge number of important variables are potentially involved. These include sedentism, storage, population density, population pressure, resource abundance, niche construction, processing and harvesting technologies, climate and environmental changes, ownership of produce and resource localities, potential domesticates, competition, wealth accumulation, inequality, risk reduction, nutritional requirements, choice, chance, and a receptive social/cultural context, among others.

Explanations of the origins of agriculture have sometimes been categorized as either push or pull models. Hunter-gatherers are either pushed, or forced, to become farmers or they are pulled, drawn by the benefits of a new lifestyle. Population-pressure models, for example, force human societies to find new ways to feed growing numbers of members. Social hypotheses usually involve pull, in which members of society are drawn into relationships of inequality in order to benefit from new arrangements that reduce risk or increase wealth.

Basically, however, this question of the transition to agriculture is a mystery to be solved — who, what, when, where and why? The simple fact is that we do not yet have a good grasp on the causes for the origins of agriculture. The how and the why of the Neolithic transition remain among the more intriguing questions in human prehistory. There is as yet no single accepted theory for the origins of agriculture — rather, there are a series of ideas and suggestions that do not quite resolve the question. At the same time, of course, the evidence we have is usually scanty and limited.

New Information from southern Scandinavia

Although there are many things we don't still know, the quantity of archaeological evidence on the transition to agriculture in southern Scandinavia has grown enormously in recent years. I will review some of this new evidence in the following pages as a means of summarizing what has been learned.

Changes in Diet

The Tauber study remains as perhaps the most important and dramatic piece of evidence regarding the transition to agriculture in southern Scandinavia. Tauber documented a remarkable and apparently sudden shift from marine to terrestrial foods from the Mesolithic to the Neolithic. There have been a number of follow-up studies and similar patterns have been observed elsewhere. There are problems with the study in that there are very few late Mesolithic and early Neolithic burials so that the rate of change is difficult to determine. Some modifications of those conclusions have been made because collagen presents a biased view of protein intake. Nevertheless, the evidence for a major shift in human diets within a few hundred years at the time of the transition remains.

Mesolithic Cemeteries

In the last 30 years or so the number of Mesolithic graves and especially cemeteries has had a major impact on the field. The discoveries at Vedbæk (Albrethsen and Brinch Petersen 1977) and Skateholm in the 70s and early 80s (Larsson 1988, 2004) documented permanent burials grounds, often thought to characterize more permanent settlement, and to offer a new look at the ritual aspects of Mesolithic society.

The Chronology of Pottery

The remarkable book published by Eva Koch in 1998 with the rather mundane title 'Neolithic bog pots from Zealand, Møn, Lolland and Falster' is a milestone in the study of the Neolithic of southern Scandinavia. Koch's analysis of the almost intact Neolithic pottery found in bog sacrifices documents systematic changes in the shape and decoration of the ceramics and moves the discussion of Neolithic chronology from regional groups such as Oxie, Volling, and Svaleklint to more time-sensitive criteria.

Earthen long barrows

Early Neolithic long barrows with wooden structures were first recognized in Denmark in the early 1970s (Madsen 1979). Almost 40 non-megalithic barrows are known today, predominantly in Jutland in western Denmark. The barrows show much variation both in construction and size. Usually the barrows are low (about 1-2 m high), but vary in the length from 10-50 m. Certain distinctive features are normally incorporated in their construction: rectangular or trapezoidal palisade enclosures surround the mound, the interior of the barrow is transversely partitioned by rows of stakes, and massive timber facades are usually placed at the east end of the mound associated with deposits of pottery.

Flanking ditches, well known from British long barrows, have only been recovered in few instances, but the low number may reflect lack of observations in the field prior to the recognition of this feature in Danish long barrows. Most long barrows contain one or more graves built of wood or a combination of wood and stone. Like the barrows, the construction of the graves varies greatly, as does the quantity of grave goods (Madsen 1979; Kristensen 1991). Radiocarbon dating of the facades indicate that the construction of earthen long barrows began right at the onset of the Neolithic period and may have continued throughout the EN I period, from Lindebjerg 3990 to 3635 cal BC (Liversage 1981); Bjørnsholm 3965-3650 cal BC (Andersen 1991); Rustrup 3955-3515 cal BC (Fischer 1975, Kristensen 1991).

Underwater Archaeology

The underwater investigation of Mesolithic sites in southern Scandinavia is probably epitomized by the research at Tybrind Vig (Andersen 1980, 1985), but much more has been done in the 25 years since that project was completed. Underwater archaeology carried out by both agencies and individuals in Denmark, Sweden, and northern Germany has revealed many artifacts, features, and sites dating from the Mesolithic. Enormous projects such as the Doggerland investigations are underway as the archaeological resources of the sea floor have been recognized as a remarkable source of often well-preserved information.

aDNA Studies

The application of investigation of aDNA in late Mesolithic and Early Neolithic human remains has been ongoing for several years now. The initial fears of contamination and other problems have been replaced by youthful exuberance and some errors. More archaeologists need to be collaborating on these studies. In spite of some false starts with Pitted Ware Mesolithic people (Malmström et al. 2009) and the like, a general picture seems to be emerging today of genetic differences between Neolithic farmers and Mesolithic hunter-gatherers (e.g., Barbujani 2012, Bramanti et al. 2009, Haak et al. 2005, Skoglund et al. 2012). The Skoglund study argues that 'modern Scandinavians are not descended from the people who came to Scandinavia at the conclusion of the last ice age but from a population that arrived later, concurrently with the introduction of agriculture.'

Climate Change Models

Climate models have always accompanied explanations of the transition to agriculture in southern Scandinavia. The concept of the landnam was associated with the climatic conditions at the onset of the Subboreal and the elm decline and used to explain the arrival of Neolithic farmers for many years in Scandinavia (e.g., Iversen 1943, Troels-Smith 1960). Although the lock-step sequence of the elm decline and the arrival of agriculture has unraveled (e.g., Rasmussen 2005), there is still substantial debate over the role of climate in the transition to agriculture.

More refined climatic data has become available in recent years and the details have been used to discover connections between climate and culture in many parts of the world. Bonsall et al. (2002) argue that expansion of agriculture in northwest Europe was triggered by a significant change in climate — a drier, warmer, more continental phase between c. 4100 cal BC and c. 3200 cal BC. Groenenborn (2009) would even have us believe that climate changes through the Holocene dictated the expansion of agriculture across all of Europe.

I must admit that when I hear climatic explanations for the expansion of agriculture, I am always reminded of the strong correlation between shoe size and IQ, a relationship that says nothing about causality but speaks to the age of the shoe wearer. Even if climatic change was associated with every transformation in human society, it doesn't mean that climate caused all those changes. Climate is always changing, correlations can always be found. I find it impossible to imagine that climate change was responsible for the repeated lurches in the expansion of agriculture from the Near East to northern Europe.

Neolithic Contact

A series of studies have pointed out the significant degree of contact between the last hunters of Mesolithic southern Scandinavia and the first farmers in northern Germany and Poland (Glob 1939, Anderson 1975). In recent years the identification of a number of imports from Neolithic societies and better chronological controls have confirmed the existence of interaction in some form among these groups. Shoe last adzes are a typical example, made of a material and in a style known only from the Early Neolithic of Central Europe (Fischer 1982). Other distinctive objects such as bone combs and rings and T-shaped antler axes also document this interaction and the spread of either ideas or the objects themselves. Klassen and others (2004, Pétrequin et al. (2004) have argued for the introduction of other Neolithic elements into southern Scandinavia after 5300 BC. In addition, these authors suggest that copper axes from southeast Europe and prestige Alpine jadite axes from the Mediterranean area were already present by the end of the Mesolithic.

On the other hand, Ertebølle ceramics have long been thought to have been a derivative of central European Neolithic pottery also from contacts to the south, but increasing evidence points to eastern sources for this tradition and earlier dates in Finland and elsewhere confirm an origin in that direction (Hallgren 2004, Hartz et al. 2004).

The intriguing question raised by the documentation of Neolithic imports in the late Mesolithic is of course in the face of this contact and interaction, why did it take 1000 years or more for domesticates and other Neolithic innovations to appear in southern Scandinavia. This question remains unanswered.

Archaeozoology

Recent contributions of archaeozoology to questions regarding the transition from the Mesolithic to the Neolithic are substantial. Questions concerning seasonality and site function are nearing resolution in some situations. Several studies document the likelihood of near or fully sedentary behavior in the late Mesolithic Ertebølle of southern Scandinavia. Carter's 2001 analysis of cervid teeth from the sites of Tybrind Vig and Ringkloster documented the presence of red and roe deer hunting throughout much of the year. Recent investigations published by Enghoff (2011) also document the evidence for multi-seasonal, apparently year-round occupation at larger Mesolithic settlements. Our investigations at Smakkerup Huse (Price and Gebauer 2005) and other sites in eastern Zealand, Denmark (Ritchie et al. 2012), have produced a series of faunal assemblages that clearly argue for long-term occupation. In addition to the evidence for seasonality, these faunal analyses document a significant variation in resource use among these hunter-gatherers and a remarkable degree of flexibility in adapting to local resource availability. There is a great deal of inter-site variability. While the same animals are generally found in all assemblages, the proportions change dramatically and the focus of subsistence at each site appears to represent a specialized adaptation to local conditions. Such flexibility argues strongly against environmental changes as a major causal force for the introduction of agriculture at the end of the Mesolithic period.

Early Neolithic in Central Sweden.

The discovery and documentation of early TRB settlements in eastern central Sweden north of Stockholm has made it clear that the introduction of the Neolithic in Scandinavia was a very rapid event. Sites such as Anneberg, Skogsmossen, Fågelbacken, and others are radiocarbon dated between 4000 and 3500 BC (Hallgren et al. 1997, 2008, 2011) and clearly document the arrival of Funnel Beaker farming culture in this northerly region almost simultaneously with its appearance in southern Scandinavia. This event seems to happen quickly, almost like a blanket coming down over the area.

Rather than a unique situation, however, this pattern of 'lurches' replicates the series of long pauses before sudden spreads in the expansion of agriculture that now appears typical throughout much of prehistoric Europe (Price 2000, Rowley-Conwy 2011). Similar rapid events, followed by long periods of stability, characterize the expansion of LBK, the Cardial culture, the introduction of agriculture into Ireland and Britain and very probably provide an appropriate model for southeastern Europe as well. The pattern reminds one of the land rushes in parts of North and South America as new areas were opened to settlers, or the gold rushes that populated undeveloped parts of the American West and Alaska.

Important new sites, new dates and the resolution of controversies

Various pieces of evidence over the years have been proposed as documentation of early domesticated plants and/or animals at Mesolithic sites. This confusion about agriculture in the Mesolithic has been present in Scandinavian archaeology for many years. Recent studies involving AMS dating and aDNA, however, have cleared up much of the confusion and documented the arrival of these new species largely after 4100 BC. The early cow at Rosenhof was determined to be an aurochs (Scheu et al. 2009). Early cattle at Löddesborg have been radiocarbon dated very much younger (Price and Noe-Nygaard 2010). Radiocarbon and light isotope investigation of domestic cattle and aurochs in southern Scandinavia have distinguished the two species based on diet and documented the arrival of domestic cattle after 4000 BC (Noe-Nygaard et al. 2005, Price and Noe-Nygaard 2009).

The burials from Dragsholm, Denmark, have been a point of debate and discussion since their discovery in the early 1970s (Brinch Petersen 1974). Grave I contained the skeletons of two women (A and B), interred with 144 animal tooth pendants, a decorated bone dagger (or spatula), a bone point, covered with red ochre. The published radiocarbon date of 5160±100 bp from Burial A confirmed the Mesolithic age of the two women; the two must be contemporary, found in the same grave. Stable carbon isotope ratios from the bones indicated a diet dominated by marine foods, also a Late Mesolithic hallmark.

The second grave, less than 2 meters from the first, held the bones of a twenty-year-old male (Burial D). This grave contained at least 60 amber beads, a stone battle axe, flint blades and projectile points, an antler pick or shaft, a bone spoon and a wrist guard, and a small ceramic beaker from the early Neolithic Funnel Beaker culture. The Neolithic age for this individual was confirmed by a radiocarbon date of 4840±100 bp (approximately 300 years younger than the females) and a stable carbon isotope ratio that indicated a largely terrestrial diet. The close proximity of these two burials and the very different grave goods and diets represented are remarkable.

The two graves raised many questions, usually revolving around the dating of the graves. Were they contemporaneous, or close or widely separated in time? These graves have been discussed and considered in numerous publications concerned with the transition to agriculture in Europe, often interpreted in line with an author's theoretical stance about how the transition occurred. It has been suggested, for example that the male and the younger woman were related by marriage.

The issue of chronology has been resolved, however, with the measurement of new radiocarbon samples and isotopic analyses of the remains (Price et al. 2007). New radiocarbon dates were obtained on the bone collagen from the three skeletons. Two sets of samples were run using AMS dating at laboratories in Aarhus and New Zealand. These dates resulted in a correction of the original date on the two female burials. The best estimate for the age of this grave actually comes from the date 5983±38 bp (AAR-7417) on a red deer bone artifact in the grave. The dates from the human collagen of the two females, even after calibration, remain a hundred years or so too old. The date of the Neolithic male remains essentially unchanged, ca. 4989±46 bp (AAR-7416) on human bone collagen. Thus the difference in age between the two graves is approximately 1000 years. They are in no way contemporary. The two females are clearly Mesolithic, and the single male falls squarely in the Early Neolithic period.

A coalescence of radiocarbon dates for the early domesticates and distinctive artifacts of the Early Neolithic has pointed to 4100 – 4000 BC as the initial date for many of these elements, often slightly earlier in northern Germany. It now appears that most of the characteristic Neolithic hallmarks appeared in southern Scandinavia between 4100 and 3700 BC. In spite of certain arguments to the contrary (e.g., Behre 2007), there is no convincing evidence for any significant number of domesticates in Scandinavia prior to 4000 BC. There is lots of new evidence for finds just after that date.

Heritage excavations for the Malmö City Tunnel project and for new roadways around the Aarhus area have produced some very important sites and very early dates for domesticates. Several cereals including emmer, einkorn, bread wheat and naked barley are found across the region in this 400-year period and very early at the Swedish site of Almhov in Malmö (Gidlöf et al. 2006, Hadevik and Gidlöf 2003). Chaff from emmer wheat, strong evidence of cultivation rather than simple import, has been found as temper in ceramic artifacts at Lisbjerg, near Aarhus (Skousen 2008) from this time. Plow marks beneath a long barrow near Egense, Denmark, are dated by association to ca. 3700 cal BC (Beck 2009).

Domesticated animals (other than dogs) also appear early in the Neolithic. Domesticated sheep and/or goat, cow, and pig appear in northern Europe, for the most part, shortly after 4100 – 4000 cal BC (Price 2000). These animals, with the possible exception of pig, were domesticated originally in southwest Asia (Herre and Röhrs 1990, Benecke 1994) and introduced into the European continent by the spread of agriculture. Sheep and goat have no wild ancestral forms in northern Europe and are readily distinguished as imported domesticated species. Early dates for domesticated sheep/goat include examples at the German site of Wangels (4150 cal BC, Hedges et al. 1996), at Jordløse Mose in western Zealand, Denmark (3790 cal BC, Heinemeier et al. 1996), and perhaps Lollikhuse in central Zealand, Denmark (3960 cal BC, Heinemeier and Rud 1997, Sørensen 2005).

Cattle and pigs, on the other hand, do have wild relatives present in southern Scandinavia during the Holocene. The aurochs, *Bos primigenius*, and wild boar, *Sus scrofa*, were common prey during the Mesolithic. Distinguishing these wild varieties from their domestic relatives is not a simple matter (Degerbøl 1963; Degerbøl and Fredskild 1970; Jonsson 1986; Nobis 1978; Rowley-Conwy 1995). Aurochs, however, were extinct on the Danish islands by the middle Mesolithic and probably in Sweden as well. Thus any bovids on the islands in the early Neolithic are almost certainly domesticated. These cattle are seen consistently in southern Scandinavia after 4000 BC (Price and Noe-Nygaard 2010).

Although recent genetic information suggests that pig may have been independently domesticated in Europe (Larson et al. 2005), anatomically the distinction from wild varieties is very difficult (Magnell 2005, Rowley-Conwy 1995). The criteria for domestication have been based largely on animal size; domesticated varieties are generally smaller than their wild relatives. However, sexual dimorphism often results in a great deal of overlap in size between wild females and domestic males. Moreover, interbreeding between wild and domestic pigs makes identification difficult.

The advent of flint mining and the production of polished flint axes also appear to be early hallmarks of the Neolithic in the region. Radiocarbon dates from the mines at Södra Sallerup in Scania, Sweden, document the removal of large flint nodules after 4000 BC (Olausson et al. 1980). Quern stones for grinding grain are also found in this early period at sites throughout southern Scandinavia.

Conclusions

The phantom of causality floats at the periphery of any discussions of the transition to agriculture, always there but often not addressed. This transition from hunting to farming poses one of the most intriguing questions about the human past and one of the most difficult to answer: why did hunters become farmers? Causality is such a nasty issue. Are there general causes? The almost simultaneous development of agriculture in so many different places is not simple coincidence. Should we invoke climate, environment, population, subsistence intensification, brain capacity, religion, inequality, entrepreneurs? Are there specific conditions? Are there immediate and local causes distinct from global ones? Are the origins of agriculture the results of a 'perfect storm' of factors that forced or encouraged human societies to domesticate plants and animals?

The beginnings of agriculture are about much more than cultivation, herding, or the ensuing domestication of various species. This revolution entailed major long-term changes in the structure and social organization of the societies that adopted this new way of life as well as a totally new relationship with the environment. As we learn more about this transition, it becomes clearer how complex this past was, exhibiting much more variability than we have realized or admitted.

This is nowhere clearer than in the origins of agriculture in the ancient Near East. There is more archaeological information from this region about the origins of agriculture than anywhere else in the world — more sites, more excavations, more analyses, more publications, and so for. Yet new discoveries in the past 20 years have completely altered our understanding of the transition and revealed levels of complexity in the process not even imagined two decades ago.

Three recent discoveries from the earliest Neolithic in the Near East highlight this new perspective, change our understanding of this period in human prehistory, and raise enormous new questions. Excavations at Gobekli Tepe in southern Turkey have revealed a series of remarkable structures; possible shrines, associated with large stone architecture and art from the Pre-Pottery Neolithic A period ca. 10,000 years ago (Schmidt 2006, Schmidt and Hauptman 2003). Gobekli Tepe documents larger scale of architecture, religious activity, and social organization than previously imagined. The regional burial ground of Kafar HaHoresh in Israel documents enormous new variation in the treatment of the dead and indications of emerging social inequality by the PPNB period ca. 8500 BC (e.g., Goring-Morris 2005). The economic intensification and competition reflected in the cemetery finds were apparently frequent companions of the Neolithic revolution society (Price and Bar-Yosef 2010). Finally, the colonization of the Mediterranean island of Cyprus by Late Pre-Pottery Neolithic A and Pre-Pottery Neolithic B people carrying domestic plants and domestic and wild animals to the island by boat is an extraordinary story (Guilaine et al. 2000, Peltenburg and Wasse 2004, Vigne et al. 2011) and documents the very early spread of the Neolithic from its homeland.

At a recent conference on the origins of agriculture (Price and Bar-Yosef 2011) some intriguing conclusions regarding the transition to agriculture were reached. One of the most interesting phenomena we noted was not pattern, but variation. In the few places where data on the transition are relatively rich, there appears to have been a 'zone of variability', a time of chaos at the origins of agriculture (Weiss, Kislev, and Hartmann 2006). There seems to have been an 'auditioning' of many possible new options for human adaptation. This time of chaos marks the beginning of a new way of life.

I would suggest that a very similar situation pertains to the transition in southern Scandinavia (as well as Ireland and Britain, the Cardial Culture, and probably a number of other examples). One of the most striking features of the transition to the Neolithic in southern Scandinavia is the absence of pattern and the lack of clear evidence for the events, contexts, and relationships that were taking place. There are very few sites from this period of 4100 – 3700 BC, there are very few human burials, it is not clear precisely when polished axes appear, when TRB pottery is first produced. The fine details of the transition have been remarkably difficult to pin down.

I have been looking for very Early Neolithic sites in western Sjælland for 20 years. We do have sites with radiocarbon dates from the time of the transition and only the slightest indications of Neolithic involvement — a few cow bones at Smakkerup Huse, some unusual pottery at Asnæs Havnemark, radiocarbon dates from the time of the transition at Fårevejle shell midden. Part of the reason for the obscurity of this transition may be the vague or inappropriate questions of archeologists, but certainly a large part reflects the nature of the archaeological evidence itself. This does seem to be a time of chaos, of variation, of auditioning, between the last of the Mesolithic and the fully Neolithic farmers building megaliths after 3600 BC.

The question of course is how to understand this chaos, how to make sense of what is happening at the transition. Explanations of the origins of agriculture (and many other phenomenon) often consider a number of different variables. It is essential to segregate such variables among conditions, causes, and consequences. Conditions for agricultural society would include sufficient population, sedentism, adequate growing conditions, domesticates and certain knowledge. Consequences of agricultural transitions include population growth, population aggregation, increased trade and craft production, inequality, organized religion, and innovation.

Research has focused on settlements and burials, artifacts and domesticates. Perhaps the answer lies more in a shift in focus from things to behavior, toward social and group activities, and toward the consequences of the new arrangements. A more intensive consideration of the Neolithic following the time of chaos may be informative with regard to the changes that were instituted. Moreover, the transition to agriculture takes place repeatedly in Europe (and elsewhere) and the fundamentals of the transformation must be quite similar everywhere. A change from community to household levels of economic organization, for example, may have accompanied the transition to agriculture, including a shift from communal sharing to familial or individual accumulation. Economic activities such as the production of polished flint axes or battle axes may become more specialized. Clearly these consequences of the agricultural transition reflect the changes that took place through the black box of the transition itself.

References

Albrethsen, S. E., and E. Brinch Petersen. 1977. Excavation of a Mesolithic cemetery at Vedbæk, Denmark. *Acta Archaeologica* 47, 1-28.

Andersen, S. H. 1975. Ringkloster, Early Neolithic jysk inlandsboplads med Ertebølle kultur. *KUML* 1973-74, 10-107.

Andersen, S. H. 1980. Tybrind Vig. *Antikvariske studier* 4, 7-22.

Andersen, S. H. 1985. Tybrind Vig. A preliminary report on a submerged Ertebølle settlement on the west coast of Fyn. *Journal of Danish Archaeology* 4, 52–69.

Andersen, S. H. 1991. Bjørnsholm. A stratified køkkenmødding on the Central Limfjord, North Jutland. *Journal of Danish Archaeology* 10, 59-96.

Barbujani, G. 2012. Human Genetics: Message from the Mesolithic. *Current Biology* 22, R631-R633.

Beck, M. R., 2009. Lå Danmarks første pløjemark ved Egense? *Svendborgs Museums Årbog* 2009, 7-16.

Behre, K. E. 2007. Evidence for Mesolithic agriculture in and around central Europe? *Vegetation History and Archaeobotany* 16, 203–219.

Benecke, N. 1994. *Der Mensch und seine Haustiere.* Stuttgart: Theiss Verlag.

Bonsall, C., Macklin, M. G., Anderson, D. G., and Payton, R.W. 2002. Climate change and the adoption of agriculture in northwest Europe. *European Journal of Archaeology* 5, 9–23.

Bramanti, B., Thomas, M. G., Haak, W., Unterlaender, M., Jores, P., Tambets, K., Antanaitis-Jacobs, I., Haidle, M. N., Jankauskas, R., Kind, C. J., Lueth, F., Terberger, T., Hiller, J., Matsumura, Forster, P., Burger, J. 2009. Genetic Discontinuity Between Local Hunter-Gatherers and Central Europe's First Farmers. *Science* 326, 137-140.

Brinch Petersen, E. 1973. A survey of Late Paleolithic and Mesolithic in Denmark. In *The Mesolithic of Europe*, edited by S.K. Kozlowski, 77-128. Warsaw: University Press.

Brinch Petersen, E. 1974. Graverne ved Dragsholm. Fra jægere til boner for 6000 år siden. *Nationalmuseets Arbjedsmark* 1974, 112-120.

Carter, R. J. 2001. Dental indicators of seasonal human presence at the Danish Boreal sites of Holmegaard I, IV and V and Mullerup and the Atlantic sites of Tybrind Vig and Ringkloster. *The Holocene* 11, 359-365.

Degerbøl 1963. Prehistoric cattle in Denmark and adjacent areas. In: A. E. Mourant, F. E. Zeuner (eds.), Man and cattle: Proceedings of a symposium on domestication at the Royal Anthropological Institute. 24-26 May 1960. Occasional Paper no. 18. 69-79. London, Royal Anthropological Institute.

Degerbøl and Fredskild 1970. *The Urus (Bos Primigenius Bojanus) and Neolithic Domesticated Cattle (Bos Taurus Domesticus Linné) in Denmark: Zoological and Palynological Investigations.* Copenhagen, Munksgaard.

Enghoff, I. B., 2011. *Regionality and biotope exploitation in Danish Ertebølle and ajoining periods.* Scientia Danica, series B. Biologica 1. Copenhagen, The Royal Danish Academy of Science and Letters.

Fischer, A. 1982. Trade in Danubian Shaft-Hole Axes and the Introduction of Neolithic Economy in Denmark. *Journal of Danish Archaeology* 1, 7-12.

Fischer, A., 2002. Food for Feasting? An evaluation of explanations of the neolithisation of Denmark and southern Sweden. In *The Neolithisation of Denmark - 150 Years of Debate,* A. Fischer and K. Kristiansen (eds.), 341-393. Sheffield, J. R. Collis Publications.

Fischer, A., and Kristiansen, K. (eds.) 2002. *The Neolithisation of Denmark.* Sheffield, J. R. Collis Publications.

Fischer, C. 1975. Tidlig-neolitiske anlæg ved Rustrup. *Kuml* 1975: 29–72.

Gidlöf, Kristina, Karina Hammarstrand Dehman, and Tobias Johansson. 2006. *Citytunnelprojektet Almhov – delområde* 1. Rapport över Arkeologisk Slutundersökning 39. Malmö, Kulturmiljö.

Glob, P. V. 1939. Der Einfluss der vandkeramischen Kulture in Dänemark. *Acta Archaeologica* 10, 131-149.

Goring-Morris, N. 2005. Life, death and the emergence of differential status in the Near Eastern Neolithic: evidence from Kfar Ha- Horesh, Lower Galilee, Israel. In *Archaeological perspectives on the transmission and transformation of culture in the Eastern Mediterranean.* J. Clarke (ed.), 89–105. Oxford, Council for British Research in the Levant/Oxbow.

Groenenborn, D. 2009. Cllimate fluctuations and trajectories to complexity. Towards a theory. *Documenta Praehistorica* 36, 97-110.

Guilaine, J., Briois, F., Vigne, J. D. and Carre`re, I. 2000. Decouverte d'un neolithique preceramique ancien chypriote (fin 9e debut 8e millenaires cal. BC), apparente au PPNB ancien/moyen du Levant nord. *Earth and Planetary Sciences* 300, 75–82.

Haak, W., Forster, P., Bramanti, B., Matsumura, S., Brandt, G., Taänzer, M., Villems, R., Renfrew, C., Gronenborn, D., Werner Alt, K., and Burger, J. 2005. Ancient DNA from the First European Farmers in 7500-Year-Old Neolithic Sites. *Science* 310, 1016-1018.

Hadevik, Claes, and Kristina Gidlöf. 2003. *Rapport 22. Öresundsförbindelsen. Fosie 11A-D and Boläge Larsbovägen.* Malmö.

Hallgren, Fredrik. 2004. The introduction of ceramic technology around the Baltic Sea in the 6th millennium. In *Coast to Coast, Arrival. Results and Reflections*, H. Knutsson (ed.), 10, 123–142. Uppsala, Coast to Coast Books.

Hallgren, F. 2008. *Identitet i praktik. Lokala, regionala och överregionala sociala sammanhang inom nordlig trattbägarkultur.* Coast to Coast-books 17. Uppsala,Uppsala University.

Hallgren, F. 2011. The early 'Trichterbecher' of Mälardalen, eastern Central Sweden. In *Early Pottery in the Baltic – Dating, Origin and Social Context*, S. Hartz, F. Lüth, and T. Terberger (eds.), 111-134. Bericht der Römisch-Germanische Kommission 89. Frankfurt, Römisch-Germanischen Kommission.

Hallgren, F., Djerw, U., af Geijerstam, M., and Steineke, M. 1997. Skogsmossen, an Early Neolithic settlement site and sacrificial fen, in the northern borderland of the Funnel-beaker Culture. *Tor* 29, 49–111.

Sönke, H., Heinrich, D. and Lübke, H. 2002. Coastal farmers – the neolithisation of northernmost Germany. In *The Neolithisation of Denmark. 150 Years of Debate*, A. Fischer and K. Kristiansen (eds.), pp. 321–340. Sheffield, Sheffield Archaeological Monographs 12.

Sönke, H., Lüth, F., and Terberger, T. (eds.) 2004. *Early Pottery in the Baltic – Dating, Origin and Social Context, Bericht der Römisch-Germainische Kommission* 89. Frankfurt, Römisch-Germanischen Kommission.

Hedges, R., Rupert A., Housley, R., Pettitt, C., Bronk, R., and van Klinken G. J. 1996. Radiocarbon dates from the Oxford AMS system: Archaeometry datelist 21. *Archaeometry* 38, 181-207.

Heinemeier, J., Rud, N., and Heier-Nielsen, S. 1996. Danish AMS radiocarbon datings of archaeological samples, Aarhus 1995, 318-325. *Arkaeologiske udgravninger i Danmark.*

Heinemeier, J., and Rud. N. 1997. Danish AMS radiocarbon datings of archaeological samples. *Arkæologiske udgravninger i Danmark 1997*, 301-312.

Herre, W., and Röhrs, M., 1990. *Haustiere — zoologisch gesehen. 2. Auglage.*

Hinz, M., Feeser, I., Sjögren, K. G., and Müller, J. 2012. Demography and the intensity of cultural activities: an evaluation of funnel beaker societies (4200-2800 cal BC). *Journal of Archaeological Science* 39, 3331-3340.

Iversen, J. 1941. Landnam i Danmarks Stenalder: En pollenanalytisk Undersøgelse over det første Landbrugs Indvirkning paa Vegetationsudviklingen. *Danmarks Geologiske Undersøgelse* II 66, 1-68.

Johansen, K. L. 2006. Settlement and land use at the Mesolithic-Neolithic transition in southern Scandinavia. *Journal of Danish Archaeology* 14, 201–223.

Jonsson, L. 1986. From Wild Boar to Domestic Pig - A Reassessment of Neolithic Swine of Northern Europe. In *Nordic Late Quaternary Biology and Ecology*, ed. L. K. Königsson, 125-129 (Striae 24).

Klassen, L., 2004. *Jade und Kupfer Untersuchungen zum Neolithisierungsprozess im westlichen Ostseeraum unter besonderer Berücksichtigung der Kulturentwicklung Europas 5500-3500 BC.* Århus, Jysk Arkæologisk Selskabs Skrifter.

Koch, E. 1998. *Neolithic bog pots from Zealand, Møn, Lolland and Falster.* Nordiske Fortidsminder, Ser. B16. København, National Museum.

Kjær, K. I. 1991. Storgård IV. An Early Neolithic Long Barrow near Fjelsø. *Journal of Danish Archaeology* 8, 72-87.

Larsson, L. (ed.) 1988. *The Skateholm project I. Man and environment.* Stockholm, Almqvist and Wiksell International.

Larsson, L. 2004. The Mesolithic period in Southern Scandinavia: with special reference to burials and cemeteries. In *Mesolithic Scotland and its neighbours,* Alan Saville (ed.), 371-92. Edinburgh, Society of Antiquaries of Scotland.

Liversage, D. 1981. Neolithic monuments at Lindebjerg, northwest Zealand. *Acta Archaeologica* 51, 85-152.

Madsen, Torsten. 1979. Earthen Long Barrows and Timber Structures: Aspects of the Early Neolithic Mortuary Practice in Denmark. *Proceedings of the Prehistoric Society* 45, 301 – 20.

Magnell, O., 2005. *Tracking wild boar and hunters. Osteology of wild boar in Mesolithic South Scandinavia.* Studies in Osteology I. Acta Archaeologica Lundensia Series in 8o No 51, 1-151. Stockholm, Almqvist and Wiksell International.

Malmström, Helena et al. 2009. Ancient DNA Reveals Lack of Continuity between Neolithic Hunter-Gatherers and Contemporary Scandinavians. *Current Biology* 19, 1-5.

Olausson, D., Rudebeck, E., Säfvestad, U. 1980. Südschwedischen Feuersteingruben – Ergebnisse und Probleme. In *Die 5000 Jahre Feuersteinbergbau. Die Suche nach dem Stahl der Steinzeit,* G. Weisberger (ed.), 183-204. Bochum.

Peltenburg, E., and Wasse, A., eds. 2004. *Neolithic revolution: new perspectives on Southwest Asia in light of recent discoveries on Cyprus.* Oxford, Oxford University Press.

Persson, P. 1999. *Neolitikums början. Undersökningar kring jordbrukets introduktion i Nordeuropa.* Göteborg, Göteborg University Press.

Pétrequin, P., Alison, S., Cassen, S., Errera, M., Gauthier, E., Klassen, L., Le Maux, N., and Pailler, Y. 2008. Neolithic Alpine axeheads, from the Continent to Great Britain, the Isle of Man and Ireland. In *Between Foraging and Farming,* H. Fokkens, B. J. Coles, A. L. Van Gijn, J. P. Kleijne, H. H. Ponjee, and C. G. Slappen (eds.), 261-280. Analecta Praehistorica Leidensia. Leiden, Rijksuniversiteit.

Price, T. D. 2000. The introduction of farming in northern Europe. In *Europe's first farmers.* T. D. Price, (ed.), 260–300. Cambridge, Cambridge University Press.

Price, T. D., and Gebauer, A. B. 2005. *Smakkerup Huse. A Late Mesolithic Coastal Site in Northwest Zealand, Denmark.* Aarhus, Aarhus University Press.

Price, T. D., and Noe-Nygaard, N. 2009. Early Domestic Cattle in Southern Scandinavia. *From Bann Flakes to Bushmills,* N. Finlay, S. McCartan, N. Milner, and C. Wickham-Jones (eds.), 198-210. Oxford, Oxbow Press.

Price, T. D., and Bar-Yosef, O. 2010. Traces of Inequality at the Origins of Agriculture in the Ancient Near East. In *Pathways to Power. New Perspectives on the Origins of Social Inequality,* Price, T. D., and G. M. Feinman (eds.), 147-168. New York, Springer.

Price, T. D., and Bar-Yosef, O. 2011. The Origins of Agriculture: New Data, New Ideas. *Current Anthropology* 52, S4.

Price, T. D., Bennike P., Noe-Nygaard, N., Ambrose, S., Richards, M. P., Petersen, E. B., Vang Petersen, P., and Heinemeier, J. 2007. The Stone Age graves at Dragsholm: New dates and other data. *Acta Archaeologica* 78(2), 193-219.

Rasmussen, P. 2005. Mid-to late-Holocene land-use change and lake development at Dallund Sø, Denmark: vegetation and land-use history inferred from pollen data. *The Holocene* 15, 1116-1129.

Ritchie, K., Kurt, C., Gron, J., and Price. 2012. Flexibility and Diversity in Subsistence during the Late Mesolithic: Faunal Evidence from Asnæs Havnemark. *Danish Journal of Archaeology.* In press.

Rowley-Conwy, P. 1995. Wild or domestic? On the evidence for the earliest domestic cattle and pigs in South Scandanavia and Iberia. *International Journal of Osteoarchaeology* 5, 115-126.

Rowley-Conwy, P. 2011. Westward Ho! The Spread of Agriculturalism from Central Europe to the Atlantic. *Current Anthropology,* Vol. 52, No. S4, *The Origins of Agriculture: New Data, New Ideas,* S431-S451.

Scheu, A., Hartz, S., Schmölcke, U., Tresset, A., Burger, J., and Bollongino, R. 2008. Ancient DNA provides no evidence for independent domestication of cattle in Mesolithic Rosenhof, Northern Germany. *Journal of Archaeological Science* 35, 1257–1264.

Schmidt, K. 2006. *Sie bauten den ersten Tempel: das rätselhafte Heiligtum der Steinzeitjäger: die archäologische Entdeckung am Göbekli Tepe.* Munich, Beck.

Schmidt, K., and Hauptmann, H. 2003. Göbekli Tepe et Nevali Cori. *Dossiers d'Archéologie* 281, 60–67.

Skoglund, P., Malmström, H., Raghavan, M., Storå, J., Hall, P., Willerslev, E., Thomas, M., Gilbert, P., Götherström, A., and Jakobsson, M. 2012. Origins and Genetic Legacy of Neolithic Farmers and Hunter-Gatherers in Europe. *Science* 336, 466-469.

Skousen, H., 2008. *Arkæologi i lange baner. Undersøgelser forud for anlæggelsen af motorvejen nord om Århus.* Højbjerg, Forlaget Moesgård.

Sørensen, L., and Karg, S. 2014. The expansion of agrarian societies towards the North - new evidence for agriculture during the Mesolithic/ Neolithic transition in Southern Scandinavia. *Journal of Archaeological Science* 51, 98–114.

Sørensen, S. 2005. Fra jægere til bondere. In *Arkeologi och Natuurvetenskap*, C Bujnte (ed.), 298-309. Krapperup: Gyllenstiernska Krapperupstiftelsen. Stuttgart, Gustav Fischer Verlag.

Tauber, H. 1981. d^{13}C evidence for dietary habits of prehistoric man in Denmark. *Nature* 292, 332 – 333.

Troels-Smith, J., 1960. Ivy, mistletoe and elm: climatic indicators – fodder plants: a contribution to the interpretation of the pollen zone border VII–VIII. *Danmarks Geologiske Undersøgelse* 2, Series 4: 4, 1–32.

Vigne, J. D., Carre`re, I., Briois, F., and Guilaine, J. 2011. The early process of mammal domestication in the Near East: new evidence from the Pre-Neolithic and Pre-Pottery Neolithic in Cyprus. *Current Anthropology* 52(suppl. 4), S255–S271.

Weiss, E., Kislev, M. E. and Hartmann, A. 2006. Autonomous cultivation before domestication. *Science* 312, 1608– 1610.

Chapter 10

In Dialogue: From Social Analysis to Epistemological Concerns

Irene Garcia-Rovira

University of Manchester, UK

Is scale a useful analytical device in archaeology? This article assesses the viability that flat approaches have to untangle the complexities inherent in the transition to the Neolithic. In doing so, the discussion addresses a broader concern with the dynamics of current archaeological theory. It is suggested that alongside our renewed interest in the study of the nature of reality, archaeology should be concerned with the ways in which we acquire insights about the past. This argument does not seek a return to anti-realist frameworks. Instead, it develops from acknowledging that the very notion of historical past exists insofar as human beings conceptualise it. Ontology and epistemology are not antagonised and related either to realist or to anti-realist frameworks but considered as two theoretical branches that may be conjoined to help resolve the fragmentation currently observed between archaeological theory and practice.

Keywords: Scale, epistemology, flat ontology, human geography, assemblage theory, emergence, archaeological record, historical past

Introduction

This article develops from the enduring question of how the transition to the Neolithic should be addressed in ways that challenge traditional research focused on its mechanisms of transmission (see Garcia-Rovira 2013a; 2013b, in press). The latter approach is not considered to be redundant. However, it may be necessary to temporarily displace this question, as its dominance has led research to depict human beings as the engine triggering this context of change.

In the latest contribution to the topic (Garcia-Rovira 2013a), I suggested that the transition to the Neolithic is best defined as a multidimensional process. Whilst at a local level the introduction of new practices triggered a myriad of responses, in exploring the process in 'historical depth and geographical breadth' (Barrett 2001:142), the transition exhibits a sense of directionality or, as Robb puts it (2013; in press), irreversibility. This differential response has led to the suggestion that, despite obvious differences, the transition to the Neolithic is akin to the contemporary process of globalisation in that whilst triggering global effects, its responses vary greatly from region to region (see Roberston 1995). Following this line of thought, I concluded by noting how our understanding of the Neolithic transition would be enhanced by the development of multi-scalar research.

This conclusive statement brought a number of methodological challenges to subsequent research. For instance, the question was raised of how to formulate past narratives in a way that encompasses the insights observed through examining a process from different scalar perspectives. However, an encounter with a debate over the validity and usefulness of the notion of scale in social analysis emerging within the field of human geography (e.g. Marston et al 2005; Leitner and Miller 2007; Escobar 2007) forced me to revisit the soundness of the aforementioned positioning on the topic.

This article stems from an initial reflection on the usefulness of the notion of scale in archaeology and more specifically for the study of the process of change traditionally defined as the transition to the Neolithic. It is suggested that even as contemporary archaeological theory continues to be concerned with the nature of reality, it should pay more attention to the ways in which the past is constructed from the very moment the *pastness* of an object is revealed to the human eye.

Human geography without scale?

'The two extremes, local and global, are much less interesting than the intermediary arrangements that we are calling networks' (Latour 1993: 122)

In recent years, the subject of globalisation has regained ground in debates within human geography. In its study, adherents of flat ontologies have raised questions with regard to the nature and usefulness of the notion of scale. The critical point of this discussion can be found in the polemic article 'Human Geography without Scale' (Marston et al 2005). In this paper, the authors demarcate the flaws of traditional accounts of globalisation with the aim of delineating an approach to social processes that conforms to a flat view of the world deployed within the ontological turn in the social sciences (Deleuze and Guattari 2004; de Landa 2002, 2005; Latour 1993, 2005).

Their point of departure is founded upon a critique to traditional approaches to the process of globalisation. Despite their efforts to deconstruct top-down approaches - e.g. through the implementation of globalisation/ glocalisation (see Robertson 1995) – in retaining a distinction between the global and the local, vertical analyses fail to overcome frowned-upon binaries such as agency/structure, contingent/abstract or place/ space (Marston et al 2005; Jones III et al 2007). More importantly, they denounce how the global (or structure) is often portrayed as the force that triggers change at the local level. Following from this discussion, Marston and her colleagues (2005; 2007) exclude vertical notions of scale from social analysis, as they necessary evoke a sense of hierarchy.

The article continues by expressing differences with fluid-based ontologies incorporated in recent globalisation analyses (e.g. Smith 2003a, 2003b). Latourian in character, these approaches decentre the traditional focus of study, locating research on the analysis of networks. In doing so, their concern is founded on the definition of dynamical processes. Their quest for dynamism is expressed by Smith (2003a), who defines the world as:

> '[…] always in the process of being made through a multiplicity of different materials […] that are enrolled and mobilized to form the very relations and connections of the heterogeneous activities that make up any network' (Smith 2003a: 34).

Despite being closer to their own contribution to the debate, the authors challenge notions of fluidity, indicating how the dynamic properties of matter often lead to clustering and redundancy.

Discarding the effectiveness of the notion of scale – be it vertical or horizontal – they proceed to outline a flat ontology that aids the exploration of social processes. The structural components of their methodology are founded upon the disassociation of social theory from anti-realist frameworks. Reality is not simply disclosed by a transcendent being; it is autonomous, independent of the human mind (de Landa 2002). Following from this axiom, their analysis of the social moves away from conceptualisations that only exist insofar as human beings conceive them. It therefore follows that globalisation, capitalism or world economy are not suitable elements of study for social theory. This view maintains that the world is flat.

Similarly to fluid-based ontologies, the authors draw attention to the interplay that is triggered through relationships among the dynamic properties of matter. However, they promote an understanding of dynamical processes which, following de Landa's assemblage

theory (2002; 2005) and Schatki's (2003) site ontologies, disperse and cluster through processes of territorialisation and deterritorialisation (see de Landa 2005: 13). This is conceived as an innovative research framework for it allows disassociating social analysis from epistemological constraints. Assemblages are not conceived as analytical devices but as real temporal associations. Social processes can then be examined by exploring the emergent properties of given assemblages. With this, it follows that our understanding of globalisation processes should be promoted by an analysis directed at the ground.

The story so far: flat ontology and the transition to the Neolithic

The adoption of insights developed in flat ontologies is beginning to have a clear impact on the subject of the transition to the Neolithic (e.g. Harris 2013, in press; Robb 2013, in press). These bodies of theory have allowed us to question the transcendent role given to human beings in this process of change and have progressively led to the definition of novel research frameworks intended to develop new interpretive exercises.

Harris (in press) has recently drawn attention to the potential that relational thought has to challenge traditional dichotomies established between our conceptualisation of the Mesolithic and the Neolithic. Domestic/wild, culture/nature binaries lose their definitional status when the examination is focused on the dynamic properties of matter that emerge in worldly engagements; a position that is further discussed by drawing attention to the middening activities evidenced at Cnoc Cnoig (Oronsay) and under the Neolithic mound at Ascott-under-Whychwood (Oxfordshire). Furthermore, in his theoretical engagement, Harris (in press) stresses the potential that assemblage theory (de Landa 2002; 2005) has to overcome the limitations of epistemological ordering as it allows the projecting phenomena that can be said to exist in reality.

Robb (2013a; in press) perceives the potential that assemblage theory has to explicate the threefold process characteristic of the transition to the Neolithic, that is, transformation, convergence and irreversibility. Drawing attention to the close-knitted relationships that exist between human and non-human entities within a given assemblage, he proposes a study that traces how the introduction of new practices triggers the formation of novel relationships, which ultimately give, rise to situations of emerging causation. Since these associations happen in the ground, Robb suggests the development of studies localised in historical landscapes of action. Interestingly, in his discussion, Robb (2013a) proposes a study of the transition that conflates human agency with deep time.

Flat ontology: from theory to practice

As we have seen, flat ontologies have triggered new research directions into the topic of the transition. The influence of these bodies of theory can be observed in an array of recently articles published (e.g. Harris 2013, in press; Robb 2013, in press, Garcia-Rovira 2013a; Barrett in press). Whether or not realist frameworks directly influence them, these publications present novel research directions, which differ from the previous wave of research in which practice theory had dominated methodological and interpretive accounts of this context of change (e.g. Cummings and Harris 2011; Whittle 2007). Theoretically speaking, elements from flat ontologies have revolutionised our understanding of the transition to the Neolithic. However, the challenges that these theoretical frameworks trigger for interpretive studies remains unknown, especially with what concerns a scalar (less) approach to this context of change. In this section, I wish to initiate an enquiry into the suitability of these bodies of theory to archaeological practice.

Despite containing many differences of approach, existing proposals for the development of flat approaches to the transition lean towards the definition of scenarios of dynamism and clustering taking place in the relationships that exists among all sorts of entities that exist on an equal plane (see de Landa 2002, 2005). What appears important in these analyses is the definition of the changing relationships that are triggered with the introduction of new things and practices; changes that eventually give rise to a situation of emergence, defined in this context as new forms of sociality. But what kind of assemblage is suitable for this kind of analysis?

To date, the only attempt at developing an interpretive scenario influenced by flat ontologies in the context of the Mesolithic-Neolithic transition is provided in Harris' examination (in press) of the middens at Cnoc Coig (Oronsay) and Ascott-under-Whychwood (Oxfordshire). In this study, Harris adopts de Landa's (2002) conceptualisation of a 'phase transition' to explain how minor changes occurring in the transition can, in the long run, have significant effect in the dynamics and thus the composition of the assemblage in question. However, as he stresses, he is not seeking here to engage into a discussion of the character of the transition as a whole but is presenting a 'non-dichotomous position' (Harris in press).

The selection of the two aforementioned middens for the case study suits the kind of insights sought by Harris in the article in question. However, in being geographically distant, they do not allow us to trace the changing relationships that take place with the introduction of new elements within the assemblage. In the hope of testing the viability and potential of notions of assembling and emergence in our conceptualisation of the transition to the Neolithic, attention has to be turned to what could potentially be a suitable context to undertake such analysis.

The spread of the Neolithic in the North West Mediterranean coast has been dated to c. 6500-6000 BP (Zilhão 2001; Oms et al in press) and, as the evidence currently stands to date, it is possible to suggest the existence of associated clusters generally localised near river basins and estuaries.

One such clustering is located near the Llobregat River Basin (Barcelona, Spain) in which 14 sites have so far been recovered (Oms et al in press). Researchers working in the area define this cluster as a cultural group given its association with Cardial pottery and its engagements within a given landscape (see Oms et al in press).

However, studies of procurement and landscape mobility allow us to posit relationships that go beyond inter-group affairs. These groups appear to inhabit landscapes such as the characteristic marshlands of the lower courses of the Llobregat River, along with mountain and coastal environments, engaging in a range of subsistence activities as well as the procurement of materials such as jasper and *Glycimeris* and *Columbella rustica* (Oms et al in press). Human and non-human relationships can be attested in this area through the avoidance of marshlands as places for settlement (note risk of infection in this area) or by the selection of caves as habitation spaces. Given the closed-knitted relationships that can be traced among groups that inhabited these areas contemporaneously, they may be defined as an assemblage.

As discussed, theoretical models shaped to account for the Neolithic transition (e.g. Robb 2013, in press; Harris 2013, in press) highlighting the necessity of tracing this assemblage in time in order to understand how these introduce of new practices, or rather, relationships, trigger processes of territorialisation and emergence. With it follows that examining the changes that occur in the impasse from the Mesolithic to the Neolithic would enhance our understanding of the transition. Unfortunately, the context presented, as with many other European contexts, lacks Late Mesolithic antecedents. The latest Mesolithic evidence recovered in this area dates to c. 7300 BP at Cova de Can Sadurní (Begues) (see Fullola et al 2011). By contrast, the earliest evidence for Neolithic dates to about the 6450 BP at the same site (Oms et al in press). Whether this is evidence for the Neolithic colonisation of an empty landscape, or could be explained as the erasure of Late Mesolithic activity by coastal dynamics is a matter of debate. In any case, this situation can be used to reflect on the interpretive inclinations of those who have posited the possibility of using assemblage theory to untangle the complexities inherent in the transition to the Neolithic. It may be said that the application of this theoretical paradigm overestimates notions of acculturation and continuity.

Let us return to the main discussion of the article. At the beginning of this text, I outlined the analytical path that took Sally Marston and her colleagues (2005, 2007) to getting rid of the notion of scale. In it, they emphasised the fact that the separation of the global and the local in globalisation studies has triggered an understanding by which the global seems to the acting force that triggers changes at the local level. Instead, they argue that the process of globalisation should be examined from the ground up. For the sake of the argument, let us imagine that in the context of the Llobregat region, Late Mesolithic evidence was well attested. This hypothetical context would enable us to trace the changing relationships that appear with the introduction of new elements, ranging from domesticated plants to novel ideological forms. In this situation, it would be possible to reveal the forces triggering the transition to the Neolithic of this area and would enhance our understanding of how these forces produce contexts of transformation and emerging causation (Robb 2013a). This study would certainly provide a more coherent picture of this process of change and would displace the role given to human beings. However, would it allow us to draw inferences that can be used to explain the Neolithic transition as a whole?

Whilst this approach challenges many traditional conceptual barriers, it should be noted that in translating insights engendered in an analysis focused on the local to explain the process as a whole triggers a series of problematic issues that may to date have gone unnoticed. Deleluze and Guattari (2004), de Landa (2002, 2005) and Latour (1993, 2005) theoretical frameworks are sustained through a non-essentialist axiom by which individuals are not characterised by their properties but by the capacities that are engendered in their relations of exteriority. This is revealing for it implies that, even if though in a flat approximation one may have determined that, for instance, new forms of society were engendered mostly through the kind of effects that domesticated cattle had over human communities[1], this kind of information would not generalizable to explain the Neolithic transition as a whole, as doing so, would inherently prioritise essences over relationships. In order to overcome this theoretical roadblock, it is therefore necessary to conduct comparative studies to discern the kind of relationships that at once triggered contexts of transformation which are different from place to place but also that gave rise to the development and consolidation of new societal forms. This kind of study requires the development of inferences, which can only be obtained by conducing scalar analyses.

This methodological strategy is furthermore informed by *a priori* conceptualisation of the immediate causes of such changes and the situations of emerging causation that are observed in deep time. This, in turn, poses questions on the selection of the assemblage. Should we choose Llobregat group as an example from which to examine this context of change, one of the central characteristics of the transition, its irreversibility (Robb 2013a, in press; Garcia-Rovira 2013a, in press) would be understated. Should we instead pose that a suitable assemblage encompasses the transition as a whole, the multiplicity of responses that the transition triggers at a local level would be neglected. A plea for a study that incorporates information obtained at different scales of analysis has been defined by Robb (2013a, in press) in recent contributions to the topic. As he notes, the real challenge is to work 'between human agency and deep time' (Robb 2013a: 658). However, as he emphasises, whilst in the last few decades, studies on material culture and archaeology have drawn heavily upon theoretical frameworks located on the local scale (see next

section for discussion), not much thought has been given to the methods that we use and the insights we obtain in establishing macro-scale observations; a remarkable problem when considering that archaeology's main strength is the capability to illuminate understanding of deep time processes (see Robb 2013a; Robb and Pauketat 2013 for discussion).

The post-processual tendency to develop studies contained in the local scale may be ratified through a renewed interest on the local – this time understood as a real temporal association – and through a repeated questioning of the usefulness of the notion of scale as defined by flat ontologies. In this section, I hope to have illustrated that despite the soundness of these theoretical approaches, they present a series of challenges when applied to archaeological practice. With regards to the study of the Neolithic transition, the questions posed relate to issues of size and time depth, thus taking us back to the necessity to account for scale in social analysis. This poses an interpretive dilemma: is it possible to conduct a study which considers all sorts of entities at an equal plane but that does not reduce the value of scalar analysis? A response to this enquiry is offered here by highlighting the need to cease prioritising ontological matters over epistemological concerns.

Discussion and conclusion

[…] we have a set of diverse and lively theories about fieldwork and data collection, formation processes, and materiality, but none of these theories seems to be talking to others. This kind of fragmentation has created serious problems for archaeological stories, notably in what I have called a new interpretive dilemma, in which our explanation often hover between vacuity and incommensurability (Lucas 2012:169).

As has been discussed, in 'Human Geography without Scale' (2005) the authors critique how in establishing a demarcation between the local and the global in globalisation studies, the global is often portrayed as force which triggers changes at a local level. Influenced by flat ontologies, they emphasise how any 'social structure needs to operate somewhere, by someone, involving some kind of materialities' (Latour 2005: 220; Fahlander 2012). Similar approaches have begun to appear in archaeology. For instance, in his 'Articulating Hybridity' (2012), Fahlander proposes an analysis of social processes, which develops from the bottom-up. This framework, Fahlander suggests, is particularly well suited to archaeology for archaeologist's primary data 'consists of localised material traces of action' (Fahlander 2012: 59).

This theoretical outlook challenges the very foundations of social analysis for, in stressing flatness, they force us to expel notions such as 'world economy or capitalism' from social analysis. These are conceptual constructions rather than real entities and therefore should be dismissed from ontological enquiry. However, whilst the study of

---

[1] Note that this is just a hypothetical example.

the past obviously requires critical understandings of about the nature of reality, these insights cannot be fully utilised unless we show concern over the ways in which we construct knowledge about the past. Rethinking the nature of our object of study can elucidate this statement.

In his 'Understanding of the Archaeological Record' (2012), Lucas examines the correspondences that exist between the social theories that archaeology deploys and the nature of our object of study. In reading his reflections one may point at the unbalanced weight given to ontological matters over epistemological concerns in recent archaeological theory. Some issues that have to be confronted with the application of assemblage theory in the study of social processes have been discussed here by using a number of hypothetical examples. Nevertheless, his approach examines these complications further by emphasising how the archaeological record is not only composed of material traces of action. In short, an understanding of the archaeological record has to necessarily problematize issues of inscription and erasure and to dwell upon the distinctive ways in which archives are produced (Lucas 2012).

Should this equation continue to play an important role in the way in which we theorise about the nature of our discipline, we will only feed the increasing fragmentation that seems to exist between archaeological theory and practice. This problem is further accentuated in thinking about the very idea of 'pastness'. Realist frameworks emphasise the necessity to theorise about reality, challenging any conceptualisations that arise from the human mind. However, one may consider the following question: does the past, in its historical sense, exists outside the contents of the human mind? So for as long as one agrees with the latter, then it is fundamental to remember that at the same time that we speculate about the nature of reality and inform our displace about it, we also need to think about the ways in which knowledge about reality, or in this case the past, is constructed. This takes us back to the issue of scale.

A number of authorities have defined the ontological turn nowadays affecting our discipline as a move from epistemology to ontology (see Harris in press). Yet it may be misleading to characterise post-processual archaeologies as concerned with epistemological matters. Indeed, the adoption of hermeneutics in our discipline triggered questions of the nature of archaeological interpretation. However, very little concern was given to the critical examination of the value of the methods and practices that archaeology employs in the definition of past narratives. This can be exemplified in the way agency theory turned its back om issues of typology, categorisation and style. Patterning was contemplated as bringing forward rigidity and it was therefore thought important to move away epistemological concerns through a development of archaeologies of practice (see Robb and Pauketat 2013; Garcia-Rovira in preparation for discussion). Concerns over agency and situated practice gradually moved

archaeological analysis from the big picture to studies focused on the local context, seeking to depict the world 'as lived' by individuals and small groups' (Collis 2008, 35). These changes enabled an understanding of the ontological soundness of the local context in contrast to the rigidity imposed by examinations focused on larger scales of analysis. A similar situation is found nowadays in flat approaches in that a preference is given to the analysis of local contexts over that which is found at other scales of analysis.

In considering this approach, it becomes possible to disassociate scale from ontological matters and deploy it as an analytical device that allows us to untangle the complexities of past processes. 'Archaeology gives us the chance to develop arguments about material culture and history on unprecedented scales' (Robb 2013: 32). In this situation, it is possible to infer that whilst macro-scale observations do not plot real social entities, it offer us possibilities to observe 'things not patently visible' (Robb 2013b: 79) in reduced scales of analysis and that are of crucial importance to understand the complexities of given processes.

I want to conclude by re-emphasising how the philosophical move from anti-realist to realist frameworks, which is currently affecting the very constitution of our discipline, should not be likened to a move from epistemology to ontology. Theoretical archaeology should continue enquiring into the nature of reality whilst it begins to devote more the ways in which archaeologists constitute knowledge about the past.

Acknowledgements

I would like to thank Mats Larsson and Julian Thomas for including me in the project 'North-West Europe in transition: the Early Neolithic in Britain and Scandinavia'. I also would like to thank Fredrik Fahlander and Tove Stjärna for inviting me to present a short version of this paper at Nordic TAG 2014. My gratitude goes to Robert Matthew for proofreading the text. Any errors are of course my own.

Bibliography

Barrett, J. 2001. Agency, the duality of structure, and the problem of the archaeological record. In: I. Hodder (ed.) *Archaeological Theory Today* (1st edition) Cambridge, Cambridge University Press, 141-164.

Barrett, J. in press. Some possible conditions necessary for the colonisation of Europe by domesticates. In: A. Whittle and P. Bickle, (eds). *Early Farmers: A View from Archaeology and Science*. London, British Academy.

Collis, J. 2008. The Celts as 'Grand Narrative'. In: A. Jones (ed.), *Prehistoric Europe. Theory and Practice*, 35-53. Chichester, Wiley.

Cummings, V. and Harris, O. 2011. Animals, People and Places: The Continuity of Hunting and Gathering

Practices across the Mesolithic–Neolithic Transition in Britain. *European Journal of Archaeology* 14, 361–393.

de Landa, M. 2002. *Intensive science and virtual philosophy*. London, Continuum.

de Landa, M. 2005. *A new philosophy of society: assemblage theory and social complexity*. London, Continuum.

Deleuze, G. and Guattari, F. 2004. *A thousand plateaus: capitalism and schizophrenia*. London, Continuum.

Escobar A. 2007. The 'ontological turn' in social theory. A Commentary on 'Human geography without scale', In S. Marston, J. P. Jones II and K. Woodward, NS 32, 106-111. *Transactions of the Institute of British Geographers.*

Fahlander, F. 2012. Articulating Hybridity. Structurating situations and indexical events in North-European rock art. In: N. M. Burström and F. Fahlander (eds.) *Matters of Scale. Processes and courses of events in the past and the present.* Stockholm, Stockholm Studies in Archaeology 56.

Fullola, JM.., Garcia-Argüelles, P., Mangado, X. and Medina, B. 2011. Paleolític i epipaleolític al Garraf - Ordal. On érem i on som…. In: A. Blasco, M. Edo, and M.J. Villalba (eds.) *La cova de Can Sadurní i la prehistòria de Garraf. Recull de 30 anys d'investigació*, Actes Jornades Internacionals d'Arqueologia, Begues, 5-7 de desembre de 2008. Milano, EDAR Arqueología y Patrimonio, Hugony Editore: 227-243.

Garcia-Rovira, I. in press. Dialogues in transition. Between entanglements and hybridities. In: T. Clark (ed.) *Archaeologies, syncrestism, creolisation.* Oxford: Oxford University Press.

Garcia-Rovira, I. 2013a. The Indian behind the artefact or the artefact behind the process? Humans non-humans and the transition to the Neolithic. *Current Swedish Archaeology* 21, 73-91.

Garcia-Rovira, I. 2013b. *'In-between: re-thinking the context of the British Mesolithic-Neolithic transition Preliminary Results'* In: M. Larsson and J. Debert (eds.) *North-West Europe in Transition,* 29-36. Oxford, British Archaeological Reports.

Harris, O. J. T. 2014. Revealing Our Vibrant Past: Science, Materiality and the Neolithic. In: A. Whittle and P. Bickle (eds). *Early Farmers: A View from Archaeology and Science.* London, British Academy.

Harris, O. J. T. 2013. Relational Communities in Prehistoric Britain. In: Watts, C. (ed.). *Relational Archaeologies: Humans, Animals, Things,* 173-189. London, Routledge.

Jones III, J. P., Woodward, K., Marston, S. A. 2007. Situating Flatness. *Transactions of the Institute of British Geographers 32*: 2, 264-276.

Latour, B. 1993. *We Have Never Been Modern.* Cambridge, Mass, Harvard University Press.

Latour B. 2005. *Reassembling the social: an introduction to actor-network-theory.* Oxford, Oxford University Press.

Leitner H. and Milner B. 2007. Scale and the limitations of ontological debate: a commentary on Marston, Jones and Woodward. *Transactions of the Institute of British Geographers* 32, 116–125.

Lucas G. 2010. Time and the Archaeological Archive. *Rethinking History* 14:3, 343-359.

Lucas G. 2012. *Understanding the Archaeological Record.* Cambridge, Cambridge University Press.

Marston S., Jones J. P. III, and Woodward, K. 2005. Human Geography without Scale. *Transactions of the Institute of British Geographers* 30, 416-432.

Robb, J. in press. The future of the Neolithic. A new research agenda. In: A. Whittle and P. Bickle (eds). *Early Farmers: A View from Archaeology and Science.* London, British Academy.

Robb, J. 2013a. Material Culture, Landscapes of Action, and Emergent Causation: A New Model for the Origins of the European Neolithic. *Current Anthropology* 54: 6, 657-683.

Robb, J. 2013b. History in the Body. Scale of Belief. In: J. Robb and T. R. Pauketat (eds.) *Big Histories, Human Lives. Tackling Problems of Scale in Archaeology,* 77-99. School of Advances Research, Advance Research Seminars, Santa Fe, N. M.: School for Advanced Research Press.

Robb, J., Pauketat, T. R. 2013. From Moments to Millennia. Theorizing Scale and Change in Human History. In: J. Robb and T. R. Pauketat (eds.) *Big Histories, Human Lives. Tackling Problems of Scale in Archaeology,* 3-33. School of Advances Research, Advance Research Seminars, Santa Fe, N.M: School for Advanced Research Press.

Robertson, R. 1995. Glocalization: Time-Space and Homogeneity-Heterogeneity. In: M. Featherstone, S. Lash, and R. Robertson (eds). *Global Modernities,* 25-45. London, Sage.

Schatzki, TR. 2003. A New Societist Social Ontology. *Philosophy of the Social Sciences* 33, 174-202.

Smith, RG. 2003a. World city actor-networks. *Progress in Human Geography* 27, 25-44.

Smith, RG. 2003b. World city topologies. *Progress in Human Geography* 27, 561- 582.

Oms, X. in press. A new E. Neolithic Group in the Neolithisation of the NW Mediterranean Coast (c.6500-6000 BP): The Llobregat River Estuary (Barcelona). *Journal of Archaeological Sciences.*

Whittle, A. 2007. Going Over: People and Their Times. In: A. Whittle and V. Cummings (eds). *Going Over: The Mesolithic-Neolithic Transition in North-West Europe.* Oxford, British Academy, 144, 617-628.

Zilhâo, J. 2001. Radiocarbon evidence for maritime pioneer colonisation at the origins of farming in west Mediterranean Europe, *Proceedings of the National Academy of Sciences* 98: 24, 14180-14185.

www.ingramcontent.com/pod-product-compliance
Lightning Source LLC
Chambersburg PA
CBHW051305270326
41926CB00030B/4735